# Slave Society in Cuba
## *during*
## *the nineteenth*
## *century*

# Slave Society in Cuba
## *during*
## *the nineteenth*
## *century*

### Franklin W. Knight

THE UNIVERSITY OF WISCONSIN PRESS

Madison, Milwaukee, & London

1970

*Published 1970*
THE UNIVERSITY OF WISCONSIN PRESS
Box 1379, Madison, Wisconsin 53701

The University of Wisconsin Press, Ltd.
27–29 Whitfield Street, London, W. 1

Printed in the United States of America
Kingsport Press, Inc., Kingsport, Tennessee

ISBN 0–299–05790–9; LC 76–121770

*for*
Ingeborg Bauer Knight

# Contents

# List of Maps and Tables

*Maps*

*Tables*

# Acknowledgments

THE ARCHIVAL RESEARCH for this book was carried out during 1967 and the summer of 1969, with the support of funds supplied by the Graduate School and the Comparative Tropical History Program of the University of Wisconsin, the Government of Jamaica, and the Research Foundation of the State University of New York. The Graduate School of the State University at Stony Brook paid for typing the manuscript. I am grateful for their support.

I wish also to express my gratitude to the staffs of the Memorial Library of the University of Wisconsin, Madison; the Consejo Superior de Investigaciones Científicas, and the Biblioteca Nacional, Madrid; and the New York Public and the Hispanic Society libraries of New York City.

I would like to thank especially, John Leddy Phelan, who directed my graduate studies; Philip D. Curtin, who kindly allowed me to use the galleys of his book, *The Atlantic Slave Trade: A Census* (Madison: University of Wisconsin Press, 1969); and Horacio Fuentes Martínez, Eugene D. Genovese, Sidney W. Mintz, Bernard Semmel, Peter Smith, David Trask, and above all, my wife, Ingeborg Bauer Knight. My manuscript derived considerable benefit from their advice, comments, corrections, and criticism. Nevertheless, I accept full responsibility for the entire work and all errors therein.

FRANKLIN W. KNIGHT

*State University of New York at Stony Brook*
*February, 1970*

# Note on Archival Sources

THE SECTIONS of the Archivo Histórico Nacional (AHN), Madrid, papers most frequently quoted are the Sección de Estado, Subsección Esclavitud, and the Sección de Ultramar, Papeles de Ultramar. Papers in both sections are grouped in *legajos* (bundles) which are themselves sometimes grouped into smaller bundles, also called legajos. Neither in the Estado nor in the Ultramar sections of the archives is there a consistent or sequential numbering scheme for folios or letters. In the footnotes I have recorded any identifying number that a document bore, as an aid in retrieval, but for many I had no option but merely to cite the legajo number.

The following terms and abbreviations have been used:

leg.    legajo
ind.    índice (roughly, "file no.")
fol.    folio (these do not run consistently where they occur)
exp.    expediente (case file)
carta   letter

# Introduction

THE STUDY OF SLAVERY and its effect on society has developed considerably during the last quarter of a century. One of the most interesting aspects of this development is the strong inclination, especially in the
United States, to broaden the perspective by a comparative approach to
the subject. The justification has been that the best way to understand
the phenomenon in any particular area is to look at a number of cases.
One cannot simply state that the slave system of the United States was
the most rigidly structured in the world without a broader look at the
phenomenon of slave societies. But what really gave further impetus to
the comparative approach was the sudden rise of interest in the racial
situation in the United States after World War II. The black minority
started moving north in the United States, and the urgent need for universal application of the civil rights of this people became more and more
apparent. At the same time, the political impact of other black people
throughout the world became more pronounced. European colonial rule
in Africa started its rapid demise—even though the Portuguese continued
seemingly oblivious of the portents—and predominantly black nations
appeared in the West Indies. With these essentially political achievements
among nonwhite peoples all over the world, the old impression that there
might be a fundamental difference between the black people of the United
States and black (and other nonwhite) people elsewhere began to resur-
face. The experience of slavery in the United States offered the best starting point in the examination of social differences between the United
States and, say, the West Indies and Latin America.

Yet comparisons between slave societies in the New World existed for a very long time before the end of slavery in the region. It was commonplace for the Spanish to boast about the "humanitarian character" of their form of slavery even while their strongest advocates sought the abolition of slavery in the Spanish colonial world at the end of the nineteenth century. Both the Cuban planter, Cristóbal Madan, and the Spanish parliamentarian, Rafael María de Labra, seemed agreed on that point, though they were poles apart on the problem of slavery and its role in the Cuban social system. And the conviction of an essential difference among New World slave societies continued into the twentieth century. In 1910, Sir Harry Johnston in his book, *The Negro in the New World,* purported to offer some proof of this by claiming that he had been told by "intelligent travellers" that conditions in the New World under slavery ranged across a wide spectrum with the Anglo-Saxon variant at one end and the Iberian variant at the other—the obvious assumption being that conditions "improved" as one moved along the line toward the Spanish and Portuguese possessions. It is now generally held that Johnston suffered from a flight of fantasy when he wrote about those rather remarkable travellers who spoke in terms of slavery as if they were sampling various cuisines. The most unfortunate aspect of all was the fact that Johnston's view gained wide currency, even though, as Noel Deerr points out in his monumental work on the history of sugar (vol. 2, p. 359), the original assertion was "undocumented and unsupported."

In 1946, Frank Tannenbaum produced a little book, *Slave and Citizens: The Negro in the Americas,* which brought Johnston's immature hypothesis into scholastic repute. Tannenbaum's thesis has been much maligned recently, but at the time that his book was written it provided a considerable step forward in a debate which had demonstrated signs of stagnation. Tannenbaum focused on the legal aspect of slavery, and affirmed that "the attitude toward manumission is the crucial element in slavery; it implies the moral status of the slave, and foreshadows his role in case of freedom [p. 69]." Tannenbaum's valiant argument does not stand up to comparative inquiry. Not the least of its weaknesses is the untenable assumption that the Anglo-Saxon Protestants methodically denied the humanity of their slaves, and that this led to the peculiar situation of the society in the southern United States. But the real problem was the refusal of the Anglo-Saxon Protestants of the Caribbean to follow the pattern of their continental companions. Slavery and post-emancipation race relations differed significantly between any of the slaveholding states of the continental United States, and any island in the Caribbean, regardless of the cultural and religious inheritance derived from their separate metropolitan powers. Nevertheless, Tannenbaum's thesis gained wide currency and refinement from later writers, particularly Gilberto Freyre, Stanley Elkins, Harry Hoetink, and Herbert Klein.

Without examining closely all of the various subvarieties of the Tannenbaum thesis, it is probably fair to say that their main focus was on an attempt to explain the observed present-day differences between race relations in the United States and those in the rest of the hemisphere. These scholars tended, therefore, to concentrate their attention either on institutional differences, such as Elkins's and Klein's emphasis on the role of the Church, or on the peculiar sociohistorical development of the Iberian people, such as Freyre's Lusitanian cosmopolitanism and Hoetink's somatic norm image, based on the way people look at themselves and others. (Hoetink contended that southern Europeans were more swarthy than northern Europeans, and so tended to accept a greater variation of "whiteness.") The main points raised by these eminent scholars all had some validity, but they failed uniformly to explain some obvious inconsistencies in the pattern of behavior within the areas they had defined. To take one example, no theory adequately accounted for the alarming loss of life among the slaves in the regions of the most paternalistic slave societies, while the reproduction rate in the United States exceeded by far that found elsewhere in the plantation zones of the New World.

This situation did not pass unheeded. As early as 1944, in *Capitalism and Slavery,* Eric Williams had produced an economic interpretation of the rise and fall of the slave system based on the growth of industrial capitalism. To simplify his theory is to do it great injustice, but the convenience is irresistible. Williams's major premise was that slavery created capitalism, which developed and destroyed its creator. And Williams insisted that racism was a consequence rather than a cause of slavery. Like Frank Tannenbaum, Eric Williams had a number of disciples and revisionists, most notably Marvin Harris, who accepted Williams's thesis in general but revised certain aspects of it. He also made an attempt to explain away the uncomfortable positions of the Tannenbaum-Elkins-Freyre-Klein thesis. But the relationship between capitalism and slavery is far more complicated than Williams and Harris have suggested. This does not mean that the economic relationship has no merit, but rather that men do not act from simple, single motives. David Brion Davis made the most cogent appreciation of this point in his book, *The Problem of Slavery in Western Culture,* when he wrote: "we should greatly oversimplify the problem if we were to see too close a correlation between economic profit and social values, or to conclude that antislavery attitudes were a direct response to economic change." Davis's insight gains support from the Cuban experience of the nineteenth century. No other slave society was more attuned to the influence of industrial capitalism than the Cuban, and from the earliest period of the large-scale sugar industry on the island the planters showed an outstanding awareness of the need to invest not only in more slaves to boost production, but also in machines. At the same time, considerable investment was made in research and technology, enabling them to maximize profits beyond the capacity of an operation based entirely on slave labor. By 1850 the Cuban sugar industry was the most advanced the world had ever experienced. Why then did abolition of slavery take so long? Surely, the combined influence of internal capital application and external humanitarian pressure should have been able to terminate slavery in the island before 1886. Obviously there were many other factors at work in the Cuban case, and we can only get an insight into them by analyzing the dynamics of the society and the nature of the industry.

Even a superficial reading of the history of the Cuban slave society of the nineteenth century gives the impression that the conditions of its development gave it certain peculiarities. Here was a society which had a very long tradition of slavery, among the oldest in the Americas. Yet it was only when most other societies were turning away from slavery as an economic system and a form of labor organization that the Cubans became involved in the agricultural revolution that had entered the Caribbean Sea in the early seventeenth century. In short, the so-called South Atlantic System, by which European capital and African labor combined to operate tropical American plantations, was dying when it manifested its belated presence in that Spanish colony. In a certain sense, this lateness redounded to the benefit of the Cubans, who could begin competing with the latest techniques of production and therefore attain an efficiency beyond the capacity of their rivals. To take one example, the Cubans, unlike producers in the other West Indian islands, seldom sold their unfinished sugar abroad. With the refining process done at home, sugar sales brought greater profits than elsewhere in the

Caribbean and Brazil. But on the other hand, the Cuban planters had the peculiar problem of getting slaves at a time when the British and others had already agreed to stop the slave trade. After 1820, therefore, the greater number of the Africans who became slaves in the island arrived there contrary to international treaty and law.

Cuba developed a robust slave society in the face of the strong criticisms of the humanitarians of the nineteenth century, and even against the active efforts of the British government to end the transatlantic slave trade and to generate other forms of "legitimate" trade in Africa. Of course, the defensive arguments of the Cuban planters were in the tradition of the racist and ethnocentric propositions which had found their most classic expression in the invective of Juan Ginés de Sepúlveda at Valladolid in the middle of the sixteenth century. But of great importance was the reality that religious and secular humanitarians had, by 1838, scored the remarkable achievement of convincing a powerful nation that slavery was morally objectionable, economically, unsound, and a regressive step in the advance of civilization. The Cubans and Spaniards of the middle and later nineteenth century were particularly sensitive to the third point.

Confronted with the confidence of the antislavery crusaders of the time, Cuban slave owners and planters, it is reasonable to assume, could not engage in this labor system with the complacency of their ancestors. Appearances had as much relevance as reality; slavery had to appear to be a better situation for the Africans than their homeland provided. But no amount of window dressing could disguise the essential barbarity and inhumanity of the system. The Spanish court in Madrid could spend long hours debating whether more female slaves would stem the disastrous decline in the black population of Cuba, but as long as nobody really thought—and nobody did—that slavery rather than the lack of procreation was the cause, their discussion was a waste of time. Yet the important point lies not in the details of slavery in Cuba, or whether it was better or worse than any other slavery at any time, but rather in the fact that many external factors were militating against the continuance of slavery. The humanitarian attackers had support from the technical inventiveness of the era as well as from new ideas about society.

I have tried to trace the various new developments that subjected the operation of Cuban slave society to internal and external pressures that affected the role and position of Cuban slaves. I have not dealt at length with the abolitionists and humanitarians as a group partly because that has already been done, and partly because I think that they did not significantly affect the conditions and persistence of slavery in the island. Moreover, the abolitionists were all in Madrid. It would be an unfair criticism to conclude that they were lone voices crying in the wilderness, but to concentrate on official actions, especially when such were centered in Madrid, is to miss the erosive forces built into slavery. But although a society cannot endure forever half-slave and half-free, it certainly can endure a long time in that condition. The Cuban planters by their efforts propped up the institution, which ultimately became completely redundant in an age when steam and the railroads and the improved technical competence of sugar production had made the industry a scientific enterprise bereft of its former charm, cruelty, guesswork, or paternalistic considerations. After abolition, the workers who had once been slaves were still exploited, but at least they were promoted to some form of ruralized proletariat.

My study of the Cuban slave society of the nineteenth century grew out of dissatisfaction with the earlier theories, which had used Cuba as an example of the modifications that the Roman Catholic Church and an Iberian cultural heritage wrought in any society, especially those in the New World. My evidence suggests that these theories themselves need modification.

It is undeniable that the Cuban plantation society of the nineteenth century had some peculiarities—as indeed did every slave society. Yet it seems to me that what is really important is the way in which the development of the sugar plantations created stresses within both the society and its traditions. As Cuba became a sugar colony it became increasingly similar to other earlier sugar islands, or to the plantation society in the United States.

This study is just a beginning of much-needed new work on the Cuban slave society, and in doing it I found myself raising all sorts of questions which I had neither the time nor the material on hand to pursue. Our knowledge of Cuban slave society is still in its infancy. We need to know, for example, far more than we now do about the new class of planters who emerged as the operators of the vast plantations in Cuba at the time. We still need much information on the sources of the new capital, whether it came from the French refugees arriving from St. Domingue and Louisiana, or New York, or Boston, or London. We are still ignorant of the day-to-day operation of the sugar estates on the island, which we could compare with say, Worthy Park Estate in Jamaica. We need these records to ascertain the extent of sickness and mortality on the average estate, the cost of food for the slaves, the amount of work done by slave labor, free paid labor, or contract labor, and the effect of epidemics and economic recession on the operation of the estate. As far as I could find out, these types of data are not available in Spain. But there exists ample material in Cuba. The *Guía del Archivo Nacional* (Havana: Academia de Ciencias, Serie Archivos No. 1, December, 1967) give details of the resources, which include very significant sections that have already been catalogued or inventoried.* The section dealing with judicial records (Protocolos) contains at least 10,000 volumes, the oldest dating from 1578. There is an uncatalogued document collection for sugar estates, as well as material covering a wide range of pertinent subjects. Unfortunately, I was unable to gain access to these records while I was undertaking the research for this book. The pity is that no satisfactory investigation can be made on any aspect of Cuban history without recourse to the National Archive in Havana. May the present restraints prove temporary, so that further research may enlighten us about this very significant experience in New World society.

* I am indebted to Dr. Magnus Mörner for a copy of this publication.

# Slave Society in Cuba
*during*
*the nineteenth*
*century*

# 1

# The Transformation of Cuban Agriculture, 1763–1838

*There is no doubt about it. The era of our happiness has arrived.*

Arango y Parreño, 1793.

OVER THE YEARS from 1763 to 1838, Cuba changed from an under-populated, underdeveloped settlement of small towns, cattle ranches, and tobacco farms to a community of large sugar and coffee plantations. Any full understanding of the history of slavery in the island after this date must perforce take into account the revolutionary changes in the structure of Cuban society and economy that preceded.

Although Cuban political life had not overcome, by 1838, the uncertainty and corruption which were its bane, the economic condition of the island was extremely promising. The island had "arrived" among the world's sugar producers. While the other producers of the West Indies complained bitterly about "rack and ruin," the Cuban sugar cane planters merely complained about the acute shortage of workhands of any color for their estates. The island had become the foremost producer of the world's sugar, but there still remained an abundance of fertile, unworked land of inestimable potential for the growing of sugar cane. The frequent changes of local political leadership in Havana and the incessant alternation of Spanish court parties had hardly affected the steady spread of the plantation throughout the island. From a minor colony in the Spanish imperial domain, Cuba had become the most valuable member of Spain's diminished overseas empire. Indeed, while Isabel II (1833–68) reigned unsteadily in Spain, sugar became "king" in Cuba. But Cuba was important not merely because it was beginning to make substantial contributions to the Spanish treasury, but also because by the very nature of Cuban production at this time, it had joined the wider world community; metropolitan Spain knew only too well the dire consequences of this development.

The history of the sugar plantation goes as far back as the late sixteenth century in Cuba.[1] The early settlers had continually produced small quantities of sugar on the island. And indeed, there were scattered examples of larger plantations, with probably as many as one hundred slaves, both in Cuba and Hispaniola from the late sixteenth century.[2] The technique of production may have been as efficient as that employed anywhere else in the world at that time. Nevertheless, it is important to point out that sugar production was geared exclusively toward internal consumption, and very few producers thought of sugar as a lucrative enterprise.[3] Moreover, the demand for sugar at that time in Europe was adequately supplied from the islands on the other side of the Atlantic and Brazil.

Cuban society at that time was not dominated by the plantation of any sort. It was, instead, an underpopulated island, a settlement colony existing on small ranches, *vegas* (tobacco farms), and in small towns, with a few plantations and a few slaves. Until the second half of the eighteenth century, Cuban agriculture consisted of alternating attempts at monoculture and a mixed economy, neither of which was distinguished in the activities of the overseas Spanish empire taken as a whole. This is not to say that the island was not an important part of the Spanish empire in the New World. It was valuable as a meeting place for ships and men from the diverse parts of the mainland, and it represented a springboard for the colonization attempts on the mainland before it lost its place to the ports and cities of New Spain and New Granada. A few colonists, however, remained in Cuba braving the elements and making a living by raising cattle and planting tobacco. Tobacco was the main export crop; but leather, meat, and dyewoods became important commercial supplements, especially in the immensely valuable inter-

1. José Antonio Saco, *Historia de la esclavitud de la raza africana en el nuevo mundo* . . . (4 vols.; Havana: Cultural, 1938), 2:96–97.

2. Hubert H. S. Aimes, *A History of Slavery in Cuba, 1511–1868* (New York: G. P. Putnam's Sons, 1907), p. 13.

3. Actually, sugar cane growing had declined markedly by the end of the seventeenth century. See H. E. Friedlaender, *Historia económica de Cuba* (Havana: Montero, 1944), pp. 28–31.

island trade.[4] The most important aspect of early Cuban society was the fact that, in accordance with the general pattern of Spanish colonial expansion, the majority of the inhabitants of the island colony lived in towns. Life in Cuba at that time for freedman or slave centered upon the town, the hacienda, or the vega.[5]

As long as the society remained predominantly dependent on the growing of tobacco and the raising of cattle, the labor requirements were low. Since tobacco was not grown as a plantation crop, but as a small-scale cash crop—as indeed it was in the English colonies of the eastern Caribbean before the sugar revolution—and ranching does not require regimented labor, Cuba could remain an island settlement of preponderantly white persons.[6] It is folly to expect that such a society would generate high racial tension, whether or not the whites were racists. The white sector maintained its substantial majority and probably as a result exhibited little or no racial fear of the nonwhite sector of the population. There was, and could be, little tension of any kind. The society just did not have the kind of divisions which yield strife: no foreigners of note, no Indians, no very rich people, few African slaves. As far as the lack of racial tension went, this resulted less from the benevolence of Spanish legislation or the doctrine and intercession of the single, all-encompassing Roman Catholic Church, than it did from the realities of the situation. In Cuba at this time the African simply represented little economic value and even less economic competition. In terms of services and obligations, therefore, white and nonwhite complemented each other.[7]

In the preplantation era of Cuban slavery, the enslaved persons could live with few rigorous rules. A large number of the slaves were obviously in domestic service, while the others worked in the fields. Often white masters and their slaves worked together in the tobacco vegas, or on the cattle haciendas. In any case, the farms were small and their pro-

4. Francisco de Arango y Parreño, *Obras* (2 vols.; Havana: Dirección de Cultura, 1952), 1:81; Elizabeth Donnan, ed., *Documents Illustrative of the Slave Trade to America* (4 vols.: New York: Octagon, 1965) 2:204–5, 211–12, 254; Allan Christelow, "Contraband Trade between Jamaica and the Spanish Main, and the Free Port Act of 1766," *Hispanic American Historical Review*, 22 (1942), 309–43.

5. See Ramiro Guerra y Sánchez, et al., ed., *Historia de la nación cubana* (10 vols.; Havana: Ed. Hist. de la Nación Cubana, 1952), 1.

6. Aimes, *Slavery in Cuba*, p. 8.

7. See Herbert S. Klein, *Slavery in the Americas: A Comparative Study of Virginia and Cuba* (Chicago: University of Chicago Press, 1967), pp. 131–33.

prietors poor. Tobacco plantations such as the ones found in Virginia and other areas of the southern United States were the exception in Cuba, where the farmers had few slaves and a lower social position than the cattle rancher. The cattle ranchers tended to be richer than the tobacco growers, but this was not really important since they both used small numbers of slaves and supervised them rather laxly. Regardless of where master and slave found themselves, the relationship tended toward intimacy and patriarchy. In comparison with the other islands of the Caribbean before the late eighteenth century, the relations between masters and slaves were relatively personal. This apparently amiable situation derived less from the differing cultural heritages of the various Caribbean islands than from their varying stages of economic development.

But the placidity and lethargy of Cuban society did not last forever. Between 1762 and 1838 the relatively mixed economy based on cattle-ranching, tobacco-growing, and the small-scale production of sugar gave way to the dominance of plantation agriculture based on the large-scale production of sugar and coffee. There was no single factor which engendered the change in the nature of Cuban society and its agriculture. Instead, a bewildering series of interrelated events and forces over which the Cubans themselves had no control, and which they often did not understand, imposed the radical transformation into a plantation society. Among these powerful agents of change in the history of Cuban society at this time must be included the shifts in international market demands, the English occupation of Havana in 1763–64, the farreaching economic and administrative reforms of Charles III (1759–88), the sudden destruction of the French colony of St. Domingue, and the disruptive wars of the Latin American independence movement. All these events, occurring in the last decades of the eighteenth century and the early years of the nineteenth, resulted in a truly revolutionary change in the nature of Cuban society.

Once the Cuban agricultural revolution took place, other equally fundamental changes were irrepressible. The entire society began to readjust itself to the new demands of the plantation and the economy. More slaves resulted in a new method of organizing slave labor. More intensive agriculture meant wider markets and greater dissatisfaction with the restrictive measures of Spanish colonial commerce. Greater participation in the international market brought new ideas of economic and political relationship. The Cuban elite which had long complacently accepted Spanish colonial rule began to demand greater intercourse with other countries, particularly France, Great Britain, and the United States. The illegal trade with the British which had always been conducted clandestinely assumed prominent proportions. And the United States became a large market for Cuban sugar as well as the best source of the manufactured goods, skilled laborers, and enlightening ideas so seriously lacking in the island.

The most convenient starting point for this intensification in Cuban agriculture may be taken as the year 1763, when the English captured and occupied Havana for a period of ten months. Of course, seen in isolation, that event may not have been crucial for the island's agriculture.[8] The English did nothing that the Cubans were not already doing before they arrived on the scene.[9] Nevertheless, the large number of merchant vessels which visited Havana during the months of the occupation and the importation and sale of more than 10,000 slaves in such a short time constituted a tremendous stimulus to a process already under way. Among other things, the English occupation of Havana emphasized the gigantic gap between the prevailing Cuban demand for slaves and its effective supply. It also convinced Charles III and his ministers that the entire colonial situation was ready for the rational reforms which they had already been contemplating.[10]

The real importance of the reforms of Charles III lay in the fact that they were the first major official attempt to integrate the island of Cuba into the mainstream of the wider world. Cuban changes, however, were only a small part of the large scheme of physiocratic ideas to bring Spain up to date by the thorough overhaul of her relations with her overseas colonies. Nor by focusing on the official acts of the Spanish Crown should one lose sight of the important fact that the entire eight-

8. Aimes quite correctly points out that the English occupation did not "cause" the awakening and economic development of Cuba (*Slavery in Cuba*, p. 33). He does, nevertheless, agree that it marks a period of significant change (ibid., p. 69).

9. Donnan, *Documents*, 2: xlv; Aimes, *Slavery in Cuba*, pp. 22–25.

10. J. H. Parry, *The Spanish Seaborne Empire* (New York: Knopf, 1966), pp. 314–25; John E. Fagg, *Latin America: A General History* (New York: Macmillan, 1963), pp. 292–303. My information on the reforms of Charles III is condensed principally from the following: Cayetano Alcázar Molina, *Los virreinatos en el siglo XVIII*, 2nd ed. (Madrid: Salvat, 1959); R. A. Humphreys and John Lynch, eds., *The Origins of Latin American Revolutions, 1808–1826* (New York: Knopf, 1965); Salvador de Madariaga, *The Fall of the Spanish American Empire*, rev. ed. (New York: Collier, 1963); R. J. Shafer, *The Economic Societies in the Spanish World (1763–1821)* (New York: Syracuse University Press, 1958).

eenth century was a period of general European economic progress and enlightenment. To a certain extent, therefore, Charles III was as much the servant of his age as he was the master of his deeds.[11] The island of Cuba was of paramount importance in the imperial plans of Charles III, as a testing ground for the measures that he subsequently applied to the rest of the empire.

Before the late eighteenth century, Cuban property owners had bought their slaves from the English, the French, the Dutch, and the Portuguese.[12] Indeed, before 1792 Spain had never been able to provide her colonies with the required human cargoes, since she lacked the necessary African factories. At first she farmed out the awards for the supply in a series of *asientos,* or contracts. These contracts gave the right to any individual of any country to deliver for sale a stated number of slaves in the Spanish empire. Later the asientos were given to the emerging joint-stock companies of the Portuguese, French, and, after 1713, the British.[13] The companies, like the individuals earlier, promised to transport a specific number of slaves to the Spanish colonies, and to pay a specified tax into the Spanish treasury.

However the awards were made, they were totally inadequate to supply the Spanish colonies. The official asientos were supplemented by a lively, mutually beneficial, interisland trade throughout the Caribbean. English privateers, often acting on their own initiative, made sporadic trips among the Spanish islands, and by force or judicious bribes sold their cargo of slaves for specie.[14] But there were also well-established markets in Jamaica and Dominica, in which the Cubans regularly made their purchases. Condemned strongly by the Spanish crown, but welcomed openly by the islanders, this interisland trade fulfilled two acute needs: the Cubans got their slaves, and the English and the French obtained cash, dyewoods, and hides. Spanish silver, dyewoods, and leather products not only enabled the Jamaican and other West Indian merchants to become solvent, but found their way into English domestic industry, and English trade with the Far East.

11. Richard Herr, *The Eighteenth-Century Revolution in Spain* (Princeton: Princeton University Press, 1958).

12. J. H. Parry and P. M. Sherlock, *A Short History of the West Indies* (London: Macmillan, 1956), pp. 95–107.

13. Aimes, *Slavery in Cuba,* pp. 35–37; Jerónimo Becker y González, *La política española en las Indias* (Madrid: Martin, 1920), pp. 412–15.

14. Allan Christelow, "Contraband Trade," pp. 309–43; Parry and Sherlock, *The West Indies,* p. 103.

The Spanish government was always aware of the unsatisfactory conduct of the asiento, and the formation of their own chartered companies in the early eighteenth century was an attempt to rectify the situation. In the case of Cuba, the Real Compañía Mercantil de La Habana was the first attempt to boost the trade in slaves and to stir the waning interest in agriculture.[15] The company was formed in 1740 to take over the transportation to and sale of Africans in the island. It disposed of its slaves for cash, credit, or pledged crop returns. In this way the company dominated, though it never monopolized, the island's major exports of sugar, tobacco, and hides before 1763. In the first twenty-six years of its operation the company brought into Cuba and sold officially 9,943 slaves. But of this number, more than 50 per cent were sold in the three years immediately following the British occupation.[16]

The Real Compañía had other counterparts in Spanish America. The Caracas Company, chartered in 1728, monopolized the trade of the Venezuelan coast. A company from Galicia received a charter to trade with the Campeche region in 1734, and the Barcelona Company, chartered in 1755, intended to carry on trade with Puerto Rico and Hispaniola. Most of these new companies had the financial backing of the merchants from the northern provinces of Spain. Only the Caracas Company proved successful over the long run. Nevertheless, the organization of the companies represented Bourbon attempts to liberalize trade in the empire and to break the monopoly of Andalusia.

The organization of the Real Compañía was extremely important, but from the planter's point of view it proved more a liability than an asset. On the one hand it failed to supply an adequate amount of goods or slaves at reasonable or satisfactory rates. On the other hand, it bought the planters' products at the lowest possible prices. Under these conditions, contraband trade became probably the largest outlet for Cuban products and the best method of obtaining necessary imported goods. But the prevalence of the contraband trade made it monumentally difficult to arrive at credible estimates for the island's commerce, or its slave population and annual rate of slave importation. This study takes into account the possibility that the official figures represent the minimum for any particular time. Nevertheless, I think that the earlier figures may

---

15. Aimes, *Slavery in Cuba,* pp. 29–30; Donnan, *Documents,* 2:xlv.
16. Aimes, *Slavery in Cuba,* pp. 23, 36.

not be too inaccurate since the demands were low; and the later figures at least represent an index of volume.

On the basis of official estimates and intelligent guesswork, Hubert Aimes set the total number of slaves imported into Cuba between 1512 and 1761 at about 60,000—a figure which seems eminently reasonable for the period.[17] For 1762–1838, the same author put the total at somewhere in the region of 400,000.[18] The mean annual import figure for the first period of nearly 250 years comes to about 250 slaves per year. The mean annual figure for the 76 years prior to 1838 comes to nearly 5,000 slaves per year. These figures dramatically reflect the demographic changes which were brought about in the society as a consequence of the transatlantic slave trade. But the trade, for its part, was merely a local response to the agricultural demand. Cuban planters wanted more adult Africans to provide the labor for the cultivation of their land. And even though they knew that it meant a fundamental change in the composition of their island's population, they were quite prepared for that eventuality. The demand, after all, preceded the fateful events in St. Domingue and France at the end of the century, and so there was less need for worry.

The commercial importance of Havana increased tremendously after the British occupation. During the eighteen years after 1760, the number of ships calling at the port rose from six to more than two hundred per year.[19] As part of the system of modified free trade which had been instituted during the reforms of Charles III, the port became a focal point for the entire gulf area, handling larger and larger quantities of European manufactured goods and slaves. Commodities which were usually scarce became more available, and in the case of slaves a greater supply seemed to be consistently below the local requirements. As far as the Cuban planters were concerned, African laborers were the most valuable commodity which could be imported into the island at that time. The liberalization of the trade afforded by the crown unwittingly paved the way for a succession of unforeseen events towards the end

17. These figures are taken from Aimes, *Slavery in Cuba,* p. 269, who derived them from Alexander von Humboldt, *The Island of Cuba,* trans. by J. S. Thrasher (New York: Derby & Jackson, 1856), pp. 216–24. Cuban import figures for this period compare closely with those for Jamaica during its heyday of slavery. See Orlando Patterson, *The Sociology of Slavery* (London: Macgibbon & Kee, 1967), pp. 290–91.

18. Aimes, *Slavery in Cuba,* p. 269.

19. Parry, *Spanish Seaborne Empire,* p. 316; Aimes, *Slavery in Cuba,* p. 35.

of the eighteenth century which would begin the promotion of the island of Cuba as the foremost producer of sugar in the world.

Once the Creoles in Cuba had begun the agricultural transformation of the island, the supply of slaves became the main concern. For at this time the international competition in the production of tropical staples depended on a sufficient labor force. The continuous agitation by the Cubans led to the complete reexamination of the island's slave supply. Not surprisingly, the consensus was that the means and measures by which the Cubans procured their slaves were totally inconsistent with the agricultural requirements of the island. Over a period of years, therefore, the crown granted permission for an unrestricted number of slaves to be brought to the island.[20] Finally, a royal cedula of February 28, 1789, permitted foreigners and Spaniards to sell as many slaves as they could in a specified number of free ports, including Havana.[21] This was exactly what the Cuban planters had been anxious to achieve for more than a decade. The royal order removed all the previous restrictions on the trade of slaves, suspended all taxes for a period of three years, and allowed the merchants to sell at any price determined by the local market conditions. Indeed, the planters were so delighted by the new situation that they persuaded the royal court in Madrid to extend the free trade beginning in 1792 for a further period of six years.[22] And so great was the interest in Cuban agriculture and the commerce in slaves that a total of eleven royal pronouncements was made between 1789 and 1798 expanding the trade in black workers to the Spanish Indies.[23]

This declaration of a virtual free trade in slaves at the end of the eighteenth century, then, provided the necessary impetus for the development of the plantation society. Nevertheless, the greater trade must also be seen against the general background of events in the Caribbean and elsewhere at that time. For exactly during this period of time international events favored the growth of Cuba's economy and importance. And perhaps the most significant single event was the

---

20. Aimes, *Slavery in Cuba,* pp. 45–48; Becker y González, *Política española,* pp. 412–15.

21. *Real cédula por la que Su Majestad concede libertad para el comercio de negros con las islas de Cuba, Sto. Domingo, Puerto Rico, y provincia de Caracas a los españoles y extranjeros* (Madrid: Impr. Nacional, 1789).

22. Aimes, *Slavery in Cuba,* p. 50.

23. Manuel Moreno Fraginals, *El ingenio* (Habana: Unesco: 1964), p. 8.

destruction of the sugar-producing capacity of the French colony of St. Domingue, and the later creation of the independent republic of Haiti.

Until 1789, St. Domingue was the most highly developed plantation society in the world. It was the paragon among sugar islands of the West Indies. Situated on the western part of the island of Hispaniola, and comprising a total area of only 10,700 square miles, the colony's population of 40,000 white persons and 480,000 slaves and free persons of color had long become the ideal of, and comparison for, every other colony in the area that hoped to become rich by growing sugar cane and coffee. The Cubans reasoned that with four times the land area of St. Domingue, and undoubtedly greater soil fertility, they could easily outproduce their neighbors. The only handicap they had was the acute shortage of slaves, which, however, was being rectified at last. And like the sugar producers in St. Domingue a little before, they would have faced the unhappy restrictions of their own exclusive imperial commercial system.[24] But before they could worry about that, there was the immediate concern of raising their sugar production to a competitive level.

The extension of the French revolution to the Caribbean brought two unexpected results beneficial to the Cuban producers. In the first place, the principal producer of the world's sugar and coffee was almost instantly and completely destroyed. The price of sugar on the European market rose sharply as the demand outstripped the available supply, and brought a windfall to producers elsewhere. But in the immediate aftermath of the events in St. Domingue, the Spanish crown was hesitant to sanction the creation of a new slave society in Cuba, even though it would give permission to the continued increase in the number of Africans imported into the island. Nevertheless, the Cuban planters won a resounding victory over the crown when they got a concession in 1792 for the first Spanish ship ever to sail directly from Africa to Cuba bringing Africans to the slave market in the Antilles. In the second place, from St. Domingue came a number of refugees who brought their skills, their slaves, and an uncertain amount of capital, and initiated the plantation agriculture of coffee in the eastern sections of the island.[25] It seemed, despite the confusion of that era, very

---

24. Arango y Parreño, *Obras*, 2:134.

25. Francisco Pérez de la Riva y Pons, *Origen y régimen de la propiedad territorial en Cuba* (Havana: El Siglo XX, 1946), p. 136; Humboldt, *Cuba*, p. 46.

clear to Don Francisco de Arango y Parreño, the intelligent, articulate representative of the Cuban planters in Madrid, that the age of their happiness had indeed arrived.

From its very inception, the Cuban plantation agriculture depended upon imported skills, imported capital, and an imported labor force. An uncertain part of the skills and capital came from the early immigrants from St. Domingue. These were joined later by other French emigres from Louisiana who preferred to go into exile than to endure life under the Anglo-Saxons after Napoleon sold the territory to the United States of America. And even some defeated royalist supporters of the mainland Latin American wars settled in Cuba, bringing at least their initiative, if they had no cash.[26]

Cuba derived enormous benefits from the unsettling external situation at the beginning of the nineteenth century. Wars in the area considerably augmented the available supply of capital devoted to agriculture. This led to other necessary changes as well. For since tropical agriculture depended at this time on the availability of land and slaves, intensified agriculture necessitated a fundamental change in the pattern of landholding and land use, and in the demographic composition of the island. In short, to accommodate the newcomers, black and white, the Cubans had to alter the basic structure of landholding in their island.[27]

The old tobacco and cattle holdings rapidly gave way in certain areas to the sugar and coffee plantations. Specific zones developed for each particular form of activity. Tobacco became the principal crop in the region mainly west of Havana. Sugar dominated the central plains and the lowlands around Santiago de Cuba in the eastern end of the island. Coffee, after failing to hold its own on the plains against the inexorable expansion of the sugar plantation, retreated to the mountainous area of the eastern division. But before this pattern attained its final form, it was imperative to abolish the antiquated nature of landholding and land use in Cuba. Only then could valuable land be free for new settlements and new crops.

26. Antonio Gallenga, *The Pearl of the Antilles* (London: Chapman and Hall, 1873), pp. 10–11; Juan Pérez de la Riva, "Documentos para la historia de las gentes sin historia. El tráfico de culies chinos," *Revista de la Biblioteca Nacional José Martí*, 6 (1965), 77–90.

27. Moreno Fraginals, *El ingenio*, pp. 18–19; Pérez de la Riva y Pons, *La propiedad en Cuba*, p. 91; Duvon C. Corbitt, "Mercedes and Realengos: A Survey of the Public Land System of Cuba," *Hispanic American Historical Review*, 19 (1930), 262–85.

To understand the revolution in landholding which took place at this time, it is necessary to go back to the early days of Spanish colonization in the new world and to trace the complicated growth of a system of landholding fettered by lethargic, ancestral latifundism. This system, incidentally, was common throughout Latin America before the nationalist wars of liberation in the early eighteenth century. The general pattern was the enormous hacienda with its ill-defined boundaries. Designed to be self-sufficient as much as possible, these estates also produced a few cash crops to meet the royal tax and support the luxurious life of their occupants. This type of hacienda had its roots far back in the frontier conditions of Spanish society, but it underwent some modification when it was transplanted to the New World.

After America was discovered, all land became the personal domain of the Castilian monarch, who had the prerogative to dispose of it either in usufruct or outright grant to any deserving person. Both methods of distribution were used. Originally, each occupied territory was divided into towns which had contiguous boundaries. Within the towns, the land was parceled among the settlers, and enclosed by a common pasture. Beyond this common pasture, the royal lands (*realengos*) were distributed in haphazard, often overlapping grants called *mercedes,* of usufructal tenure.[28] It must, however, be emphasized that the royal grants were modest in size. Latifundism was certainly not the intention of the crown and had its own peculiar historical genesis in the following years.

Each merced was given for the cultivation of a particular crop. Recipients of these mercedes were forbidden to change the designated crop for which they had originally received their parcel of land. The usufructal landlords paid a special annual fee that was determined by the size of the plot or its agricultural purpose. And although the land could be inherited, it could not be sold, sublet, or subdivided. This, then, was the system, which, fraught with abuses and legal complications, prevailed throughout the centuries and was to provide the basis for Creole wealth by the early nineteenth century in Cuba. Over a period of time marriage, as well as other agreements of local interest and dubious legality, converted the modest holdings into larger farms, sometimes of astonishing dimensions.

The absence of a real estate market was only one handicap to the

28. Pérez de la Riva, *La propiedad,* pp. 20–21; Corbitt, "Mercedes and Realengos," pp. 262–78.

accumulation of wealth by the landholding group. For although a planter may have had the use of his land, he could not cut a large number of the hardwood trees on his hacienda without express royal permission. Until the late eighteenth century, the crown had first lien on all hardwood trees in the island in order that the fleet construction continually taking place at Havana would not be jeopardized.[29] But as the years passed, the rise of the large sugar plantation and the preservation of the hardwood forests became mutually antagonistic. Part of the entire scheme to change the pattern of landholding, therefore, was an alteration of the system of hardwood forest preservation. The sugar revolution—indeed, the entire structure of Cuban society in the nineteenth century—cannot be understood without recognizing the importance of the fundamental change in landholding and land use between the late eighteenth and the early nineteenth century.

The big opportunity for the landholders came with the gradual insolvency of the Spanish crown. As the resources of the treasury decreased the crown ceded for cash the land which its representatives— or the local municipal councils—had offered in usufruct. By these means, a small number of wealthy colonists had persevered in the time-consuming legal disentanglements, and finally bought titles in fee simple, to use the Anglo-Saxon term, to the land they used or hoped to own. Nevertheless, by the end of the eighteenth century there had been few concrete achievements in the way of legal security for land. As more immigrants came the demand for land dramatically grew. In order to capitalize on the new source of wealth from land, it became urgent to straighten out the existing confusion or uncertainty over land. That, therefore, became the first obsession of the Sociedad Económica de Amigos del País, or the Havana Economic Society.

The Havana Economic Society, founded by twenty-seven Creole landholders, received its royal sanction in 1791.[30] It was not the only such organization in the island, but another attempt to form a group by the Creoles of Santiago de Cuba ended in failure leaving the Havana group as the only dynamic social and economic association dominated by the Creoles. Despite the fact that the Havana group later expanded into a body with a membership of nearly two hundred persons, at no

29. Pérez de la Riva, *La propiedad,* pp. 137–48.
30. Shafer, *Economic Societies,* pp. 151–54, 183–98; R. Guerra y Sanchez, *Sugar and Society in the Caribbean,* trans. Marjorie M. Urquidi (New Haven: Yale University Press, 1964), pp. 56–57.

time did its influence and activity extend beyond a small enthusiastic core mainly domiciled in Havana. Of the 126 members registered in 1793, 113 resided in the capital city, Havana. The Economic Society was, in every respect an exclusive club, a tightly organized elite group bent on the pursuit of economic power and political influence.

The formation of economic societies was a common response in Latin America to the ideas of the European Enlightenment, although this development was interrupted by the wars of separation from Spain in the early nineteenth century. But in Latin America, unlike in Europe, there was a greater emphasis on the pure and applied sciences than on philosophy.[31] In Cuba, the emphasis was on scientific activity and economic interests. The program of the Havana Economic Society encompassed science and arts, commerce and industry, beautification, and agriculture and education. Nevertheless, throughout the long life of the society, agriculture remained its consuming passion.

The Economic Society became the chief advocate for radical changes in the structure of Cuban landholding. Not surprisingly, its members were among the most articulate and influential men on the island. Yet the ultimate success of the society's pleas rested with the nature of political leadership in Havana, and the prevailing state of the Spanish treasury. Interested captains-general and impoverished monarchs were the ingredients of success.

The two most successful periods of the Economic Society coincided with the terms in office of Luis de Las Casas y Arragori (1790–96) and Alejandro Ramírez (1816–19). The supreme political head of the island was also the titular head of the Economic Society (acting in the name of the Spanish monarch) and was able to exert official influence in Madrid, helping or hindering any measure according to his fancy. Regardless of the political ideas held by both Las Casas and Ramírez, they both were themselves landholders in Cuba and probably had a personal interest in reforming the system of land ownership and land use.[32] It was evident that during the periods of office of these two men the landowners would have friends in high places.

On the other hand, the Spanish crown was hardly in a position to resist colonial requests that offered the opportunity of financial rewards. For over a century the royal treasury had barely been solvent, and the

31. See Arthur P. Whitaker, ed., *Latin America and the Enlightenment,* 2nd ed. (Ithaca, N.Y.: Great Seal Books, 1961).
32. Pérez de la Riva, *La propiedad,* pp. 127–28.

long Napoleonic wars further depleted the already slender resources. The Spanish troops and naval forces which at first fought reluctantly with the French emperor in Europe—and then, after experiencing the occupation of their homeland, turned against him—cost a lot of money to maintain. Neither Charles IV nor Ferdinand VII could be oblivious to the constant need to find new ways of securing money according to the necessities of the state. One such new way, of course, was to accept the advocated changes in the legal nature of land tenure. Unfortunately, the crown derived far fewer returns from that gesture than it had anticipated, and the poverty of the Spanish treasury remained a constant factor throughout the nineteenth century.[33]

Between 1795 and 1820, the landholders won such major concessions from the crown that they altered irrevocably the entire system of land ownership in Cuba. A royal cedula of 1800 broke up the hereditary pattern of the existing *señorios,* or large estates, and permitted the outright ownership of lands previously held in usufruct. Even crown lands became fast-selling real estate. Further royal decrees in 1815 and 1816 gave landowners the right to parcel, sell, sublet, and use their land without legal intervention. But most important of all for the future development of the sugar estate, royal approval was finally given for the destruction of the hardwood forests in the interest of agricultural expansion. After a long dispute, sugar at last took precedence over the royal navy: the Spanish crown had cleared the way for the sugar revolution in Cuba.

The immediate effect of the series of royal decrees was to open the way for real estate speculation. Land values rose rapidly, sometimes as high as five times what they had been in the late 1790's. And as the sugar belt moved out of the area around Havana, it further stimulated the rise in the market price of land. In the Matanzas sugar belt, for example, land that before the turn of the century was priced at eighty pesos per hectare was sold at prices in excess of five hundred pesos afterwards. The Economic Society of Havana bought a number of estates and resold them to the new immigrants at moderate profits.[34] Private investors such as Juan Poey, a wealthy Creole planter of Havana, dreamed of making millions of pesos in real estate speculation,

33. See Raymond Carr, *Spain 1808–1939* (Oxford: Clarendon Press, 1966), pp. 155–319.
34. Moreno Fraginals, *El ingenio,* pp. 14–15; Guerra y Sanchez, *Historia,* pp. 157–63.

though it is unlikely that they made quite that amount. Nevertheless, many new schemes produced new towns, mainly settled by immigrants, such as Guira, Alquizar, Nueva Paz, Palos, Bagäes, and Güines in the outskirts of Havana. The construction of towns was even carried on by private individuals, like Agustín de Cárdenas, Marquis of Cárdenas de Monte Hermoso, who founded the town of San Antonio de los Baños on his estate. He also leased small farms to the new immigrants. The exemption from the payment of the alcabala, or sales tax, by the purchasers of new land also served to further encourage a lively real estate market.[35]

The ability to cut and use the timber on private lands did not result in the instant deforestation of the island. Until the middle of the nineteenth century, the landowners zealously protected the forests as their primary source of fuel for their boilers, and timber for general building and the construction of the boxes in which they transported their sugar. Major deforestation only came with the advanced technological era, especially after the use of railroads had become general throughout the sugar-cane-producing area. Rail transport eventually proved so convenient and economical that the cane growers derived more profits by replacing their forests with canefields, and importing their lumber, firewood, and coal. Even the railroads, which had used locally mined coal, found it necessary to import this fuel as local supplies dwindled.[36] By the late 1860's, the central section of the island had been almost completely deforested.

The leaders of the Cuban agricultural phenomenon of the nineteenth century were extremely intelligent men, fervently desiring that Cuba should stand second to none in gross agricultural production. Francisco Arango y Parreño and Francisco Frías y Jacott, Count of Pozos Dulces, were amazingly farsighted. They knew that Cuban prosperity had come latest among the West Indian producers of sugar and coffee. Unlike the plantation owners of Jamaica, Barbados, Antigua, and St. Domingue, the Cubans lacked the numbers of slaves to catapult them into competitive production. But this liability, they reasonably assumed, was offset by the vast stretches of deep fertile land in Cuba.[37] Moreover, the Cubans were starting when science and technology offered new scope for profits and production in the sugar industry. With

35. Pérez de la Riva, La propiedad, pp. 132–34; Guerra y Sanchez, Sugar and Society, pp. 33–36.
36. Moreno Fraginals, El ingenio, pp. 74–78.
37. Arango y Parreño, Obras, 1:114–74.

no obsolete machinery on their hands, the Cubans began with the latest equipment and the most proven formula for sugar production.

The Cuban Creoles, in agriculture as in politics, were a restless group. They were always ready to grasp at any innovation which promised to boost the total output, or to cut the costs of production.[38] As the sugar industry got under way, private individuals and public commissions made long trips through the other sugar islands, reporting in detail upon every aspect of the production of sugar and coffee.

In 1795, along with Ignacio Montalvo y Ambulodi, Count of Casa-Montalvo (who died soon afterwards), Arango y Parreño made the first official trip abroad for the Cuban sugar planters. The long voyage took the indefatigable and curious representative of the city of Havana to England, Portugal, Barbados, and Jamaica. Everywhere he went, the extremely inquisitive Arango reported back to his keenly interested audience on a bewildering range of topics, with particular emphasis on agriculture and relevant proposals for adaptation to Cuban conditions.[39]

In his reports from Europe, Arango noted the superior advantage of the English and Portuguese in the slave trade. Both countries, he pointed out, had factories on the African coast. This measure facilitated a steady supply of African slaves to their colonies, and reduced the price of the slaves at the delivery point because the initial cost was lower. English industrial development impressed him most. He sent back models of the newly invented sugar mills, and a detailed description of the refining process. His opinion was that the Cubans stood to gain a far greater advantage from importing "those marvelous European machines" and thus completing the entire refining process in Cuba, than from selling muscovado (unrefined brown sugar) to the European refiners. This was, perhaps, his most valuable observation. It was partly the result of the British West Indians' failure to mechanize and to refine their sugar which weakened their competitive position in the European market.

In Barbados and Jamaica, Arango visited the foremost sugar producers among the British islands. Nothing in the political, social, and economic position of the islands escaped his careful scrutiny. Long reports relayed information ranging from the total area of land under

38. For a variety of interesting local inventions, especially designed for the sugar cane industry, see the records in Archivo Histórico Nacional, Madrid, Sección de Ultramar (hereafter AHN, Ultramar), Fomento, leg. 49(19, 27, 28).

39. Arango y Parreño, *Obras*, 1:243–47.

cane cultivation to the most minute aspect of the production of sugar and rum.

Arango's journey convinced the Cubans that soon Cuba would be the world's leading sugar producer. As a result of his persuasive advocacy new varieties of cane, particularly the Otaheiti, and new types of processing employing steam, water, and wind power were introduced to the island.[40] But along with the imported technique came a new awareness on the part of the Cuban Creole elite. They had joined the stream of ideas of the wider world. A mounting wave of criticism—carefully tendered under the guise of "suggestions"—of Spanish colonial and economic policies originated in Havana. As the Cubans realized the magnitude of their economic potential, they realized the stifling restrictions of being a part of the Spanish empire. They demanded free international trade to buy the slaves, food, and manufactured goods that Spain could not supply, and to sell in a market larger than that offered by the Iberian peninsula. The Cuban attraction towards Britain and the United States in the early nineteenth century was, therefore, one of practical economic necessity.

Arango's fact-finding tour of Barbados and Jamaica in 1795 became the first of a frequent general practice. To any Cuban sugar producer, the grand tour of the British West Indies became a source of personal prestige, establishing the traveler as an authority on the subject of sugar production. And in some cases, the trip became the prerequisite for the founding of an *ingenio* (sugar estate with factory).[41] The curiosity value aside, the trips did provide much useful knowledge of methods and machines which were brought to Cuba. The "Jamaican train," the boiling process of sugar manufacture, became standard in the early days of Cuban sugar production. Yet the true value of these trips over the long term came from the restless desire of the Cuban planters to find a process which would combine speed, efficiency, economy, and labor-saving devices. Because they were never able to stock their plantations with slaves the way the Jamaicans or Barbadians did, they had to find some alternative. In the fiercely competitive sugar market, survival depended on the volume of production. To the British West Indies and to Brazil, increased volume resulted from more slaves and more acreage under cane. But in the nineteenth century the British were waging a relentless

40. Francisco J. Ponte Dominguez, *Arango Parreño, el estadista colonial* (Havana: Ed. Trópico, 1937), pp. 84–87.

41. Moreno Fraginals, *El ingenio,* p. 24.

crusade to abolish the slave trade and, ultimately, slavery. The essential problem for Cuba, therefore, was to devise a method of increasing the total output using the available manpower or, better, less manpower.

By 1828, Cuba had clearly surpassed her British West Indian neighbors in sugar production. A commission of Ramon de Arozarena and Pedro Bauduy made a thorough tour of Jamaica in that year, and reported back to the Cuban government.[42] In a lengthy report filled with interesting and knowledgeable observations, the commissioners described their journeys through the island, and the state of its sugar, coffee, and pimento operations. There were only three aspects in which the Cubans were not as distinguished as their neighbors: in the large-scale manufacture of rum, as a byproduct of sugar; in the extensive use of guinea grass as cattle fodder; and in the possession of pimento, which was native to Jamaica. They clearly supported the immediate adoption of those three measures. But they thought that Cuba, with her vast areas of virgin land, her large forests, water supply, and mountains would always be in a position to outproduce the sugar and coffee planters of Jamaica. They were amazed, too, that English chemical developments were completely unknown in the Jamaican sugar industry, which produced only muscovado sugar. Jamaica's economic glory lay in her past; Cuba was the land with the future.

The economic and political activities resulting from the progressive reforms of Charles III initiated the complete renovation of Cuban society: a steep rise in population, agricultural production, and profits; a new political awareness as new ideas crept back along the routes of economic and educational contact. The old order slowly dissolved. The new prosperity based on land speculation, slave trading, and sugar and coffee plantations brought to the forefront of Cuban society a new economic elite which accepted the old order on its own terms. This was extremely important, especially for the race relations which were to develop from the demands of plantation management and operation. Men like Miguel Aldama, Juan Poey, Julian Zulueta, Gonzalo José de Herrera y Beltran de Santa Cruz, Count of Fernandina, and Francisco Arango y Parreño were men who had become wealthy during their lifetimes, when the island was undergoing the changes of economy and demography which made it a classic, late-flowering example of the plantation society and the

42. AHN, Ultramar, Fomento, leg. 37, fol. 91: *Informe sobre . . . Jamayca. Por D. Ramon de Arozarena, y D. Pedro Bauduy* (Havana: Impr. Fraternal de los Diaz de Castro, 1828).

South Atlantic System. But the real importance of this new slave-owning class was that they would not, and could not, be bound by the patriarchal conventions of the previous era of Cuban slavery. Their attitude to the Church, the state, and their plantations was one which they themselves worked out—an attitude which reflected the new political power position of the Cuban Creole class (see Chapter 5).

Between 1775 and 1838 the island underwent profound changes in the composition of its population. In 1775, Cuba had a population of 171,500 persons. Of this total, 96,400 were white persons; 36,300 were free persons of color; and, 38,900 were African slaves. But even then, a

TABLE 1
Cuban Population Growth, 1774–1841

| Class | 1774 | % | 1827 | % | 1841 | % |
|---|---|---|---|---|---|---|
| White | 96,440 | 56.9 | 311,051 | 44.1 | 418,291 | 41.6 |
| Free colored | 36,301 | 20.3 | 106,494 | 15.1 | 152,838 | 15.1 |
| Slave | 38,879 | 22.8 | 286,942 | 40.8 | 436,495 | 43.3 |
| Total population | 171,620 | 100.0 | 704,487 | 100.0 | 1,007,624 | 100.0 |

Sources: For the census of 1774, Guerra y Sánchez, *Historia*, 2:78. For 1827 and 1841, *Resumen del censo de la población de la isla de Cuba . . . 1841 . . .* (Havana: Impr. del Gobierno, 1842), p. 19.

large proportion of the African slaves were recently imported—a trend which was to continue throughout the period of slavery on the island. By 1841, the official census reported a permanent population of 1,007,- 624 persons, of whom 418,291 were white, 152,838 were free persons of color, and 436,495 were slaves (see Table 1). In two generations the black element of the population had risen to be a majority in the society. The phenomenal growth of the slave population—from less than 23 per cent of the total population in 1774 to more than 43 per cent in 1841—may be understood and explained only by looking at the profound concomitant change in the nature of agricultural activity. But the volume of the trade to Cuba in the nineteenth century is more surprising, because of Great Britain's hostility to the trade at that time and her attempts to put an end to it.

The volume of the trade in Africans to Cuba, had, despite fluctuations from year to year, tended to increase generally as the demand grew for workers on the island, and especially since the attempt to import white workers was not succeeding. With the abolition of the English slave trade in 1807, the most efficient suppliers of slaves in the Caribbean were removed. But from the Cuban planters' point of view, the greatest calamity was the agreement of 1817, forced by the English upon a war-weakened Spain, whereby the Spanish agreed to stop the trade to their colonies after 1820.[43] Of course, as an incentive to do so, the English government had paid the Spanish crown £400,000 as "compensation." No amount of money, however, especially when it was paid in Spain, could have induced the Cuban planters at that time to cooperate in the cessation of the slave trade. Instead, the Cubans regarded the British offer as a "monstrous, hypocritical plot" designed to undermine their expanding sugar cane and coffee plantations and eventually stifle their economic progress.[44] The Anglo-Spanish agreement had the effect of increasing the numbers of Africans brought to the island of Cuba. Indeed, with the fear that the trade might be terminated in 1820, the mean annual importation figures between 1816 and 1820 were more than three times the figures for the period between 1812 and 1815.[45] Despite their awareness of the racial tragedy in St. Domingue, and despite the foreboding of the metropolitan power, the Cubans gambled on the risks: the plantation society had, by then, become the *sine qua non* in the Caribbean for wealth, stability, civilization, and patriotism.[46]

Yet, after the establishment of the independent republic of Haiti in 1804, slaveowners in the area could never be as complacent as they used to be in the unquestioned days of the eighteenth century. And after about 1817, the official relations between the metropolis and the colony, between Cuba and Spain, changed considerably as a result of the increased inflow of Africans. The white population suddenly became more and

43. Ibid., Esclavitud, leg. 3547, fol. 1333: governor of Cuba to minister of war and colonies, July 2, 1861 (confidential).

44. Justo Zaragoza, *Las insurrecciones en Cuba* (2 vols.; Madrid: Hernández, 1872–73), 1:512.

45. Aimes, *Slavery in Cuba*, p. 269, gives the imports as follows:

| | |
|---|---|
| *1812:*6,081 | *1816:*17,737 |
| *1813:*4,770 | *1817:*25,841 |
| *1814:*4,321 | *1818:*19,902 |
| *1815:*9,111 | *1819:*15,147 |
| | *1820:*17,194 |

Since these figures are based on official calculations, they probably represent the lowest import statistics.

46. Arango y Parreño, *Obras,* 1:148–50.

more aware of the heightening possibilities of a racial confrontation in the island.[47] Some white persons became fearful. The planters began to see the Spanish government—and especially the Spanish military power on the island—as the best guarantee of their personal safety and the security of their property.[48] Even the native Cubans began to see self-interest and self-preservation as the overriding concerns of the moment. Cuba would remain a faithful colony as long as the planters needed Spain.

47. Rafael M. de Labra y Cadrana, *La abolición de la esclavitud en el orden económico* (Madrid: Noguera, 1873), p. 251; AHN, Ultramar, Esclavitud, leg. 3552(2), ind. 6, fol. 3: confidential despatch of Captain-General O'Donnell, Sept. 30, 1844.

48. Ibid.

# 2

# The Sugar Revolution of the Nineteenth Century

*The change from coffee plantations to sugar plantations—from the cafetal to the ingenio, has seriously affected the social, as it has the economic condition of Cuba.*

R. H. Dana, *To Cuba and Back*, 1859.

THE SUGAR CANE INDUSTRY had a most profound influence on the course of Cuban history during the nineteenth century. The widespread cultivation of the sugar cane provided a new economic base, created a new society—the plantation society—and carved out a more important political and economic position for Cuba in the history of the western world.

The rise of the sugar industry not only affected the traditional relations of the various groups within the society, but also engendered an incompatibility within the framework of the Spanish empire. For a long time many Creoles supported the Spanish connection as the best line of defense against their oppressed slaves. Yet the friction between metropolis and colony was bound to increase as long as the mother country could not supply the enormous capital requirements, the improved technology, and the receptive consumer market which the production of sugar necessitated. For with sugar and sugar products amounting to more than 70 per cent of all Cuban exports, the colony would have to look elsewhere for its trade relations.[1] An increasing part of this trade was

1. Robert P. Porter, *Industrial Cuba; Being a Study of Present Commercial and Industrial Conditions* (New York: G. P. Putnam's Sons, 1899), p. 256. José García de Arboleya, *Manual de la isla de Cuba* (Havana: Impr. del Tiempo,

with the United States of America, from which most Cuban imports, especially food, lumber, and agricultural implements for the sugar estates came. Toward the end of the century, the Spanish connection had little more than sentimental value. As the Cuban society and economy became progressively subject to international events and pressures, the planters became more and more disenchanted with a metropolitan government that had little to offer in return for severe taxation, inefficient and ineffective political management, and virtual exclusion from the political process.

All these changes and the concomitant dissatisfactions were the byproducts of the sugar revolution in the island, and a description of the plant, its cultivation, and the whole complex of production provides an appropriate background against which to view the new society that unfolded.

The sugar cane is a succulent grass belonging to the same family as the bamboo, sorghum, Indian corn, and a wide variety of forage grasses. It thrives best in moist tropical or subtropical soil rich in humus content and adequately drained—requirements wholly satisfied throughout almost the entire island of Cuba. The cycle from planting to harvesting takes from twelve to fifteen months. On maturity the plant attains a height anywhere from five to fifteen feet, with a robust, jointed stalk filled with a dark green, sticky liquid high in sucrose content. When cut, the roots sprout again and continue to produce new plants—called "ratoons"—for a number of years. The mature sugar cane contains about 18 per cent sugar, 10 per cent cellulose, 70 per cent water, and 2 per cent other mineral matter.[2]

Until the late nineteenth century, each plantation owner grew and produced his own sugar cane and sugar. Every estate principally dedicated to this end was called an ingenio, and was not only an agricultural-industrial complex, but was also a small, self-contained, almost self-sufficient township. The ingenio in Spanish America was the sugar hacienda, complete with social divisions and captive labor force.

---

1859), p. 238, gives the percentage for sugar and its byproducts from 1851–55 at 83.78% of all Cuban exports, with tobacco and coffee contributing 7.15% and 1.85% respectively.

2. For sugar cane growing, see Noel Deerr, *The History of Sugar* (2 vols.; London: Chapman & Hall, 1949–50); William Reed, *The History of Sugar and Sugar Yielding Plants* (London: Longmans, Green, 1866); and George T. Surface, *The Story of Sugar* (New York: Appleton, 1910). Many descriptions of the process of sugar manufacture in Cuba rely on Arboleya's *Manual,* pp. 133–36.

The factory for producing sugar was usually set up in the center of the fields of cane, for before the wide-spread use of railroads equidistant transportation from the farthest extremes of cane cultivation assumed great importance. The factory compound comprised areas of forty acres on sizable holdings, and held all the buildings: the residences, often resplendent palaces, of the owner; the living quarters for white supervisory staff, skilled and semiskilled staff of any color, and slaves or indentured laborers (these last were known as *bohíos* or *barracones*); an infirmary; a chapel (usually built adjoining the great house); and the *batey,* with its complex of boiling and drying houses.

Canes coming from the field were first crushed in a mill (*trapiche*) operated by animals, steam, or water power. The juice, collected in a gutter below the press, flowed to a series of sunken boiling pans, where it was heated, clarified, and purified. This system was the famous "Jamaican train" (*tren jamaiquino*), a process originally developed in Barbados in the mid-seventeenth century.

When the heated syrup began to crystallize, the workers removed it to a separate two-storied building called the *casa de purga,* or purging house. This enormous building had a series of holes—sometimes as many as twenty thousand—in the floor of the upper story, for placing the funnel-shaped containers of tin, sheet-iron, or zinc through which the molasses drained off the sugar into troughs below. The containers, called *furos,* had a piece of cloth covering one end; this the attendants removed as soon as they inserted the containers in the molds. The trough below drained the molasses into huge vats (*bocoyes*) with a capacity of between twelve and fifteen hundred gallons. In the casa de purga the various qualities and colors of the sugar were determined. Most manufacturers spoke only of two basic colors—white, or clayed sugar, and brown, or muscovado—but they could grade their sugars into nearly ten colors, each having a different price.

Some Cuban mills, particularly in Oriente, did not make sugar for the export market. Instead, their obsolete machinery restricted their production to only a hardened syrup, called *raspadura,* used entirely for local consumption. Many authors did not include these small mills, some of which had existed for more than a century, among the sugar producers of the island, a neglect which resulted in wide variations in the total number of mills estimated at any time.

There could be no doubt that the island of Cuba was extremely well endowed with all the natural requirements for the large-scale production of sugar. And it was rather surprising that it took the Cubans so long to achieve prominence in that form of enterprise. The reasons for the neglect lay in the politics of the Spanish empire. Had Cuba not been a part of the Spanish empire, it would undoubtedly have followed the earlier path of St. Domingue, Barbados, or Jamaica. Despite the fortuitous geographical conditions, Spanish imperial politics and economics decided how the land in Cuba should be used, and how and where the products should be sold. In addition, neither Spaniards nor Cubans had the capital and supply of slaves required for large-scale sugar production. Only toward the end of the eighteenth century did the Cubans begin to adopt plantation agriculture on a large scale, and to take advantage of the great demand for sugar on the world market. The collapse of the sugar industry in St. Domingue, and the exhaustion of the soils in the leading British West Indian islands, provided part of the powerful initial impetus to the Cuban sugar cane grower.[3]

The traditional requirements for an ingenio were land, oxen, forests, and slaves.[4] The sugar planter needed suitable land to grow canes, oxen to provide transportation, firewood for fuel in the boiling processes, and slaves to supply the labor.

Land, oxen, and firewood were abundant in Cuba. The island had an area of 44,000 square miles, most of which was either flat or gently undulating, and all of which was adequately drained. In area, therefore, Cuba was more than ten times the size of Jamaica, the largest of the British West Indies, and at the beginning of the nineteenth century the leading producer of sugar in the Caribbean.[5] Cuba also had an adequate supply of oxen for agricultural purposes, thanks to the long-standing tradition of ranching in the island. Most plantations had their own ranches, or *potreros,* in order to eliminate the expense of renting draft animals.[6] Royal protection of the forests, originally in the interest of

3. On the decline of the British West Indies, see Lowell J. Ragatz, *The Fall of the Planter Class in the British Caribbean, 1763–1833* (New York: Century, 1928), esp. chapter II. For the effect of the destruction of St. Domingue on the Cuban sugar industry, see Francisco de Arango y Parreño, *Obras* (2 vols.; Havana: Dirección de Cultura, 1952).

4. *Cartilla práctica del manejo de ingenios ó fincas destinadas á producir azúcar* (Irun: Impr. de la Elegancia, 1862); Manuel Moreno Fraginals, *El ingenio* (Havana: Unesco, 1964), pp. 15–16.

5. Reed, *Sugar,* p. 74.

6. *Cartilla práctica,* pp. 46–48: "The livestock is the second element on an ingenio which comes after the Negroes, and merits particular attention both for its own value, as well as the high cost its absence creates."

ship-building, had had the salutary effect of preserving an abundant supply of firewood for the boiler houses.

The island was not equally fortunate in its possession of slaves. In 1827, Cuba had only 286,942 slaves in a total population of 704,487, a figure deemed highly inadequate for the successful pursuit of sugar cane growing. The usual method of obtaining slaves was through purchase from the itinerant vendors, whose ships called frequently at the many ports of the island. Some planters bought their slaves in other islands (or in extreme cases in Brazil or Africa), and transported them to Cuba. But as mentioned before, the British abolition of the slave trade in 1807 eliminated the most proficient vendors, while the abolition of slavery in 1838 throughout the British colonies further reduced the available supply. Moreover, Anglo-Spanish agreements in 1817 and 1835 made the slave trade illegal and greatly increased the price of slaves. In the early years of the century, the price of a sturdy male slave averaged nearly 350 Spanish dollars. By 1860, the price for such a slave had climbed to over 1,000 dollars. After 1840, the most efficacious method of obtaining slaves was usually a private expedition to Africa.

Of course, there were many hazards in fitting out a vessel in Cuba for the illegal trade in slaves. Not the least of these were the cruisers which the British navy stationed off the coast of Cuba and along the West African coast. These vessels readily intercepted any ships suspected of participating in the trade. When the squadrons captured any such ship, they turned over the crew and vessel to a court of Mixed Commission situated either in Sierra Leone, or, for a time, in Havana.[7] Between 1824 and 1866, the squadrons stationed off the Cuban coastline captured 107 slave ships with a total of 26,026 Africans on board.[8] Legally, these Africans should have been declared free. In practice, very few ever obtained their freedom. Instead, by various subterfuges, they were added to the growing slave population of the island.[9] In June, 1855, the British consul at Havana, James F. Crawford, wrote in despair to the earl of Clarendon that nearly 4,000 *emancipados* (as the Africans were called) had been converted into slaves in a devious system of fraud involving many high officials.[10] Neither repeated British protests to Spain,

7. See AHN, Estado, Esclavitud, leg. 8048–50.
8. AHN, Ultramar, Esclavitud, leg. 3554: "Estado de las expediciones de negros bozales capturados en las costas de la isla de Cuba."
9. AHN, Estado, Esclavitud, leg. 8048: Bulwer to Sotomayor, Jan. 15, 1848.
10. Ibid.: Crawford to Clarendon, June 1, 1855.

nor the risks of capture by the cruisers, deterred the slave traders. The demand for slaves in Cuba was so great that the illegal trade continued until after 1865. In the interest of the sugar industry, the trade was both necessary and profitable, even though it added a racially dark stratum to the population.

Few significant innovations were introduced in the sugar industry before the late 1830's. The ingenio continued as a basic agricultural unit rather than an agricultural-industrial complex, with greater emphasis on the plantation aspects. The major investment remained the initial cost of purchasing land, slaves, oxen, and agricultural implements, and the construction of the batey.[11] With the prevailing price of slaves fluctuating between 350 and 400 pesos[12] (the peso at the time was on a par with the United States dollar), the cost of the labor force alone amounted to between 25 and 40 per cent of the total initial costs.[13] Once the ingenio was set up, the highest recurrent operating cost was that of replacing the slave force. For, with the sexual imbalance (see chapter 6) and the extreme regimentation of plantation conditions, the slaves proved incapable of reproducing themselves sufficiently to maintain a stable population. And as the cost of slaves kept on increasing, it resulted in higher operating costs for the planter, who needed both replacements and additional hands for expansion.[14]

Steam power had, of course, been used in the industry from the early years of the century, largely owing to the advocacy of Francisco de Arango y Parreño.[15] The large-scale adoption of steam, however, took a very long time. The Cuban planters encountered two severe handicaps:

11. Moreno Fraginals, *El ingenio,* pp. 9, 15–16; Julio Le Riverend Brusone, "Sobre la industria azucarera de Cuba durante el siglo XIX," *El Trimestre Económico,* 11 (1944), 52–70.

12. For the prices of slaves between 1528 and 1875, see Fernando Ortiz Fernández, *Hampa afro-cubana, los negros esclavos* (Havana: Revista Bimestre Cubana, 1916), pp. 173–74.

13. Le Riverend Brusone, "La industria azucarera," p. 53, n. 3. As the price of slaves increased, the value of the labor force reached nearly 50% of the total value of some estates. This was not unusual elsewhere. In 1861, the total capital invested in the Louisiana sugar industry amounted to approximately $194,000,000, of which $100,000,000 was in slaves—an investment completely wiped out by the Civil War. See J. Carlyle Sitterson, *Sugar Country: The Sugar Cane Industry in the South, 1753–1950* (Lexington: University of Kentucky Press 1953), p. 226.

14. Le Riverend Brusone, "La industria azucarera," p. 56.

15. Arango y Parreño, *Obras,* 1:126–27.

the new machines were heavy, difficult to transport, and technically deficient; and the costs of setting them up were exorbitant.[16] To popularize the use of their machines, many of the manufacturers went to Cuba to assist in the assembly of their products. Nevertheless, as long as the price for slaves remained relatively low, it was usually possible to outproduce the steam-powered mills using the old, familiar methods of oxen or water power. But as the Europeans gradually eliminated the major defects of the steam machines, the Cubans began to realize their greater efficiency, particularly in crushing the newer, harder type of Otaheiti canes.[17]

Notwithstanding its potential, the adoption of steam did not by itself create a full-scale revolution within the Cuban sugar industry. In the initial stages before 1838 increased production depended on the proliferation of small units. The Cuban planters considered the optimum size of an ingenio to be that giving an annual production of one hundred long tons of sugar, with a labor force of one hundred slaves.[18] Having attained that ratio of production to labor force, the planter simply established another independent ingenio elsewhere. In this way, the total number of ingenios rapidly increased from 400 in 1800 to more than 1,570 in 1857.[19]

Proliferation, however, presented an enormous problem for the profit-conscious planters. It greatly increased their transportation costs, while cutting deeply into anticipated profits. The first phase of expansion, therefore, kept close to the northern coastal ports, where the planters could take advantage of water transport for their bulky product.[20] Yet even though they could move their finished products by sea to Havana they could not entirely evade the problem of overland transportation to the ports or, in some cases, to the storage depots in Havana.

Overland transportation of goods and supplies to the estates and of sugar to the markets was both labor-consuming and costly. Planters

16. Le Riverend Brusone, "La industria azucarera," p. 46; Moreno Fraginals, *El ingenio*, p. 70.

17. Heinrich E. Friedlaender, *Historia económica de Cuba* (Havana: Montero, 1944), pp. 195–97.

18. Moreno Fraginals, *El ingenio*, pp. 15–16.

19. See Justo Germán Cantero, *Los ingenios, colección de vistas de los principales ingenios de azúcar de la isla de Cuba* (Havana: Marquier, 1857), unnumbered pages.

20. Moreno Fraginals, *El ingenio*, p. 9.

found that the distance involved required unduly long absences of the slaves, draft oxen, and carts. Depending on the proximity to the port (or, later, the railroad station), the repair of carts and the replacements of oxen became additional high expenditures. Coastal transportation to Havana was also exorbitant. In an attempt to reduce costs, some estates built larger, heavier carts, hoping that they would endure much longer.[21] But since production was constantly rising the newer carts did not prove economical. Nor did they reduce the time lost by absent slaves. In addition, they hastened the already rapid deterioration of the streets of Havana and the main thoroughfares of the island.[22] For the first four decades of the nineteenth century, the Cuban planters found themselves in the perplexing position of trying to increase the sugar yield while at the same time holding down the concurrently mounting costs of production and transportation. Even when moderate gains accrued from the use of more efficient mills which displaced a few slaves, the victory was not won. More efficient mills demanded more canes, which meant a greater area under cultivation, hence a need for more slaves. It was a vicious circle broken only by the introduction of railroads, and by the scientific revolution within the sugar-making process.

In 1830, just about five years after the first steam-driven railway began to function in England, the Real Junta de Fomento (a sort of local development board, or chamber of commerce) initiated the negotiations for the first railroad to be constructed in Cuba to assist "in the development of agriculture and commerce." Work on the first line from Havana to Güines began in 1834 and was completed in 1838.[23] Although it covered only fifty-one miles, it was the first railroad laid in Latin America and the Caribbean, and was completed long before the first track was laid in Spain. The first part of the line, from Havana to Bejucal, became operative in November 1837, a year before the line finally reached its proposed terminal at Güines. Its first year of operation was enormously successful, and it stimulated the formation of private companies to boost the extension of small, often unconnected railroads throughout the sugar cane growing areas of the island.[24] Within a short time, railroads were

21. AHN, Ultramar, Fomento, leg. 27, exp. 22, fol. 2.
22. Ibid., leg. 42: "Memoria que acompaña al Plano general de los ferrocarriles de la isla de Cuba." Also Moreno Fraginals, *El ingenio,* p. 73.
23. AHN, Ultramar, Fomento, leg. 42, fol. 102.
24. Ibid., leg. 33: *Diario de La Habana,* Sunday, Nov. 25, 1838.

in service in all the major sugar producing areas of the island. The capital to found the enterprises came principally from England, raised under the auspices of the Cuban Junta de Fomento.[25]

The widespread depression of 1857 in Cuba hit the railroad companies very hard, and many suffered heavy operational losses for the first time.[26] The multiplicity of competitive lines had reached the point of chaos. The operating companies themselves urgently petitioned for a special law governing the development and use of railroads, submitting at the same time their own vague proposals and ideas. The companies called for less competition between lines, and asked that the government create a master plan of railways to cover the entire island. In this way the island could be methodically exploited, and the railroad system economically dovetailed.[27]

In 1858, a law came into effect standardizing the future establishment of railroads in the island, and regulating the use of equipment. Further hardship, brought on in part by the Civil War in the United States, led to a series of mergers after 1860.[28]

The construction and operation of the railroads increased the demand for an already scarce supply of local labor. The government authorized the railroad companies to import their own labor, in order that they would not compete with the sugar planters who were their best customers. The railroads, therefore, began the system of foreign contract labor in Cuba.

The railroads mixed three types of laborers: white skilled and semi-skilled operators with Asians and rented or bought Afro-Cuban slaves.

Imported white laborers were used in the initial stages of construction, and came principally from Ireland. Engineers and other skilled operators also came from England, France, Germany, and the United States. White labor, however, was expensive, since many of the contracted parties either died or returned to their native lands. Notwithstanding, white contract laborers were indispensable in the establishment

25. Ibid., leg. 42, fol. 102.
26. Ibid., Presupuestos, leg. 3443.
27. Ibid., Fomento, leg. 42, fol. 103.
28. For example, the merger between the Cienfuegos-Villa Clara Co. and the Sagua Co. in 1860–61. See ibid., Presupuestos, leg. 3443: *Memoria de la junta directiva del ferrocarril de Sagua la Grande en . . . 1860* (Havana: Impr. del Tiempo, 1860).

of the railways in Cuba, and continued throughout the period as a recurrent expense item.[29]

The available records of the railway companies show that they owned very few slaves. Instead, they depended upon the services of the emancipados (whom they probably considered as purchased slave property), and indentured coolies. In 1861, the report of the Havana railroad listed some interesting details on that branch of its labor force (Table 2).

The problems of the indentured Asians on the plantation, it should be noted, were similar to those of the slaves. This is reflected especially in the death rate and in the inclination to escape. Obviously, it was the conditions under which Africans or Asians labored which constituted the primary desire to escape.

The emancipados had a very ambiguous position in Cuba. Legally they were supposed to be free men, contracted out to labor for a specific number of years (the idea being to "civilize" them), after which they were free to remain in Cuba, or leave for some other island. In some cases this was actually done, and the five expired emancipado contracts listed by the Havana Railroad Company suggest that those slaves might have received their freedom. In general, however, the emancipados were not so fortunate. Their periods of contract were constantly renewed as new owners signed them for successive eight-year terms of service. One extraordinary case was that of the African woman Trinidad Carabelí, whose case came up in Madrid in July, 1857. It turned out that she had

29. See the various annual reports of the Cuban railway companies, ibid. White labor was also used in the sugar industry on a very large scale. Ibid., Fomento, leg. 39, fol. 46, 1858, gives the following information about foreign white labor on the Cuban railroads in 1858:

| Company | Irish | English | USA | German | French | Total |
|---|---|---|---|---|---|---|
| Güines-Matanzas | 319 | 36 | 5 | 54 | 15 | 429 |
| Havana | 146 | — | 15 | 9 | — | 170 |
| Regla-Matanzas | 28 | 1 | 1 | 3 | — | 33 |
| Sabanilla-Maroto | 70 | — | — | — | — | 170 |
| Total | 663 | 37 | 21 | 66 | 15 | 802 |

| Company | Total | Died | Returned | Remaining |
|---|---|---|---|---|
| Güines-Matanzas | 429 | 70 | 45 | 314 |
| Havana | 170 | 71 | 45 | 54 |
| Regla-Matanzas | 33 | 8 | 1 | 24 |
| Sabanilla-Maroto | 170 | 82 | 33 | 55 |
| Total | 802 | 231 | 124 | 447 |

been on a slave ship captured by the British cruiser, "Pincher," in 1836, and declared an emancipado. At the end of eight years her master supported her request for freedom, only to have it refused by the Cuban captain-general on the ground that to grant such a request would create

TABLE 2

Colored Labor in a Cuban Railroad, 1861

| Status | Asians | Emancipados | Slaves |
|---|---|---|---|
| In possession, 9.30.1860 | 146 | 16 | 7 |
| Subsequently returned by police | 5 | — | — |
| Captured | 2 | — | — |
| Newly contracted | 200 | — | — |
| Recently escaped | 1 | — | — |
| Handed over to police | 2 | — | — |
| Expired contracts | 13 | 5 | — |
| Died | 15 | 1 | 2 |
| In possession, 9.30.1861 | 322 | 10 | 5 |

Source: AHN, Ultramar, Fomento, leg. 81: *Informe presentado por la junta directiva de caminos de hierro de la Habana a la general de accionistas en 27 de Octubre de 1861* [pamphlet] (Havana: Impr. del Tiempo, 1861).

"umbrage among those emancipados enduring slavery for a longer period of time than she."[30]

It was not surprising, therefore, that emancipados like slaves should have been regarded as commercial assets, and were so used. The Trinidad Railroad Company in 1861 made a contract with the Cienfuegos Railroad Company, whereby a loan of 5,000 pesos made by the latter company was repaid, with interest, by the rental of fifteen emancipados at a rate of seventeen pesos per month.[31]

The railroads were created to serve the sugar industry. And after the novelty wore off and the number of pleasure riders decreased, the dependence of the companies on the plantations for their success became quite pronounced. In 1840, the then government-operated Güines Railroad reported a gross income of more than 346,000 pesons, of which fully 50 per cent came from passenger fares, and 23 per cent from the

30. Ibid., Estado, Esclavitud, leg. 8046(13), fol. 10.
31. Ibid., Ultramar, Presupuestos, leg. 3443: *Compañía del camino de hierro de Trinidad. Memoria que la junta directiva presenta . . . el día 2 Abril de 1862* [Pamphlet] (Havana: Impr. "La Antilla," 1862). One peso = $1 American, 1862 value.

freight charge for the transportation of sugar and sugar products.[32] By 1860, however, the railroad companies were getting the greater part of their income from serving the sugar estates. The Sagua Railroad Company, a private concern—as were all the other Cuban railroad companies—received more than 121,000 pesos out of an annual gross of 235,840 pesos from the transport of sugar and molasses, while passenger fares amounted to less than 50,000 pesos.[33] In the same year, the Cienfuegos–Villa Clara Railroad Company received nearly 50 per cent of its annual gross income from hauling sugar and molasses.[34] Many of the passenger fares came from the workers on the estates, and much of the remaining income of the railroad companies came from other services such as carrying firewood, lumber, machinery, and food for the plantations.

Railroads were also valuable within the boundaries of the sugar plantation. Small private lines, often using animal-drawn equipment, revolutionized the method of conveying the canes to the mills, and transportation within the factories. One team of oxen attached to a number of railway cars was far more effective than the former large heavy carts in pulling the canes in from the fields. With the elimination of the problem of getting the canes to the mills on time, a greater area could be planted, resulting in an overall increase in the size of sugar estates.

Rapid transportation of canes was vital to the economic operation of the estates. Canes delivered to the mills later than twenty-four hours after being cut yielded less sugar, since they would begin to ferment. A good crop yielded more molasses and less sugar if it were not delivered on time, and because sugar sold at a far higher price than molasses on the market, there was, understandably, a keen desire to get the most sugar possible from a harvest of canes.

In order to take full advantage of the facilities of the railroads, however, all the land on an estate had to be fairly level. This was not a major problem in western Cuba. Justo Cantero, in speaking of the great ingenios of Cuba in the mid-nineteenth century, frequently empha-

32. Ibid., leg. 33: "Contaduría de la Real Junta de Fomento. Camino de Hierro."

33. Ibid., Presupuestos, leg. 3443: "Memoria del Ferrocarril de Sagua la Grande. . . . Estado general de sus productos y gastos en el año que termina 31.12.1860."

34. Ibid.: "Ferrocarril entre Cienfuegos y Villa Clara. Estado de sus productos y gastos en el año social que termina en 31 de Octubre de 1860."

sized the usefulness and economy of the railroads.[35] He noted that farms derived their values principally from "the number of Negroes and animals, the quality of its buildings, and its accessibility to the sea or railroad." He commented that Julian Zulueta's ingenio, Alava, situated in Cárdenas, had three ox-drawn railroads running from the extreme ends of the plantation right up to the mills. The railroads of Alava permitted the ingenio to crush canes for a record 185 days in a milling crop-time of 190—a loss of only five days. "This demonstrates," continued Cantero, "how useful it would be for the other ingenios to construct similar railroads provided the cost of construction was not too great."[36] Cantero gives the impression, indeed, that many planters found the costs of railroad construction prohibitive.

The railroads were useful not only in the fields, but also within the factory complex. Narrow-gauge tracks connecting the various sections where parts of the process of sugar manufacture took place both facilitated the job of transportation, and displaced a number of slaves. For this reason, many factories had these internal railroads even though the surrounding fields did not have any. Two cases where the use of wheels helped relieve the task of the slaves a great deal were in transporting the hot cylinders from the boiling house to the purging house, and later, the drained sugars from the purging house to the drying house. Cristóbal Madan considered these jobs quite prejudicial to the health of the slaves. He thought that the railroads (and other mechanical improvements in the factory) were doubly advantageous in minimizing health hazards and at the same time leaving extra men free for duty elsewhere.[37] By 1850, most of the richer planters in Cuba, prompted by the economy in manpower, and confronted with a dwindling supply of increasingly expensive slaves, had installed railroads in their ingenios.[38]

But the real value of the railroads was not simply in transporting canes to the mill and sugar in the factory and to the wharves, thus relieving the burden of beasts and men; the revolutionary effect of the railroads extended to the very visual and practical organization of the

35. Cantero, *Los ingenios.*
36. Ibid.
37. [Cristóbal Madan], *Llamamiento de la isla de Cuba a la nación española* (New York: Hallet, 1854), pp. 27–33.
38. See Roland T. Ely, *Cuando reinaba su majestad el azucar* (Buenos Aires: Editorial Sudamericana, 1963), pp. 625–49; Samuel Hazard, *Cuba with Pen and Pencil* (Hartford, Conn.: Hartford Pub. Co., 1871), pp. 356–57.

ingenio. Before the introduction of the railroad, every ingenio had reserved a portion of its land in forests in order to supply fuel for the boiler houses to supplement the crushed, dried cane stalks frequently used. Usually, forests took up about one-quarter of the total land area of any well-organized ingenio. The cutting of wood had been an expensive and time-consuming part of the preseason preparation for sugar production.[39] But wood could be easily and quickly brought from outside by rail. Gradually, therefore, a decreasing proportion of estates was reserved for forests, and the center of the island took on the appearance of an endless sugar cane field, punctuated by small tickets.[40] Meanwhile, the railways received more and more income from transporting firewood and lumber for building the boxes in which the sugar was sent abroad. By 1860, the Cienfuegos–Villa Clara Railroad received more than 15,-000 pesos, or 6 per cent of its total income, from hauling wood—a contribution absent from the railroad calculations of the early 1840's.[41]

Railroads broke the magical formula of ingenio production based on a specific number of slaves and a certain acreage of cane. Since the canes could be transported from farther afield quickly and easily, it was no longer necessary to limit the acreage under cane. The impact of the railroads was truly revolutionary, especially in the significant contributions they made towards solving the problems of acute labor shortage, and their help in maximizing land use and minimizing production costs. Considering simple transportation costs alone, Manuel Moreno Fraginals has estimated that the Güines Railroad reduced the costs of shipping sugar by 70 per cent during the first year of its operation. In internal transportation, the railroads made feasible the production of more than 800 tons of sugar from estates of about 300 acres of sugar cane, and therefore of a conventional capacity of merely 300 tons. Indeed, the introduction of the railroad was the first major element of the industrial revolution which initiated the transformation of the Cuban conditions of sugar production.[42]

Railroads and steam power opened a new era for the Cuban sugar

39. *Cartilla práctica*, pp. 15, 94.

40. Moreno Fraginals, *El ingenio*, pp. 74–78; also Antonio C. Gallenga, *The Pearl of the Antilles* (London: Chapman & Hall, 1873), p. 93.

41. AHN, Ultramar, Presupuestos, leg. 3443: "Ferrocarril entre Cienfuegos y Villa Clara. . . . Estado. . . ."

42. Moreno Fraginals, *El ingenio*, pp. 71, 72.

industry. They not only made the old formula for production obsolete, but also enormously increased the capital requirements for founding an ingenio. After 1838, there developed a pattern which unmistakably signalled the conversion of the island into a one-crop economy. A new type of planter emerged, for it became increasingly difficult for the smaller producers to compete with the larger ones. The economical production of a plantation became two to three thousand tons, instead of the former optimum output of one hundred tons. The general reorgani-

TABLE 3
The Largest Sugar Estates in 1857

| Ingenio | Proprietor | Total acreage | Founded or reorganized |
|---------|-----------|---------------|------------------------|
| Flor de Cuba | Sr. Arrieta | 3,105.5 | 1838 |
| Purisima | | | |
| Concepción | Sra. de Pedroso y Herrera | 3,048.5 | 1847–51 |
| San Martín | "          "          " | 7,403.7 | 1851 |
| El Narciso | Count of Penalver | 3,618.0 | 1840 |
| El Progreso | Marquis of Arcas | 6,134.0 | 1845 |
| Alava | Julian Zulueta | 4,958.0 | 1845 |
| Sta. Teresa | Count of Fernandino | 2,948.0 | 1847 |
| Finguaro | Francisco Diago | 1,876.0 | 1839 |
| La Ponira | Fernando Diago | 2,512.5 | 1843 |
| Monserrate | Count of Santovenia | 1,172 in canes | 1847 |
| Armonía | Miguel Aldama and José Luis Alfonso | 2,479.0 | 1848 |
| Acaña | José Eusebio Alfonso | 1,608.0 | ren. 1840's |

Source: Cantero, *Los ingenios.* Conversion to acres by author.

zation of the industry was reflected in the fact that all the larger and more efficient sugar plantations in the nineteenth century—every one listed by Justo Cantero in 1857—were either founded or reorganized in the years immediately following the introduction of the railroads (see Table 3).[43]

Steam power, although perhaps secondary in effect to the railroads, was also very important. As steam-powered mills became more efficient, their popularity rapidly increased. Only 2.5 per cent of the 1,000 ingenios in Cuba in 1827 were steam-powered. In 1846, 19.8 per cent of the total of 1,422 used steam. By 1861, 70.8 per cent of the 1,365 ingenios used steam, while 29.0 per cent used animal force. At the same

43. Cantero, *Los ingenios.*

time, less than 1.0 per cent, or seven plantations, had water wheels to turn their mills.[44]

But the sugar revolution also changed the zones of production. The region around the capital city of Havana, which had the finance and port facilities, was the first to experience the dramatic effects of sugar monoculture. The sugar area moved swiftly into the coffee zone in the central provinces, and rapidly displaced the small tobacco farmers. Sugar production depended as much on cattle as it did on slave labor. Hence the sugar producers also became cattle ranchers.[45]

The disastrous hurricanes of 1844 and 1846, the increasing price of slaves, and the greater competition from Brazil all combined to depress the coffee plantations.[46] As coffee production declined, the sugar planters moved in to take over the land and slaves. Besides, some coffee planters changed over to sugar cane growing. According to official estimates, more than 38,000 slaves were transferred from *cafetales* to ingenios in the years before 1843.[47] By the third quarter of the nineteenth century, tobacco remained chiefly in the region of San Cristóbal and Pinar del Río, and throughout what constitutes the present province of Oriente. Coffee flourished throughout the eastern mountains, as well as the hills of Cienfuegos, while sugar covered the central plains in much the same way that it does today.

The agricultural production figures for 1861 clearly accentuate the great extent to which the Cuban economy depended upon plantation crops. Sugar and coffee combined amounted to more than 70 per cent of the total agricultural produce value of 110 million pesos. Tobacco, although not really a plantation crop in Cuba, accounted for a further 16 per cent.[48] The predominance of sugar was even further emphasized by the figures for land use in 1861: more than 25 per cent of the 80,-000 *caballerías* devoted to all types of cultivation was in sugar cane.[49]

44. Carlos Rebello, *Estados relativos a la producción azucarera de la isla de Cuba* (Havana: Impr. del Gobierno, 1860). Raul Cepero Bonilla, *Obras históricas* (Havana: Inst. de Historia, 1963), p. 31, has slightly different figures.

45. Moreno Fraginals, *El ingenio*, pp. 8–15.

46. Francisco Pérez de la Riva y Pons, *El café: Historia de su cultivo y explotación en Cuba* (Havana: Montero, 1944), pp. 68–75.

47. Robert R. Madden, *The Island of Cuba* (London: Gilpin, 1849), p. 191.

48. Jacobo de la Pezuela, *Diccionario geográfico, estádistico, histórico de la isla de Cuba* (4 vols.; Madrid: Mellado, 1863–66), 1:38–39.

49. One caballería equals about 33⅓ acres. These figures are taken from both Pezuela and Rebello. Ingenio farmlands accounted for an additional 38,689 caballerías of land, but since it is not known what proportion of this land was

The slave population followed the cultivation pattern. In 1871, the island's slave population, according to the official estimates, stood at 287,620, of which more than 80 per cent were in the rural areas.[50] But approximately 55 per cent of the rural slaves were in the four major sugar provinces of Colon, Matanzas, Santiago de Cuba, and Sagua la Grande. And one planter estimated that fully 50 per cent of the island's rural slaves were on the sugar estates in 1869.[51]

One result of the massive concentration on the production of sugar was that by the middle of the nineteenth century Cuba had been divided for all practical purposes into two distinct zones: the sugar area and the nonsugar area. Very roughly these two zones corresponded geographically and politically to the jurisdictional divisions of eastern and western Cuba. (See Map 1). Nevertheless, neither zone presented an aspect of undiluted homogeneity. Within either section were small areas where the population and the agriculture varied from the norm. Within the western division, Pinar del Río and San Cristóbal had a combined total of 3,347 tobacco vegas, when the entire sector had just 4,228 vegas.[52] Both divisions had only a combined total of 16 ingenios, when the total for the entire region was 1,167. Other divisions also revealed aspects of strong nonsugar economic bases, qualifying any attempt to portray western Cuba as a solid sugar belt. Yet so dependent on sugar was the economy of the region as a whole that the sugar planters dictated the political and economic direction not only of their own section, but the entire island. A combination of geography, geology, agriculture, and economics created the mutually reinforcing cleavages which made the west richer, more powerful, and more vulnerable to international conditions than the east. Because the number of slaves was so much larger and more necessary in the west, it became the bastion of the pro-slavery movement.

---

used for forests, pastures, or gardening, no proper figures can be given for the total percentage of cultivated land pertaining to the ingenios. Nevertheless, these figures strongly challenge the argument of Herbert S. Klein that Cuban society and economy in the later nineteenth century were not plantation-oriented (*Slavery in the Americas: A Comparative Study of Virginia and Cuba* [Chicago: University of Chicago Press, 1967], pp. 150–51).

50. *Cuba desde 1850 á 1873* . . . (Madrid: Impr. Nacional, 1873), pp. 154–55.

51. "Fragments of a letter addressed to a distinguished Party in May, 1869," pp. 3, 14, in José de Armas y Céspedes, *The Cuban Revolution: Notes from the Diary of a Cuban* (New York: n. p., 1869).

52. Pezuela, *Diccionario*, 1:38–39.

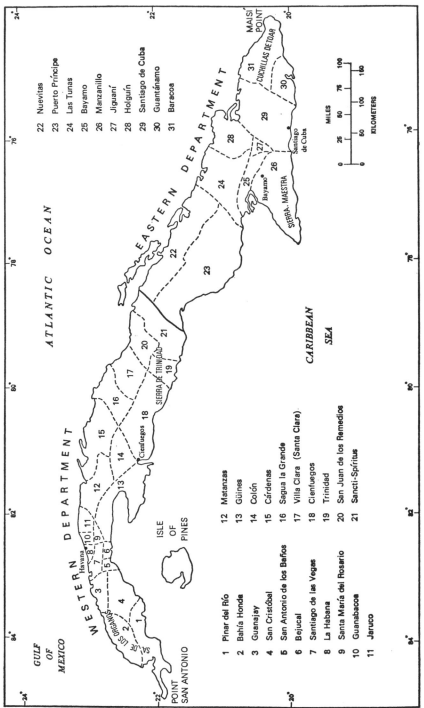

Map 1. Political Divisions in Cuba, 1860. Map Courtesy UW Cartographic Lab.

In many respects, eastern Cuba was the very opposite of the western sector. Except for the areas around Guantánamo and Santiago de Cuba, the area was mountainous, the soils were poor, the farms were small, and the economy was mixed.[53] But the east was not only inferior in population and economic resources, it was also different in outlook. Although the whites had slaves, they felt less attached to slavery than the large western planters, since their undertakings were generally much smaller. Having less need for slaves, and having a proportionally larger group of free persons of color, the white farmers of the east exhibited a lesser degree of racism in the difficult years towards the end of the century. This area bears strong comparison with race relations in Puerto Rico and the nonplantation areas of Spanish America.

In the disruptive wars between the Cubans, it was not surprising that the two factions should polarize roughly along the lines of east and west. While each region exerted centripetal tendencies on the dwellers there, it had a nearly opposite effect on those of the other region. And the individual regionalism could only be overcome by some transcendental emotional force. Cuban nationalism was one such force, as became clear during the Ten Years War.[54]

The sugar revolution in Cuba radically changed the pattern of foreign trade. Although legal free trade began in 1817, the island's commerce was not affected very much, owing to its backward economy.[55] Furthermore, the general dislocation of international politics in the post-Napoleonic period afforded little opportunity for the Spanish colony to compete for outside capital with the more attractive, recently independent Latin American countries. But toward the middle of the nineteenth century the rise of the sugar industry not only boosted foreign trade, but also made the island an important area for investors from abroad (see Table 4).[56]

As Cuban foreign trade increased in the nineteenth century, the United States played an increasingly important role in Cuban economic

53. Ramiro Guerra y Sanchez, *Guerra de los diez años 1868–1878* (Havana: Cultural, 1950), pp. 1–16.

54. Emilio Roig de Leuchsenring, *La guerra libertadora cubana de los treinta años, 1868–1898* (Havana: Oficina del Historiador de la ciudad de la Habana, 1952). It should be added that the success of the Cuban effort was closely bound up with international politics, which lie outside the scope of this work.

55. García de Arboleya, *Manual*, p. 233.

56. Grupo Cubano de Investigaciones Económicas, *A Study on Cuba* (Florida: University of Miami Press, 1963), pp. 130–31.

affairs. Partly owing to geographic proximity, but far more on account of its large merchant marine, its sturdy economy, and its huge domestic consumption of sugar, the United States steadily displaced Britain and Spain as the leading Cuban trading partner. In 1859, Cuba conducted 41.9 per cent of its foreign trade with the United States, 25.0 per cent with Great Britain, and 12.0 per cent with Spain. In 1864, the respective totals were 35.94 per cent, 22.52 per cent, and 19.48 per cent.[57] Later,

TABLE 4

Cuban Foreign Trade and Sugar Production, 1830–64

| Years | Average imports* | Average exports* | Sugar output† |
|-------|------------------|------------------|---------------|
| 1830–35 | 16.3 | 13.2 | 128 |
| 1836–40 | 24.0 | 20.4 | 150 |
| 1841–45 | 24.0 | 23.4 | 162 |
| 1846–50 | 23.0 | 25.0 | 200 |
| 1851–55 | 30.5 | 31.5 | 321 |
| 1856–60 | 37.6 | 42.2 | 415 |
| 1861–64 | 44.3 | 57.0 | 513 |

* In millions of pesos.
† In hundred thousand long tons.
Sources: Friedlaender, *Historia económica de Cuba*, pp. 545–47. Deerr, *The History of Sugar*, 2:131.

as the number of world sugar producers increased, and the European nations closed their markets to Cuban sugar cane in order to promote their domestic beet industries, the United States assumed an even more prominent role in Cuban trade. In 1865, Cuba exported 65 per cent of its sugar to the United States while only 3 per cent went to its metropolis, Spain.[58] In 1877, 82.0 per cent of all Cuban exports went to the United States, 5.7 per cent went to Spain, 4.4 per cent to Great Britain.[59]

That the United States should become Cuba's closest trading partner was not surprising. It was the eventual result of the Cuban one-crop economy. Having very little to offer besides sugar, the Cubans were

57. Cepero Bonilla, *Obras,* p. 103.
58. Herminio Portell Vilá, *Historia de Cuba en sus relaciones con los Estados Unidos y España* (4 vols.; Havana: Montero, 1939), 2:180. The remaining 7.9% of the trade was with France, Denmark, and the Latin American Republics.
59. Cepero Bonilla, *Obras,* p. 105.

hardly in a position to exercise any choice in this direction.[60] As Justo Cantero suggested, the United States was the second largest consumer of sugar in the world (after Great Britain), with the fastest rising population; even more significant was the gap between production and consumption in the United States—nearly 500 million pounds in 1855.[61] British consumption, on the other hand, was already completely satisfied from Britain's own sugar-producing colonies.

Within Cuba, the devotion to sugar production left little time or labor force to supply food requirements. In any event, the Cubans found it easier and cheaper to import their food from abroad. Almost all the flour, codfish, and food and clothing for the slaves came from the United States.[62] Machines, machine parts, and rolling stock for the railroads came from the foreign countries that made them: the United States, France, Britain, and Germany. Cubans, therefore, showed great interest in the business and commerce of the wider world, with which they were closely related and from which they suffered the usual business repercussions.

The historical importance of the sugar revolution lay in its all-pervading effect on the structure of Cuban society and economy. In social mattters, this revolution made possible the emergence of a new class—the slavocracy, which replaced the existing elite group, and had the further political effect of subordinating the bureaucracy and old-line Spanish-born residents to a new moneyed class of planters and merchants (see chapter 5). This new class was represented by men of the caliber of Julian Zulueta, Juan Poey, the Aldama brothers, Miguel and Domingo, and the new aristocrats who bought their titles toward the end of the eighteenth century. The agricultural revolution increased the African element in the population to a majority (albeit for a brief

60. García de Arboleya, *Manual,* p. 238, gives this breakdown of Cuban exports in 1855:

| | |
|---|---|
| Sugar and sugar products | 83.78% |
| Tobacco | 7.35 |
| Copper | 3.45 |
| Coffee | 1.85 |
| Timber | 1.53 |
| Beeswax | 0.80 |
| Honey | 0.25 |
| Fruits | 0.28 |
| Animal products | 0.71 |

61. Cantero, *Los Ingenios.*
62. Ely, *Cuando reinaba, passim,* and Grupo, *Cuba,* esp. part II.

period of time); it promoted plantation crops and destroyed the basis for small farm operation in most of the western part of the island. Sugar and coffee were export crops, and since Spain could not absorb the increasingly high yield of the Cuban producers, the long-term effect was the reorientation of the patterns of Cuban export trade. For the first time in its history, Cuban commerce was intrinsically connected with foreign capitalism—a connection which outlived and, indeed, eroded the colony's metropolitan connections.

# 3

# The Cuban Slave Trade, 1838–1865

*The end of the trade in bozales would create
and has created a vacuum which cannot be filled
either by the white immigrants, because of
climate; or the promoted marriage of the blacks,
owing to sexual imbalance*

Confidential letter of Captain-General O'Donnell
to Minister of State and Overseas Colonies,
February 15, 1845.

THE CUBAN SLAVE TRADE was a small part of the wider international operation through which Africans came to the New World.[1] The Africans came unwillingly, as the victims of unfortunate circumstances which they did not understand. Responding to the demands of war and trade, some Africans sold other Africans to European traders, who later resold their human cargoes in the far-away lands. After the long sea voyage, those Africans who arrived in the New World found themselves among strange peoples, strange languages, and new occupations.[2] A less unfortunate few found their way into domestic service, but those were almost entirely females. Others became traders or semiskilled

1. The best authority, by far, on the transatlantic slave trade is Philip D. Curtin, *The Atlantic Slave Trade: A Census* (Madison: University of Wisconsin Press, 1969); for Cuba see esp. pp. 30–45, 243–49. Other popular accounts are Basil Davidson, *Black Mother: The Years of the African Slave Trade* (Boston: Little, Brown, 1961); and Daniel P. Mannix and Malcolm Cowley, *Black Cargoes: A History of the Atlantic Slave Trade, 1518–1865* (New York: Viking, 1962).
2. See A. Norman Klein, "West African Unfree Labor before and after the Rise of the Atlantic Slave Trade," in Laura Foner and Eugene D. Genovese, eds., *Slavery in the New World: A Reader in Comparative History* (New Jersey: Prentice-Hall, 1969), pp. 87–95.

hired hands. But, particularly in the nineteenth century, about four out of every five slaves imported into the island of Cuba ended up on the plantations and rural farms away from the growing cities.[3] This high proportion, it must be pointed out, clearly refutes the assumptions of some that only a minority of Cuban slaves were on the estates.

The new Africans, or *bozales,* ended up on the estates for two principal reasons: there the greatest demand for workers existed; and there they could most easily be adapted. For not being able to speak or understand Spanish, the bozales performed best jobs where they could be constantly supervised. Obviously they could not handle the urban chores adequately. By the second generation, however, the acculturated Afro-Cuban was competent to move to the cities, and to assume tasks demanding less constant supervision. As a general rule, therefore, the rural slaves were predominantly bozales, while the urban slaves were criollos. Besides, the plantations—and to a lesser extent, the mines— were the areas of greatest labor demand throughout the centuries. Plantations and mines, therefore, tended to be the areas where the labor force was less mobile, and where the laborers were mainly slaves.

Most slaves in the New World originally came from the west coast of Africa, behind the region of indented coastline stretching from the mouth of the Senegal River to the territory which today (1970) roughly corresponds to the Portuguese colony of Angola. The vast majority of the slaves who came to the New World during the nineteenth century, however, came from the coastal region running from the Bight of Benin to the Bight of Biafra—from the present state of Togo in the west to Cameroon in the east.[4] But all along the coast, the European merchants and traders set up small forts and factories overlooking stockades or barracoons, and conducted their commerce, often chiefly in living human cargoes, for more than three centuries. The coastal factories and barracoons in which traders congregated the slaves prior to their transshipment to the Americas formed the overlapping point in two systems of trade, and continued to do so until the British moved in to abolish their part of the trade after 1807.[5]

3. Statistical evidence shows that more than 80% of the slaves were in the rural areas. See AHN, Ultramar, Esclavitud, legs. 3553, 3554.

4. See Philip D. Curtin and Jan Vansina, "Sources of the Nineteenth Century Atlantic Slave Trade," *Journal of African History,* 5 (1964), 185–208.

5. Christopher Lloyd, *The Navy and the Slave Trade* (London: Longmans, Green, 1949); and William L. Mathieson, *Great Britain and the Slave Trade, 1839–1865* (London: Longmans, Green, 1929). The figures in Lloyd correspond in many instances with Spanish official compilations.

One system of trade involved the Europeans. Some were primarily interested in obtaining slaves for resale in the American markets. These slave ships usually started their missions from European ports, loaded with European manufactured goods. On their arrival along the African coast, they sold or exchanged their cargoes for slaves, and set sail for the New World, where they sold or exchanged the slaves for cash, bills of credit drawn on European houses, or, in times of uncertainty, for tropical staples, especially sugar, tobacco, cotton, and hides. The return trip for a slave ship took anytime from ten to twenty months. Other Europeans traded along the African coast solely for the purpose of selling and receiving goods of mutual interest to Africans and Europeans—just as some Europeans traded with the American territories without actually dealing in slaves. The trade which linked the west coast of Africa with the lands across the Atlantic followed such a shifting, complex pattern that to describe it as a "triangular trade" is the grossest simplification of the historical reality.[6]

The other system of trade involved the Africans who exchanged their fellow men (often the unfortunate victims of local wars) for guns, gunpowder, tobacco, iron bars, rum, and cotton cloths brought by the Europeans and Americans. The exigencies of the trade resulted in severe dislocations within the structure of African communities and their legal systems, but that subject is peripheral to the transatlantic aspect of the trade that is my main concern. What is important, however, is to point out that the trade shifted as the areas of supply gradually diminished to be replaced by other areas elsewhere along the coast, or further into the interior. And by the nineteenth century, other factors which were not primarily demographic had already begun to influence the nature and conduct of the slave trade. The volume and areas of the trade began to respond to the Fulani jihad in West Africa, as well as to the attempts by Great Britain to intercept and eliminate the trade by placing naval squadrons along the African coast north of the equator before 1839, and all along the coast after that date.

The attempts of the British government to end the trade must be

---

6. For authoritative refutations of the old versions of the "triangular trade" see J. E. Merritt, "The Triangular Trade," *Business History*, 3 (1960), 1–7; Gary M. Walton, "New Evidence on Colonial Commerce," *Journal of Economic History* 28 (1968), 363–89; or Merrill Jensen, ed., *English Historical Documents, IX. American Colonial Documents to 1776* (Oxford: Eyre & Spottiswoode, 1964), esp. pp. 376–89. By the nineteenth century, of course, there was no semblance of any triangular connection. Most Cuban commercial contacts were geographically bilateral.

seen against the activity of the English abolitionists, who applied a peculiar pressure on the government to put an effective end to that commerce anywhere it existed. From the last decades of the eighteenth century, anti-slave-trade sentiment had been growing stronger in Europe and America. By 1814, Denmark, Sweden, the United States, and Great Britain had already abolished the trade among their nationals. During the twilight of the Napoleonic wars, the British abolitionists concentrated upon an effort to impress upon the allied powers the need to include a strong commitment to end the slave trade in the period after the wars, and they kept up the pressure until 1822.[7] As Betty Fladeland points out in her admirable review of the diplomatic history of the period, the abolitionists managed to persuade the British delegation to the Congress of Vienna, and by November, 1815, the French had reluctantly agreed to abolish the trade to their colonies, and even incorporated this decision into the Second Treaty of Paris.[8] The relative success at Vienna and Paris led to increased pressure by the group to convince the British government that Spain and Portugal, even though they conducted the trade south of the equator, offered a flag under which other nationals could conveniently transport slaves to the New World. These adamant abolitionists, therefore, were key elements in the treaty agreements arrived at with Spain and Portugal in 1817, setting a time to end the slave trade to the Spanish Antilles and Brazil.[9]

Yet as long as Africa had the manpower, and as long as a demand existed in the Americas, particularly in Cuba and Brazil, the transatlantic slave trade would continue, and did continue. Indeed, the Brazilians, especially from the Rio de Janeiro region, continued to demand large numbers of Africans until the 1850's, and the trade to Cuba continued rather strongly and stubbornly until the middle of the 1860's. The continuation of the trade to Cuba was, of course, the result of a series of interrelated circumstances. The most important factor, however, was the sugar revolution currently under way in the island. The intensive cultivation of the sugar cane that had started in Cuba early in the nineteenth century had not been accompanied by improvement in the manufacturing process of sugar production, and the old formula of increased manpower came into operation. For a number of reasons—not the least

7. Betty Fladeland, "Abolitionist Pressures on the Concert of Europe, 1814–1822," *Journal of Modern History*, 38 (1966), 355–73.

8. Ibid., p. 366.

9. Ibid., p. 367.

of which was the insufficiency of European migrants, who, when they came, had the idea of being landed proprietors themselves, contrary to the interests of the sugar cane planters—Africa remained the most reliable source of plantation laborers of the type demanded by the planters of Cuba.[10] The sugar revolution and the slave trade with Africa became interconnected in Cuban history as they had in the history of all the sugar-producing colonies of the Caribbean area. The experience of Barbados, Jamaica, and St. Domingue found a belated parallel in the agricultural development of Cuba. Nevertheless, the pattern was not to be simple in the Cuban case.

Three factors strongly influenced the Cuban slave trade: British diplomatic activity and naval interceptions off the African coast and around the island itself; the attitude and personal character of the local governors and captains-general; and the fluctuating labor demand based on a combination of external and internal factors, especially the price of sugar and the availability of slaves in either Africa or Cuba.

The impact of British political activity on the Cuban slave trade cannot be accurately assessed. British politicians, particularly after the 1830's, consistently appealed to the Spanish government to declare participation of Spanish subjects in the slave trade to be equivalent to piracy. Eventually, the British succeeded in forcing the Spanish to adopt a series of measures affecting the trade (see chapter 7). British squadrons cruising off the coast of Africa or around the island of Cuba had two effects. On the one hand, they intercepted and confiscated ships involved in the trade, and turned them over for adjudication to the courts of Mixed Commission established either in Havana or Sierra Leone. On the other hand, naval activity increased the risks and the costs of sending an expedition to Africa to get slaves.[11] But Cuban ships still continued to go to Africa for slaves regardless of the action taken by the British. At first the Cubans evaded the British cruisers by flying foreign flags or by getting their Africans from south of the equator, outside the effective patrol off the African coast. Moreover, until 1839, the Portuguese could legally conduct the trade south of the equator.[12]

---

10. On European population movements of the period, see William Woodruff, *Impact of Western Man: A Study of Europe's Role in the World Economy, 1750–1960* (New York: St. Martin's, 1967), pp. 60–100.

11. See Appendix I, Statistics of Cuban Slave Ships Captured off the Island of Cuba, 1824–66.

12. Curtin, *Atlantic Slave Trade,* pp. 231–33.

Gradually, treaties between Britain and France (1831), Spain (1835), and Portugal (1839), left only the American flags as a useful disguise. Increased squardron activity south of the equator after 1839 made the acquisition of slaves even more hazardous and expensive, and the Cubans finally resorted to getting their slaves from as far away as the Portuguese colony of Angola, and directly from Brazil, which still had a legal slave trade crossing the Atlantic until 1845.[13]

But the cruisers attempting to intercept slave ships in the Caribbean faced formidable handicaps. For one thing, the Cuban shoreline was long, and pitted with innumerable bays and coves in which slave ships easily hid and discharged their cargoes. For another thing, the vessels engaged in such enterprise were usually very fast, and when they used the flag of the United States were often indistinguishable from traders dealing in legitimate commerce. Furthermore, the general population of the island, dominated by the planters and merchants, connived in the trade and actively sabotaged attempts at legal investigation of suspicious activities.[14] Contrary to at least one official report, it seems unlikely that the temporary withdrawal of the squadrons from the African coast, as occurred during the Crimean war in 1853–54, led to a temporary increase in the trade.[15] Moreover, as soon as the Spanish government assumed the responsibility for patrolling the area around the island and paid ransoms for each ship captured after the mid-1850's, the number of naval interceptions increased noticeably (see Table 5).

On the local side, the attitudes of the higher Spanish officials in Cuba also affected the operation of the trade: some officials were in favor of the trade, others vigorously opposed it. The energetic attempts of some governors, particulary Gerónimo Valdés in the early 1840's, and José de la Concha and Juan Manuel González de la Pezuela y Ceballos, Marquis of Pezuela, in the 1850's, may have discouraged the more timid participants in the slave trade. But many other captains-general

13. Hugh G. Soulsby, *The Right of Search and the Slave Trade in Anglo-American Relations, 1814–1862* (Baltimore: Johns Hopkins Press, 1933), pp. 46–48. Also AHN, Estado, Esclavitud, leg. 8045: Henry Southern, Rio de Janeiro, to Palmerston, Jan. 10, 1852.

14. Joseph Liggins and James Kennedy before the Select Committee on Slave Trade Treaties, House of Commons, July 26, 1853. See *Parliamentary Papers, Reports,* vol. 419, nos. 1255–59. Also see AHN, Ultramar, Esclavitud, leg. 3548, fol. 28/22: Quesada al Consejo de Ultramar, Aug. 23, 1853.

15. AHN, Estado, Esclavitud, leg. 8045(12), fol. 11: Howden to Alcoy, Feb. 11, 1853.

were either indifferent, or actual participants. The most notorious official in this respect was Captain-General Leopoldo O'Donnell, who succeeded Valdés in 1842, and was reputed to have made a small personal fortune from the slave trade.[16] No official in Cuba, however, confronted with the general conditions prevalent there in the middle of the nineteenth century, could do much to end the trade. The higher officials in Cuba joined with the large planters, since they could not override the latter's wishes. When Captain-General Valentin Cañedo seemed to have followed the example of his predecessor, O'Donnell, the British ambassador in Madrid, Lord Howden, protested vigorously

TABLE 5

The Slave Trade, 1835–64

| Period | Slaves imported | Captured | % of total import | No. of interceptions | Average captured per interception |
|---|---|---|---|---|---|
| 1835–40 | 165,000 | 3,362 | 2.0 | 12 | 280 |
| 1841–45 | 34,357 | 1,202 | 3.5 | 10 | 120 |
| 1846–50 | 15,000 | 532 | 3.5 | 5 | 106 |
| 1851–55 | 33,232 | 3,822 | 11.5 | 21 | 182 |
| 1856–60 | 90,095 | 6,209 | 6.8 | 22 | 282 |
| 1861–64 | 49,532 | 4,967 | 10.0 | 13 | 382 |
| Total | 387,216 | 20,094 | | 83 | |
| Annual average | 12,908 | 670 | 5.0 | 2.7 | 24.2 |

Sources: Lloyd, *The Navy and the Slave Trade*, pp. 275–76. AHN, Ultramar, Esclavitud, legs. 3547, 3549, 3552, 3553.

to the Spanish minister of state, Count Alcoy, that the slave trade had doubled and as a result anti-Spanish sentiments in England had increased.[17] Lord Howden's accusation, however, should not be taken too seriously. The slave trade to Cuba depended on many factors, local as well as international, and certainly responded to greater pressures than the efforts of any captain-general. Cañedo may have been negligent in his duties but he did not have the resources to combat the planters and merchants in Cuba who wanted slaves and would do almost anything to get them. Nevertheless, the British were enthusiastic about the cessation of the slave trade, and Lord Howden's protest contained an implicit threat that Great Britain would probably acquiesce in the transfer of Cuba to any other national power if by so doing slavery in the island

16. Ibid., leg. 8040: Kennedy and Crawford to Aberdeen, 1845.
17. Ibid., leg. 8045(12), fol. 11: Howden to Alcoy, Feb. 7, 1853.

would be abolished. The Spanish government, which was extremely sensitive about losing its richest colony, became even more apprehensive when *The Times* of London echoed the sentiments of the government, and put all the blame for the continuation of the slave trade solely on the collusion of the Spanish authorities in Cuba.[18] For Spanish policy in Cuba, 1853 was a very bad year.

The underlying causes of the fluctuation in the volume of the trade, however, rested neither in the efficiency of the English cruisers in capturing slave ships, nor the inefficiency of the Spanish authorities in enforcing the letter of the laws and treaties. In any case, the Spanish government made a determined attempt to end the trade after 1850. But the slave trade continued as long as the system of slavery was accepted as the best way by which the Cubans could obtain and organize their laborers at a time when the island was undergoing a massive intensification of agricultural activity. In the significant absence of a depressed working class, the planters had no other way of replacing the enslaved workers who failed to reproduce themselves sufficiently, or to satisfy the need created by the unexpected afflictions of diseases and natural disasters. The planters had no other way, that is, which could be applied without radically restructuring the social and economic base of the society. And that they were unwilling to do in the 1850's and early 1860's.

One of the interesting facets of the Cuban slave trade in the nineteenth century, and especially after the 1830's, was the rough correlation between the periods of high annual importation and the cycles of natural disasters. During 1833 and 1834, a severe cholera epidemic ravaged the island, and according to the official report of José García de Arboleya, left a racially integrated death toll of more than 30,000 persons.[19] During 1852 and 1853, a lethal combination of cholera and smallpox devastated the slave population of the western department.[20] Furthermore, a severe wave of yellow fever hit the island in 1858 and 1859, and caused many deaths among all elements of the population.[21] After these

18. Ibid., leg. 8047(14), fol. 2: *The Times,* Aug. 19, 1853.
19. José García de Arboleya, *Manual de la isla de Cuba* . . . (Havana: Impr. del Tiempo, 1859), p. 51. These figures appear to be excessive, but they are the only ones I have seen.
20. AHN, Estado, Esclavitud, leg. 8045: Crawford to Malmesbury, Jan. 29, 1853. See also Antonio de las Barras y Prado, *Memorias, La Habana a mediados del siglo XIX* (Madrid: Ciudad Lineal, 1925), p. 23.
21. Jacobo de la Pezuela y Lobo, *Diccionario geográfico, estadístico, histórico de la isla de Cuba* (4 vols.; Madrid: Mellado, 1863–66), 3:417–18.

visitations of pestilence, the planters naturally tried to recover their lost slaves by new importations (see Appendix I).

Apart from the diseases, the planters had to contend with the frequent disruptive forces of the tropical hurricanes which pass over the island on their way from the western Atlantic Ocean to the American mainland. Two very disastrous hurricanes occurred in 1844 and 1846.[22] While diseases usually reduced the total number of slaves, hurricanes had an additional effect: even though the loss of life may have been less than an epidemic, the destruction of buildings and farm crops and the general dislocation created added pressure on a labor force already considerably overtaxed. This pressure may have indirectly fostered slave-trading activities.

British officials and some members of Parliament tried to establish some connection between the price of sugar and the increase or decrease of the slave trade. Indeed, the argument was even used as an attack on the policy of free trade after 1846.[23] *The Times* of London tried to chart the relation between the price of sugar on the English market and the fluctuations of cruiser captures off the African coast.[24] The charts and calculations were almost useless since they revealed nothing about the principles of economics or the actual situation in Cuba that affected the trade in slaves. No direct relation can be established between the increase in the volume of slaves sold in the island of Cuba and the price of sugar. For one vital consideration was the amount of sugar which the Cubans sold elsewhere, not on the London market. Moreover, the trade obviously depended upon many different factors, internal as well as external.

One observation is in order. A general decrease in the price of sugar on the world market tended to result in an increase in the volume of production since the planters calculated that, all other factors being equal, a greater output could offset the effects of a lower price.[25] This attitude might have subsequently led to an increased demand for slaves to augment production, but I have no evidence to support this hypothesis. Cristóbal Madan, a rich planter from Havana, linked the fluctuations in the trade solely to the demand of the plantations. He asserted

22. Arboleya, *Manual*, pp. 56–57.

23. *Parliamentary Papers, Reports*, vol. 419 (1853), no. 290 (Liggins before the Select Committee), and nos. 1176–1207.

24. AHN, Estado, Esclavitud, leg. 8042(10), fol. 4: Clippings from *The Times* and *The Globe* of London, 1850.

25. Manuel Moreno Fraginals, *El ingenio* (Havana: Unesco, 1964), pp. 144–47.

that the trade continued only because there existed an acute shortage of labor, and doubted that it would be necessary after the island had built up a population of peasants and workers—a kind of "rural proletariat."[26] Meanwhile, the trade got the support of the rich and politically influential men in Cuba, Spain, and Brazil who continued to support the illegal expeditions to get Africans from the Cuban plantations. Indeed, so great was the desperation of some planters that they often fitted out a ship for a single trip across the Atlantic, destroying it on the completion of its successful mission in order to avoid detection.[27] Once the evidence of trading had been destroyed, the traders themselves were safe from legal indictment since the officials were strictly forbidden to enter the estates to remove suspected newly imported Africans.

In the long run, the Cuban slave trade ended less from the exertions of the Spanish officials than from the rapid deterioration of the conditions that had facilitated its continuation. Nevertheless, the efforts of Captains-General Francisco Serrano and Domingo Dulce should not be underestimated. During their terms of office in Havana, both men made vigorous attempts to abolish the trade and to prosecute the traders in Africans.[28] In 1865, Captain-General Dulce exiled to Spain the foremost Cuban slave trader and one of the greatest planters on the island, Julian Zulueta, and removed some subordinate officers suspected of complicity in the illegal trade.[29] But the real deathblow came from other sources. It would appear that the single most effective measure which destroyed the Cuban slave trade was the abolition of slavery in the United States and the withdrawal of the Americans from the slave trade after the Anglo-American treaty of 1862.[30]

Lincoln's Emancipation Proclamation of January 1, 1863, removed the strongest psychological defense for Cuban slavery. Cuban slaveholding society was left in the uncomfortable company of Brazil, alone of the numerous countries which had once thrived on sugar and slavery. Most Cuban planters realized that the abolition in the United States fore-

---

26. [Cristóbal Madan], *El trabajo libre y el libre cambio en Cuba* (Paris: n. p. 1864), pp. 6–7.

27. AHN, Estado, Esclavitud, leg. 8048, 1853.

28. AHN, Ultramar, Esclavitud, legs. 3547, 3549, and 3550.

29. Arthur F. Corwin, *Spain and the Abolition of Slavery in Cuba, 1817–1886* (Austin: University of Texas Press, 1967), pp. 145–50. A fuller treatment of the political factors influencing the Spanish action is given in chapter 7. Zulueta was exonerated on a legal technicality.

30. See Mathieson, *Britain and the Slave Trade*, pp. 173–83; Soulsby, *Right of Search*, pp. 172–76.

told a similar fate in their nearby island. Cristóbal Madan, who only a decade earlier had staunchly defended the position of the Cuban planters, wrote in 1864, with reference to the Lincoln declaration and the Civil War in the United States: "we consider with anxiety that the terrible events which are taking place at the moment in the United States mark clearly and unequivocally for them and for us the beginning of a new era."[31]

Once the United States flag was no longer available, and once the entire institution had been abolished on the North American mainland, it was only a question of time before slavery would have to be abolished in Cuba. The Cubans could no longer continue a trade which had been deplored by all the leading powers of the western world. Had they made the attempt, the telling force of economic restraints allied to the perseverance of diplomatic approaches would have combined to humble them, in the same way that the British Parliament had acted against its own sugar colonies in the West Indies in the 1820's and 1830's. Cubans had too much to lose by openly thwarting world opinion. But, in the final analysis, the Cubans did not have to even make the attempt. The Cuban trade ended abruptly, as dealers in African slaves, in Cuba as well as in Spain, shifted their interest to the equally remunerative "trade" in indentured Asian laborers. At long last, with the end of the trade in the middle 1860's, Spain could then turn its attention to the institution of slavery itself.

The final legislative measure on the slave trade was the new "law for the suppression and punishment of the slave trade," which passed the Spanish Cortes on July 9, 1866. The law did not equate participation in the trade with piracy, as the English had desired for so long, but it did define complicity more explicitly, and it imposed far more onerous fines and imprisonment on convicted offenders. It also ordered the death penalty for those persons who resisted arrest (a distinct possibility in Cuba at that time), and those whose cruelty resulted in the death of any slave. The law further insisted that a most careful census be made of all slaves, and that any "person of color" omitted should be declared to be a free person.[32] In this way the government began a direct assault on the practice of not registering illegally imported slaves.

31. Madan, *El trabajo libre*, p. 1.
32. AHN, Estado, Esclavitud, leg. 8049(16), 1: "Disposiciones sobre le Represión y Castigo del Tráfico Negrero, mandadas observar por Real decreto de 24 Sept. de 1866."

But the victory of the bureaucracy over the wealthy planters implied by such a strong measure was more apparent than real. The law of 1866 was practicable only because, for the first time, it did not result in any conflict between the state and the planters. For essentially the Cuban planters only wanted men to work in the sugar cane fields; they did not necessarily want those men to be slaves—merely in servile conditions. After 1861, the importation of Asian coolies began to remedy the labor shortage; Africans at last became dispensable. Nevertheless, the end of the African slave trade was a significant advance toward the end of legal slavery in the island of Cuba.

The history of the Cuban slave trade in the nineteenth century is an account of the experience of a society caught midway between the transition from an essentially preplantation society to a modernized, industrialized sugar-plantation economy. As long as sugar production remained basically dependent on large numbers of unskilled or semi-skilled laborers, the producers needed continuous supplies from Africa. As far as the planters were concerned, slavery was the most efficacious way of organizing labor, especially at the times when it was most needed. Slavery, moreover, reduced the competition for scarce laborers, and permitted the planter to secure the services of those he had "broken" into the technique of sugar production. And no other source could effectively compete with Africa in supplying men who could be made slaves at that time.

# 4

# Slavery in a Plantation Society

*With twenty hours of unremitting toil,*
*Twelve in the field, and eight indoors to boil,*
*Or grind the cane—believe me few grow old,*
*But life is cheap, and Sugar, Sir!—is gold.*

R. R. Madden, *Poems by a Slave*, p. 45.

CUBAN SLAVE SOCIETY, like any other slave society, was subdivided into castes and classes. The castes corresponded very roughly to the racial divisions in which membership was hereditary and defined by laws: the white population first, and then, in descending order of social rank, the free persons of color and the slaves. A class stratification characterized each caste. The term class is appropriate in this context, referring as it does to those who had a certain degree of social mobility, and whose status and position were not necessarily either heritable or legally prescribed. This combination of caste and class provided a certain stability to the society by allowing a dynamism within the separate classes of each racial group, while retaining and constraining the various elements within the castes.

The two classes within the slave caste were the urban and domestic, and the field slaves. Arriving Africans joined either of these two classes. But the number of domestic and urban slaves in the nineteenth century was relatively small, and the chance of a recent arrival finding his way into this group was extremely slim. A small minority of the slaves lived in the towns, where they were employed mainly as domestic servants, or in minor skills and simple professions (though these services formed an important economic function in the society as a whole). The vast majority of the Africans imported during the nineteenth century—more than 80 per cent of those brought in between 1840 and 1860—ended up working on the plantations of the interior. It was precisely this preponderance of rural slaves which made Cuban slave society in the nineteenth century a plantation society, and hence distinct from Cuban slavery in the earlier period. Urban slaves were the exceptions; urban slavery could not be considered the norm for the society. Yet many visitors to Cuba, and a great many historians of Cuban slavery from 1800 to the present have probably honestly, though nonetheless erroneously, based their opnions on Cuban slavery from a limited exposure to, or inference from, this type of urban slave conditions. Any attempt to generalize about Cuban slavery must bear in mind some important distinctions, and not the least of these is the separate environment of the two slave groups. The two classes were a world apart. Urban slaves had some unique opportunities and resources which their rural counterparts lacked or were denied. Moreover, the entire organization of urban and domestic slavery in Cuba, as in other parts of the world, lent itself to moderation and liberality. Some observers did compare and comment on the vast differences evident between the two types. Fernando Ortiz, with some degree of exaggeration, insisted that the conditions surrounding urban slaves were more closely comparable to the conditions of the master group than to the conditions of rural slaves.[1]

The urban slave enjoyed advantages denied his rural counterpart in three crucial areas: in the method of labor and participation in the cash economy; in social and sexual conduct; and in the available legal resources.[2]

Urban slaves fell into three large groups. Many were domestic helpers, with some women being wet nurses for the infants of the white people, and females in general dominating the domestic occupations. Many others conducted some specific occupation—coachmen, carpenters, dressmakers, gardeners, musicians—or small trade. A third group

1. Fernando Ortiz Fernández, *Hampa afro-cubana, los negros esclavos* (Havana: Revista Bimestre Cubana, 1916), p. 320.
2. Two historical novels which clearly exemplify the gulf between rural and urban slaves are Cirilo Villaverde, *Cecilia Valdés or Angel's Hill,* trans. Sydney G. Gest (New York: Vintage, 1962), first published in 1882; and Anselmo Suárez y Romero, *Francisco. El ingenio o las delicias del campo* (Havana: Ministro de Educación, 1947), written in the late 1840s, and originally published in 1880. The latter was the basis of accounts by Medden and Fernando Ortiz, and is often compared with *Uncle Tom's Cabin.*

hired out their labor either for their own gain, or for their master's.[3] No group, however, was entirely exclusive, and sometimes circumstances superseded preferences. Ortiz remarked that within the urban slave community during a certain period in the nineteenth century it was considered somewhat ignominious to be rented, as such a gesture indicated the poverty and low social position of the owners.[4]

Writers on slavery generally conceded that the urban slaves, regardless of their occupations, established an understanding and a relationship with their masters which was completely absent elsewhere. Not only was the life of slaves in the towns far less regimented, but also the opportunities to get cash enabled them to buy their freedom with relatively greater facility than rural slaves. Urban slaves also mixed with the free colored people, and escaped from their masters with greater ease.

With far more cash and far more freedom, the urban slave both fed and dressed himself better, and enjoyed himself more. Instead of the striped, coarse clothes and simple dress of the plantation slave, the urban slave was sometimes smartly—if uncomfortably—uniformed if he were a coachman or she a preferred domestic helper. Otherwise, the slaves in the city generally dressed in the style of the whites. In the towns, too, the slaves participated in a wide variety of common attractions, ranging from membership in an Afro-Cuban *cabildo,* or lodge, to dances and drinking in their *bodegas,* or taverns.[5] Such forms of entertainment took place with their friends of the same accepted "tribe," or their *carabelas*—their shipmates from Africa. Sexual union was facilitated by the consistently larger proportion of black women in the towns. Apart from this, sexual relations with the whites were common, and often rewarding for the black parties involved. For not only did the whites offer handsome material rewards in cash or other valuables which assisted in *coartación,* the method by which the slave gained his freedom, but also, albeit quite rarely, they gave their slaves freedom in their wills.[6]

3. Ortiz, *Negros esclavos,* pp. 307–13; Herbert S. Klein, *Slavery in the Americas: A Comparative Study of Virginia and Cuba* (Chicago: University of Chicago Press, 1967), pp. 145–51.

4. Ortiz, *Negros esclavos,* p. 313.

5. See Fernando Ortiz Fernández, "La fiesta afro-cubana del día de reyes," *Revista Bimestre Cubana,* 15 (1921), 5–26; and "Los cabildos afro-cubanos," ibid., 16 (1921), 5–39. See also Villaverde, *Cecilia Valdés.*

6. Ortiz, *Negros esclavos,* p. 312.

Legal stipulations had some meaning and effect in the towns. Urban slaves were aware of their legal rights and resources, and often resorted to them. If the relationship between a particular master and his slave broke down, then either party could effect the sale of the slave. In that case, the *síndico,* or protector of slaves, intervened to see that the slave's right to permission to seek a new master was observed.

The physical punishment possible in the rural areas was not necessary in the towns. Masters with troublesome slaves either sent them to the country or sold them. Besides, slaves were more expendable in the cities than they were in the fields.

Unfortunately the mitigating influences of the cities did not extend to the vast majority of Cuban slaves, who found themselves circumscribed by the regimented requirements of plantation agriculture. Planters usually bought slaves when they wanted them, and sold them when they thought that they were redundant. In the countryside—in sharp distinction from the towns—the practice of renting slaves was frowned upon as being uneconomical and *déclassé.*[7] As a result the avenues of mobility for the rural slaves were, naturally, far more limited, and depended upon special skills. Sometimes, however, a slave possessing a light skin color and a sympathetic character might win the affection or the goodwill of a kind master, with enormous benefits accuring as a consequence of this coincidence. Such slaves— the skilled and the loved— might then be transferred to the city from the farm, and in the course of time could gain their freedom through the accustomed urban avenues.[8]

Not surprisingly, the general tendency of the slave population before the end of the slave trade was for the number of urban slaves to decline steadily, while the rural slaves, constantly augmented from Africa, increased. Since the urban slaves had a higher birthrate than those in the fields, and since there is no evidence of massive transfer of slaves from the cities to the plantations, the decrease of urban slaves could perhaps be due to manumissions. On the other hand, the steady increase in rural slaves reflected the healthy state of the illegal slave trade. Nevertheless, the cessation of the trade after the mid-1860's brought a sharp increase in the proportion of urban slaves (see Table 6).

The official declaration of an end to the slave trade agreed upon by Britain and Spain for a second time in 1835 made it impossible to

7. *Cartilla práctica del manejo de ingenios* . . . (Irun: Impr. de la Elegancia, 1862), p. 94.
8. See Suárez y Romero, *Francisco.*

TABLE 6

Cuban Slave Population, 1855–57 and 1871

| Year* | Urban | % of all slaves | Rural | % of all slaves | Total slaves |
|---|---|---|---|---|---|
| 1855 | 70,691 | 19.0 | 304,115 | 81.0 | 374,806 |
| 1856 | 66,132 | 17.8 | 305,243 | 82.2 | 371,375 |
| 1857 | 65,610 | 17.5 | 307,375 | 82.5 | 376,899 |
| 1871 | 55,830 | 20.9 | 231,790 | 79.1 | 287,620 |

* All figures are for January.
Sources: Figures for 1855 to 1857 are taken from the capitation censuses found in AHN, Ultramar, Esclavitud, leg. 3551; for 1871, from *Cuba desde 1850 á 1873* (Madrid: Impr. Nacional, 1873), pp. 152–53.

continue the former system of large barracones or slave markets in the principal cities of the island. After the last barracón was destroyed in 1836, the arrival of slaves and their distribution took place clandestinely, often at night.[9] Traders called their slaves *piezas* (pieces), and divided them into three outstanding categories: "bozales," "ladinos," and "criollos."[10]

Bozales were raw Africans who could not speak Spanish. These were also called "negro de nación," a reference to their foreign origin. Traders referred to such Negroes between the ages of six and fourteen as *muleques;* and those between the ages of fourteen and eighteen as *mulecones.* Most traders, however, had no way of ascertaining the age of the slave, and resorted to physical appearance as the best index of age. Ladinos were slaves who, although foreign born, were baptized into the Roman Catholic faith, and could speak Spanish or Portuguese, or in some cases French. Criollos were slaves born in Cuba. On the markets, criollos fetched the highest prices, especially if they possessed certain skills, and were destined for city or domestic use. Until the end of the trade in the mid-1860's, bozales fetched an ever-increasing price owing to the high demand for them on the plantations.

Most rural slaves found themselves working on tobacco farms, coffee plantations, or sugar plantations. Rural life and conditions for the slaves were so far removed from city or great house conditions that banishment to the plantation was a frequent threat against recalcitrant slaves. David Turnbull reported that the most dreadful threat which the

9. Ortiz, *Negros esclavos,* p. 168, fn.
10. Ibid., pp. 171–73.

wealthy inhabitants of Havana used to terrify their delinquent domestic servants was the hint of sending them back to the plantation under the special charge of the *mayoral,* the supervisor of slaves.[11]

There was a general consensus that conditions of labor varied according to the nature of the agricultural enterprise. The tobacco farms were thought to offer the easiest life, followed by the coffee plantations, where the work was not very arduous. Life on the sugar plantations, however, was seen in Hobbesian terms as "nasty, brutish, and short." The life and conditions of any particular group of slaves depended, of course, on the personality of the master. Notwithstanding, two factors corresponded to make the labor and living conditions on the coffee and tobacco farms more favorable than on the sugar plantations. In the first place, the nature of the tasks differed and the need for regimentation was less: only sugar demanded a great number of workers who had to accomplish their tasks in a very important and specific period of time. In the second place, many white planters lived on their farms, and often worked with their slaves in tending and reaping the harvests of tobacco or coffee.

Traditionally, tobacco-growing in Cuba was a small, cash crop undertaking on small farms, just as it had been in the Eastern Caribbean islands in the early seventeenth century, before the sugar revolution there. In the areas where the tobacco thrived best, it was a meticulous culture, as lyrically described by Fernando Ortiz. Far from being an enormous, impersonal, capitalistic enterprise, it was essentially an activity dominated by the fastidious individualist:

> The best smoker looks for the best cigar, the best cigar for the best wrapper, the best wrapper for the best leaf, the best leaf for the best cultivation, the best cultivation for the best seed, the best seed for the best field. This is why tobacco-raising is such a meticulous affair, in contrast to cane, which demands little attention. The tobacco-grower has to tend his tobacco not by fields, not even by plants, but leaf by leaf. The good cultivation of good tobacco does not consist in having the plant give more leaves, but the best possible. In tobacco quality is the goal; in sugar, quantity. The ideal of the tobacco man, grower or manufacturer, is distinction, for his product to be in a class by itself, *the best.* For both sugar-grower and refiner, the aim is *the most.*[12]

11. David Turnbull, *Travels in the West. Cuba . . .* (London: Longman, Orme, Brown, Green, and Longmans, 1840), p. 51. Also Suárez y Romero, *Francisco.*
12. Fernando Ortiz Fernández, *Cuban Counterpoint: Tobacco and Sugar,* trans. Harriet de Onís (New York: Knopf, 1947), p. 24.

By the middle of the nineteenth century, tobacco-farming was an activity of free white and free colored people, with very little use of slave labor.[13] In reality, therefore, relatively few slaves participated in the delights of the vegas, compared to those on the sugar estates. In 1846, García de Arboleya claimed that only about 4,000 slaves, or 40 per cent of the total tobacco labor force, worked in urban tobacco concerns.[14] Although the author did not give the number of rural slaves engaged in cultivating tobacco, he pointed out that the tobacco haciendas were generally found along the banks of rivers, and that the total area of the farms seldom exceeded thirty-three acres, only one-half of which was in tobacco. Tobacco farms had, in addition to the dwelling house, a drying house for curing the tobacco leaves after they had been collected. The labor force varied between four and twenty workers, who were not always blacks, since that branch of agriculture was, above all others, "the chief concern of the whites."[15]

The principal tobacco-growing areas of Cuba were in Pinar del Río, San Cristóbal, Villa Clara, Manzanillo, Bayamo, Jiguaní, Santiago de Cuba, and Guantánamo. (See Map 2.) Confined to specific zones, the tobacco farms increased in number from 9,102 in 1846 to 9,482 in 1861, while the total value of tobacco products remained constant.[16] Quite probably, the number of vegas did not suffer marked fluctuations after 1846, because tobacco no longer competed with sugar cane either for land or manpower.

Coffee, unlike tobacco or sugar cane, grew best on shaded slopes. But coffee was successfully grown on the plains of central Cuba before it was displaced by the sugar cane, in the middle of the nineteenth century. After that, the coffee areas remained in the more hilly regions of Guanajay, San Antonio de los Baños, Cienfuegos, and Matanzas in the western department, and the mountains of Santiago de Cuba and Guantánamo in the eastern department.

Large-scale coffee cultivation in Cuba began with the arrival of the French refugees from St. Domingue. The plantations were modest in size, and carefully tended by a resident proprietor, who adorned the

13. See Jacobo de la Pezuela, *Diccionario geográfico, estadístico, histórico de la isla de Cuba* (4 vols.; Madrid: Mellado, 1863–66), 1:38–39.

14. José García de Arboleya, *Manual de la isla de Cuba* . . . (Havana: Impr. del Tiempo, 1859), p. 180.

15. Ibid., p. 142.

16. For 1846, ibid., p. 144; for 1861, Pezuela, *Diccionario,* pp. 38–39.

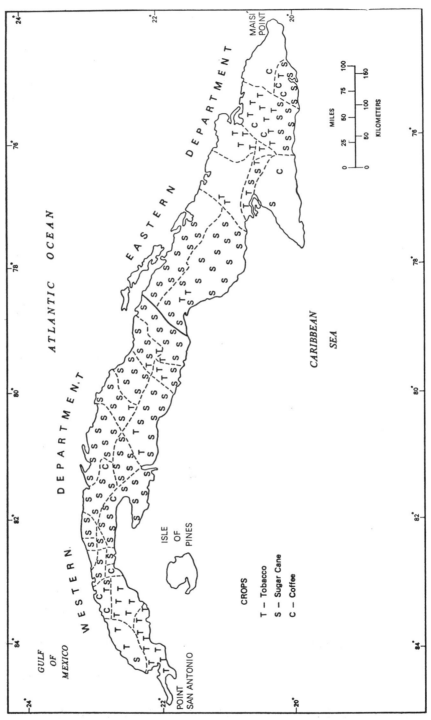

Map 2. Crop Distribution, 1861. Map Courtesy UW Cartographic Lab.

farms with exotic shade trees and valuable timber. The coffee plants grew to a height of six feet, and yielded their berries twice a year. So that the trees could be cleaned and the fruit gathered at harvest, wide wagon-trails intersected the plantation at regular distances, presenting the visual aspect of a charming garden—an idea continually in the mind of the coffee planter, who spent a very long time perfecting the picture of re-splendent beauty.[17]

When the coffee berries turned purple, they were collected, dried in the sun, and thrashed to separate the grain from the useless dried cuticle. It was not a very arduous job, and one in which females could be as adept as males. Slaves on coffee plantations did not suffer the sexual imbalance characteristic of the sugar plantations. Coffee cultivation, therefore, required no extraordinary capital outlay, no elaborate mechanical power, no large factories, and no specialized scientific knowledge beyond a simple familiarity with soils, plants, and cultivation.

In 1846, García de Arboleya stated that coffee plantations varied in size from four to twenty caballerías (133 to 666 acres), with a maximum labor force of one hundred slaves.[18] But a recent scholar of the Cuban coffee plantation, Francisco Pérez de la Riva, has pointed out that the average size of the cafetal by the later 1850's—the twilight of coffee cultivation in the island—was only eight caballerías (267 acres), employing forty slaves.[19] In short, the cafetal was the closest approximation to the cotton plantation of the United States southern belt.

Unlike the great sugar estates, coffee plantations, in common with all the other forms of small, rural, agricultural enterprises, also embodied large areas devoted to the growing of their own food crops, or the rearing of cattle and small stock used mainly for their domestic food supply. Almost all the land of the ingenio went into sugar cane or cattle, and the enormous size of its slave labor force made food importation both more desirable and more economical than domestic production.

By the late 1860's, nearly 50 per cent of all slaves in Cuba worked directly on the sugar estates, while a substantial proportion of the remainder were in some way involved in the sugar industry. And on some

17. Richard H. Dana, *To Cuba and Back: A Vacation Voyage,* new ed. (Carbondale: Southern Illinois University Press, 1966), p. 53. This book was first published in 1859.
18. Arboleya, *Manual,* pp. 140–41.
19. Francisco Pérez de la Riva, *El café: Historia de su cultivo y explotación en Cuba* (Havana: Montero, 1944), pp. 170–71.

sugar estates, the slave was considered as "little else than an item of labor raised or bought."[20] However different were the conditions outside the sugar industry, its economic influence was so great that the entire course of slavery was affected by the decisions of the sugar manufacturers.

The successful operation of the sugar plantation demanded a change in the treatment and operation of slave labor. As the size of slave gangs became larger, the slaves were more alienated from the traditional semi-extended family relationship. Apart from the change in treatment, the slaves saw and felt other physical alterations of their status. Large infirmaries became necessary to treat the real and pretended illnesses. The collection of individual huts gave way to long, connected barracks which the owners thought were more secure, since the two main doors could be locked at night.[21] The *conucos,* the small, slave-worked plots of land which had so long provided food for the hacienda and a source of private gain for the slaves themselves, gradually succumbed to economic necessity as the planters put more area under sugar cane and relied on imported flour, salt pork, and codfish to feed the laborers.[22] Naturally, therefore, the number of slave uprisings increased in the nineteenth century. And with the constant example of Haiti before them, the white planters responded with even more severe regimentation, as evidenced by the slave laws of 1842 (see Chapter 6).

The entire operation of a sugar estate was set out in a handbook written by a planter in Havana, and published in Spain in 1862. Called *Cartilla práctica del manejo de ingenios*—"practical handbook for the management of sugar estates"—it covered every aspect of sugar production: selection and required area of land, choice of cane, labor needs, and the advisability of renting laborers rather than contracting out the work in times of insufficient labor supply.

We have already seen that in Cuba, as elsewhere, the sugar industry was highly capitalized, with an inordinate need for land, slaves, and oxen. By the middle of the nineteenth century the most important planters aimed at an annual production of between 5,000 and 6,000 boxes of sugar, or a little more than 1,000 tons.[23] Cristóbal Madan, however,

20. Dana, *To Cuba,* p. 56.
21. *Cartilla práctica,* pp. 75–80.
22. Manuel Moreno Fraginals, *El ingenio* (Havana: Unesco, 1964), pp. 15–16. Of course, the conucos were never entirely abolished.
23. *Cartilla práctica,* p. 15.

thought the average size was a little less: "one of 4,000 boxes, which, while not one of the recent colossal factories, cannot be classified as small."[24] Production in this range demanded an acreage in excess of 3,000 acres, of which more than 1,300 acres were in sugar cane. Furthermore, the handbook stated that such an estate needed "a minimum of 317 slaves and 326 head of oxen."[25] To establish an estate of this sort would cost far more than $300,000, with annual maintenance costs being around $40,000, and net profits nearly $20,000 per year.[26]

The crucial role of labor in sugar production led to the wretched conditions of the slaves on the plantation. The Planter had to supervise his workers in such a way that he would have them at exactly the right time, as well as ensure maximum output.[27] Richard Dana reflected planter opinion when he wrote:

> The sugar estate is not valuable, like the coffee estate, for what the land will produce, aided by quiet manual labor only. Its value is in the skill, and the character of the labor. The land is there, and the Negroes are there, but the result is loss or gain, according to the amount of labor that can be obtained, and the skill with which the manual labor and the mechanical powers are applied.[28]

After the 1850's most large sugar estates employed a mixed group of laborers; free, wage-paid whites, indentured Asians, and slaves. The labor organization was hierarchical, corresponding to the racial divisions. Occupying the topmost administrative and skilled positions were the whites. Asians did the intermediate, semiskilled tasks. Slaves did unskilled, manual jobs.

Since most sugar estates had absentee proprietors—a characteristic common to all the Caribbean sugar islands—the operation and management of the estate devolved upon the *administrador* or overseer, who often lived in the palatial great house. Below the administrador was the mayoral, or supervisor of Negroes, and a boyero, a supervisor of animals. Other important white jobs regularly held were the *maestro de azúcar,* or boiling-house chief, noted more for his cooking ability and guesswork

---

24. [Cristóbal Madan], *Llamamiento de la isla de Cuba a la nación española* (New York: Hallet, 1854), p. 11.

25. *Cartilla práctica,* pp. 15–18, 46. I have converted the caballerías to acres, and rounded the figures. Madan gives a requirement of 300 slaves.

26. [Madan], *Llamamiento,* pp. 15–17. Prices are in U.S. dollars, 1854 value.

27. *Cartilla práctica,* pp. 31, 53–58.

28. Dana, *To Cuba,* pp. 54–55.

than for any knowledge of chemistry; the machinist, usually from Europe or the United States, and employed only for the crop-time season; and the *mayordomo,* or bookkeeper—a term applied in its most literal sense. Some estates had a part-time nurse or doctor, who paid periodical visits for an agreed sum of money.

Cristóbal Madan gave the following salaries for the white employees on a medium-sized estate at the middle of the nineteenth century:

| | |
|---|---|
| Overseer | $1,500 |
| Supervisor of Negroes | 600 |
| Supervisor of animals | 300 |
| Book-keeper | 408 |
| Nurse (part-time) | 240 |
| Doctor (part-time) | 300 |
| Maestro de azúcar and his assistant | 1,600 |
| Machinist for five months | 698.50[29] |

Apart from his basic salary the overseer enjoyed many additional perquisites, including an annual bonus, and unusually great opportunities for fraud and other means of private accumulation of wealth. With the exception of the machinist, and sometimes the maestro de azúcar, the other white people on the estates were locally recruited. In nineteenth-century Cuba, as two centuries before in Barbados and the other West Indian islands, the sugar revolution uprooted many small farmers, ranchers, and gardeners. In Cuba, these were absorbed into the labor force of the ingenios, and even dockyard workers, foundry workers, and other small artisans of the urban areas like Bejucal and Santiago followed suit—sometimes under pressure, sometimes attracted by the higher wages. The slaves suffered indirectly from the displacement of these small poor farmers: many of the *guajiros* (landless whites) developed a strong racial prejudice which they vented in severe punishments for simple misdemeanors, or brutal hunting excursions after runaways.[30]

29. [Madan], *Llamamiento,* p. 12.

30. Roland T. Ely, *Cuando reinaba su majestad el azúcar* (Buenos Aires: Ed. Sudamericana, 1963), pp. 464–72; Moreno Fraginals, *El ingenio,* p. 8; Samuel Hazard, *Cuba with Pen and Pencil* (Hartford, Conn.: Hartford Pub. Co., 1871), pp. 352–71. For comparisons with the West Indies see J. H. Parry and P. M. Sherlock, *A Short History of the West Indies* (London: Macmillan, 1957), chapter 5. Most travel books on Cuba at this time included extensive references to the white workers on the sugar estates. Dana, *To Cuba,* pp. 60–64, is the best, but see also Demoticus Philalethes [pseud.], *Yankee Travels through the Island of*

The Asians, who bridged the gap between black and white, assisted the slaves in the field and in the factories. Unlike the slaves, however, they did simple semiskilled jobs, and handled some machines.[31] Although the Asians were classified as whites, their conditions of labor tended to be identical to those of slaves. Antonio Gallenga asserted that on the few estates with an all-Asian labor force the organization and working conditions were identical to the slave-worked estates.[32]

An American visitor to Cuba in 1853 expressed the opinion that Chinese would eventually "occupy the place of the Negroes in all agricultural districts."[33] The Cubans did not seem to share that opinion. Some planters thought the Chinese a poor substitute for Negro slave labor, but admitted that they were an indispensable link in the transition from slavery to free labor if sugar production was not to be seriously disrupted. Other planters thought that the importation of the Chinese should be discontinued as they only further complicated the racial problem on the island.[34]

Both indentured laborers and slaves fell into the subordinate group of "purchased" labor, a cardinal point of calculation in the value of any estate.[35] Slaves did any kind of job in the process of sugar manufacture leading up to the machine-performed tasks, and then on afterwards.[36] Some black men became *contramayorales* or assistants to the whites, an extremely prestigious position for any slave, and one which carried some authority with it.[37]

The regimentation of the slavery system and of the system of indenture in Cuba was a logical outgrowth of the process of sugar production. It was, in fact, the most simple form of labor organization for a process

*Cuba* (New York: Appleton, 1856), pp. 33–36. For evidence of increased racial prejudice, see José J. Ribó, *Historia de los voluntarios cubanos* (2 vols.; Madrid: González, 1872), 1:21–23.

31. Moreno Fraginals, *El ingenio*, p. 118.

32. Antonio C. Gallenga, *The Pearl of the Antilles* (London: Chapman & Hall, 1873), pp. 127–28.

33. Philalethes, *Yankee Travels*, p. 75.

34. AHN, Ultramar, Esclavitud, leg. 3550: *El Correo de España*, Sept. 13–27, 1863.

35. Justo German Cantero, *Los ingenios* . . . (Havana: Marquier, 1857).

36. Moreno Fraginals, *El ingenio*, p. 118. Richard H. Dana visited an estate, however, on which one free person of color was trained to operate the machines so that he could relieve the white machinist at night. This was the highest position to which a free colored person could rise on any plantation.

37. *Cartilla práctica*, pp. 43–46.

which had extremely unbalanced labor requirements, especially in a situation of great labor scarcity. To ensure sufficient manpower for harvest, the planter had to buy and keep his slaves throughout the year. Once he had bought them and had to maintain them, it was judicious to keep them fully occupied. That was easy during the hectic months of harvest between late December and early May, when the slaves had to work for extremely long periods. After the harvest, the estate required fewer laborers, but still had its full complement of men. Every serious sugar planter, therefore, had a carefully planned annual cycle of work calculated to use his force as fully as possible throughout the entire year.

For the Cuban slave the year had two significant divisions: *zafra*, or crop-time; and *tiempo muerto*, or dead season. These two divisions not only composed his yearly cycle but also decided his daily activities.

The beginning of the calendar year often coincided with the beginning of the harvest. All the slaves were given the first of two changes of clothes (the other being given at the end of the harvest).[38] Each man received one loosely-fitting cotton shirt, and one pair of pants, which reached just below the knees, a woolen cap, a short, thick flannel jacket, and a blanket. Each woman received one striped cotton dress and a cotton scarf (*pañuelo*). At the end of the harvest, the rations were almost identical, except that the men were given straw hats instead of woolen caps. A holiday usually followed this first distribution of clothing, the signal that the harvest was about to begin.

Before the actual work began, however, it was important that all the slaves knew precisely where they worked, and the order of their rotation. At the first session on a new estate, this was done by an assembly of the entire working force, and their division.[39] First the men for the boiler house were called forward. They were the strongest men in the force, and were handed over to the maestro de azúcar. The number of boilers determined the number of men. Each boiler needed about 7 attendants, with an additional 4 or 5 for odd jobs. A factory of 5 boilers had about 39 men.

The cartmen who hauled the canes were next selected. If the estate lacked its own domestic railroad, the number of cartmen was equal to the number of men in the boiling house, since they took over the first

38. Ibid., pp. 75–76.

39. This pattern is taken from ibid., pp. 43–46: "Fuerzas que se necesitan para la zafra y distribución de ellas."

night shift from these men, after their own day's work in the fields. For that reason they had to be the second strongest team of men.

Following in descending order of strength came the cutters. Numbering about fifty for a medium-sized estate, they had to be taught the way of cutting in order to achieve maximum safety and maximum output. The cutter held the cane in his left hand, then first cut off the leaves with one swift stroke of his machete. He then cut the cane as near as possible to the ground with a second stroke of the machete, and threw the stalk behind him. At nights the canecutters relieved the men in the purging house, and those carrying the bagasse on the compound.

Lesser duties followed in this order of selection: 25 men for the purging house; 50 women and boys to collect the cane, stack it, and help to load the carts; 4 boys to change the teams of oxen; 2 older men and women to collect the cane which fell from the carts or railway wagons along the way; 8 men to take away the green bagasse (crushed canes) from the mills; 10 men to carry the dry bagasse and tend to the fires; and 60 additional women and a few boys to attend to the cooking, and to serve water to the men in the fields.

Harvest was the time of work for everyone on an estate. It presented a scene of concentrated and determined labor.[40] During these months, the slaves averaged a workday of nearly twenty hours, even on the best-run estates.[41] The slaves worked almost to the maximum of their physical ability:

> The hour for ringing the morning bell should be so arranged that nothing from a full day's work is lost. On the other hand, the Negroes should not be unnecessarily disturbed, depriving them of that part of their rest which they may enjoy without jeopardizing their labor.[42]

In order to keep the slaves awake, and as a stimulus to work, the whip became the chief instrument of the mayorales and contramayorales. Sometimes, the slaves were flogged owing to the sadism of the supervi-

40. Dana, *To Cuba,* pp. 48, 56–59.
41. The slave laws of 1842 stipulated that the crop-time work should be "16 hours daily with 2 for rest in the days, and 6 at nights to sleep." These became the minimal requirements observed only on the very best estates. Many travellers remarked that during crop-time the slaves got no more than 3 hours of sleep per day. Edwin F. Atkins, *Sixty Years in Cuba* (Cambridge: Riverside Press, 1926), p. 98, states that the Negroes on his estates worked regularly for 18 hours during the harvest, and that some became crippled by their work.
42. *Cartilla práctica,* p. 58.

sory personnel, but during crop-time, whipping was, by some reports, almost incessantly employed to keep the slaves on the job and to prevent their malingering or falling asleep.[43]

Indeed, the need for continuous labor was so great at this time that the handbook recommended that the men in the boiler house be given their night meals on the job.[44] Nevertheless, despite the rigorous regime of crop-time, many reporters remarked that the slaves not only survived, but even displayed a robust physical appearance.

The second distribution of clothing signalled the end of harvest. The slaves cleared the land and planted new fields of sugar cane, weeded the old fields of "ratoon" cane, and cut wood to prepare for the next harvest. These occupations were time-consuming and made reasonably heavy demands on the labor force.

Planting the canes involved a system of digging holes or trenches in the cleared land. The land was divided into small squares, and in each square two slaves, working together, opened a furrow with a hoe. The strongest men did this work, which could be very difficult in soils laced with stones or roots or lowland soils of plastic mud. The rest of the slaves were divided into sowers and carriers. The sowers placed the canes longitudinally in the holes and covered them with loose soil hauled from the banks. The carriers supplied the canes from the stockpiles. Later, as the canes began to grow, the male slaves moved in to weed the fields and loosen the soil around the young plants.[45] The planting season usually lasted from September to December. More often, however, the scarcity of labor forced the planters to continue the operation long after the close of the conventional season. At such times the planters might be forced to hire additional slaves to cut wood or tend the cattle.[46]

The great fertility of Cuban soils allowed a lengthy ratooning of canes. Nevertheless, the soils became exhausted eventually, and the farmers had to move on to new plots. Many attempts were made to popularize the use of manures, but those met with little success while land was available at reasonable cost. Some of the richer producers such as Miguel Aldama, Pedro Diago, and Joaquín de Ayesterán, however, made serious efforts to get fertilizers from abroad, either in the form of crushed

43. Hazard, *Cuba*, p. 360; for other contemporary reports, see Noel Deerr, *The History of Sugar* (2 vols.; London: Chapman & Hall, 1949–50), 2:359.
44. *Cartilla práctica*, p. 58.
45. Ibid., p. 31.
46. Moreno Fraginals, *El ingenio*, pp. 90–94; *Cartilla práctica*, p. 94.

bones from New York, or guano from Peru.[47] Not until the end of the century and the arrival of the large corporation did fertilizers play an important part in Cuban agricultural practices.

Many attempts were made to use steam-driven plows to replace the hand plows used by the slaves. But although the machines were far more efficient, their high cost, coupled with the fact that they could not be easily operated by slaves, tended to make them prohibitive for all but the richest planters. The first steam-driven plow was demonstrated on Friday, April 24, 1863, on the ingenio Concepción, owned by Miguel Aldama.[48] Many farmers traveled very far to view the plow which promised a new breakthrough in the labor-land dilemma. They were impressed by the speed and efficiency of the machine. Its cost and the additional requirement of an imported, salaried operator and mechanic considerably dampened their enthusiasm. Following the path of least resistance, many planters preferred to take fullest advantage of the wretched system of slavery while it still existed, or sought simply to replace their slave labor by equally wretched indentured Asians.

One of the innovations of plantation agriculture in Cuba, at least in the history of slavery there, was the provision of facilities for medical care for the sick, and a nursery for the small children. The sick room, or miniature hospital, catered to the small eventualities of the estate. It possessed all the medicines required for the frequent injuries, small infections, or the colds and influenza epidemics which accompanied the rainy summer months.

Many slaves used the facilities of the infirmary as an excuse for procrastination. The result of this was that some planters were particularly skeptical about admitting the illnesses of their slaves.[49] In the earlier days of slavery, some plantation owners had held the assumption that it was more economical to work a slave to death as quickly as possible and then replace him with a new purchase than to care for the slave properly and encourage reproduction.[50] Cristóbal Madan openly confessed that the care given to a slave was generally related to the costs of production: the lower the price of slaves, the less was their general welfare considered, and vice versa. "The reduction in the trade with Africa and

47. *Ely, Cuando reinaba,* pp. 569–75.
48. Moreno Fraginals, *El ingenio,* p. 91.
49. *Cartilla práctica,* pp. 82–83.
50. Alexander Humboldt, *The Island of Cuba,* trans. J. S. Thrasher (New York: Derby & Jackson, 1856), pp. 227–28.

the consequent reduction in the facility to replace the work-force at a low cost, has forced some proprietors to take better care of their slaves, and to promote their well-being and comfort," he wrote in the 1850's.[51]

According to the handbook for slave-run sugar estates, pregnancy and birth were not classified as illnesses.[52] Forty-five days after giving birth, a mother went back to work, often in the fields, while the offspring was given to the *criollera,* an old slave woman who supervised the nursery.

Under the arduous conditions of labor, the rural slave population found it impossible to maintain its own equilibrium of births and deaths. One important factor, of course, was the tremendous imbalance of the sexes on the plantations, where productive males outnumbered productive females by over 2:1, as very few planters made any attempt to supply an adequate number of females to satisfy the males on their estates.[53] Women were considered to be less productive than men. Apart from the sexual imbalance, women could not produce healthy babies under conditions of labor entirely devoid of hygiene, and where they often had to do field work for the entire time of their pregnancy. The practice of having women in their ninth month of pregnancy working alongside men and cutting canes in the field perhaps contributed to a number of deformed or stillborn babies.[54] Many women lost their babies during the terrible punishments they underwent for individual misdemeanors.[55]

Corporal punishment was at once a measure of discipline and of intimidation for the slaves. The slave code of 1842 sanctioned the more popular forms—flogging, stocks, shackles, chains, and imprisonment—which were administered on the estates.

Flogging was the most common and the most convenient form of punishment. It was legally limited to twenty-five lashes, but was often given on a brutal installment plan called the *novenario* which consisted of nine strokes daily over a period of nine days. Not only was the legal limit exceeded, but the slave did not run the risk of an immediate loss of life during the procedure. Some estates had a special flogging section

51. [Cristóbal Madan], *El trabajo libre y el libre cambio en Cuba* (Paris: n.p., 1864), p. 3. See also AHN, Ultramar, Esclavitud, leg. 3552: Serrano al M. de la Guerra y Ultramar, April 15, 1862 (confidential).

52. *Cartilla práctica,* pp. 82–83.

53. See census returns in AHN, Ultramar, Esclavitud, legs. 3553–54.

54. Moreno Fraginals, *El ingenio,* pp. 157–58.

55. Ortiz describes, with illustrations, the wide variety of corporal punishments used by the masters to ensure discipline, in *Negros esclavos,* pp. 245–69.

called a *tumbadero*. Flogging, however, was dealt to the slaves anywhere and everywhere, either as a consequence of the anger of a white person, or as an incentive to work harder.

Next in popular use on the plantations came the stocks and shackles (*cepo* and *grillete*). Both forms had many styles. The most common form of stocks consisted of an enormous, fixed board with holes through which fitted the head, hands, and feet of the delinquent slaves, either separately, or in any combination. Left in the open in a number of uncomfortable positions, the slaves suffered from the weather as well as from the many varieties of insects found in the tropics without being able to protect themselves.

Shackles varied from simple chains and padlocks attached to the ankles or wrists and fastened around the neck to the types that were attached to a large log, which the slave had to lift whenever he desired to move from one place to another. The heavy iron of the shackles sometimes chafed the skin, resulting in serious infection of the wounds. That such forms of punishment should have led directly or indirectly to miscarriages among pregnant females was not surprising.

The degree to which these measures operated depended on the individual slave master and the supervisory personnel on the estate, who had the authority to inflict punishment in the absence of the proprietors. All the above forms of physical abuse remained on the law books until 1882.[56]

The slaves never remained indifferent or acquiescent to their conditions. Not many were literate and therefore able to leave a written account of their impressions and experiences, although at least one probably did.[57] Instead, the reactions of the slaves must be deduced from their actions.

As long as the Cuban economy had remained relatively underdeveloped, and the increase of Africans small, the social problems of a multiracial society were neither obvious nor frightening. Both elite and subordinate groups had the kind of close, personal relationship characteristic of patriarchal societies. On the one hand, the number of slaves held by any one master was unlikely to be very large. On the other hand,

56. AHN, Ultramar, Gobierno, leg. 4815, 1880–82: "Exposiciones abolicionistas a las Cortes, 1881–1882"; and leg. 4814, fols. 279–80, 1883.

57. See, Robert R. Madden, *Poems by a Slave on the Island of Cuba recently liberated* . . . (London: Ward, 1840), which contains the poems supposedly written by the exslave Juan Francisco Manzano, along with his autobiography.

the absence of any great economic incentive on the part of the master permitted him to be fairly liberal in his regimentation of the lives of the slaves. Besides, as Herbert Klein has revealed, the diversification of the economic system in the rural areas and the growth of urban zones lent themselves to quite a relaxed form of slavery.[58] Nevertheless, the slaves, despite the often vaunted "Spanish Catholic kindness," consistently and in a variety of ways expressed their opposition to their servitude. And with the harsher conditions of a plantation type of slavery, such resistance became more widespread. The slaves resisted slavery in many ways. Some simply poisoned their masters, destroyed machines, or set canefields on fire.[59] Such manifestations of resistance, however, neither alleviated their suffering nor affected their status, and represented individual responses of anger, jealousy, or revenge in particular situations.

Far more serious reflections on the general state of slavery came from the evidence of voluntary abortions, suicides, and runaways. Many women practiced abortion by drinking a brew concocted from wild herbs, in order to save their offspring from undergoing the life that they themselves were leading.[60] Suicide was so frequent that the problem was taken up by the highest authorities in Madrid in 1847, and continued under active consideration until 1855.[61] Initially, the Cuban captain-general proposed that more religious instruction offered the most efficacious method of fighting a practice inimical to the "propagation and conservation of that caste not only necessary to the country, but also difficult to replace by any other."[62] Eventually the officials realized that something else had to be tried. A royal order in 1855, noting that males outnumbered females on some estates by a ratio of 4:1, insisted that all proprietors be forced to balance the sex ratio on their farms. It also suggested that tax rebates could be used as incentives for the successful procreation of the slaves on the estates.[63] The figures given in the royal order, however, are not borne out by an examination of the census returns for slaves. The incidence of such one-sided masculinity

58. Klein, *Slavery in the Americas,* pp. 142–50. In a personal communication, Sidney W. Mintz of Yale University has suggested the term "lagging capitalistic" to describe this earlier period of Cuban history.

59. Philalethes, *Yankee Travels,* pp. 14–15, and Dana, *Cuba,* p. 61.

60. Moreno Fraginals, *El ingenio,* p. 157.

61. AHN, Ultramar, Esclavitud, leg. 3550: "Expediente sobre los medios de evitar los frecuentes suicidios de los esclavos." Also Ortiz, *Negros esclavos,* pp. 391–423.

62. AHN, Ultramar, Esclavitud, leg. 3550(1), ind. 17.

63. Ibid., ind. 18: "Proyecto de importación de mugeres esclavas en la Isla de Cuba."

among the slave populations on estates was extremely rare. Among all the rural slave population, the ratio of males to females was far nearer the proportion of 2:1—which even then represented an exaggeration of the male sector.

Wherever the plantation society existed—as indeed, wherever slavery existed—slaveowners faced the recurrent problem of escapees. Herbert S. Klein noted in his study of slavery in both Cuba and the state of Virginia that the occurrence of runaways in the island was "far out of proportion to anything experienced in Virginia," and was so serious a

TABLE 7
Slaves: Sex and Age Groups, 1855–57

| Year | Males | | | Females | | | Total |
|------|----------|-----------------|----------------|----------|-----------------|-------------------|-------|
| | Under 12 | Useful 12–60 | All males* | Under 12 | Useful 12–60 | All females* | |
| **1855** | | | | | | | |
| Urban | 6,991 | 21,438 | 33,140 | 7,911 | 26,111 | 37,551 | 70,691 |
| Rural | 32,566 | 143,767 | 192,919 | 30,128 | 78,456 | 111,196 | 304,115 |
| **1856** | | | | | | | |
| Urban | 7,083 | 22,616 | 30,303 | 7,975 | 26,561 | 36,820 | 67,123 |
| Rural | 35,476 | 143,183 | 190,327 | 32,719 | 77,749 | 114,916 | 305,243 |
| **1857** | | | | | | | |
| Urban | 7,673 | 21,478 | 30,838 | 7,743 | 25,649 | 34,762 | 65,600 |
| Rural | 35,147 | 144,310 | 193,187 | 33,160 | 75,416 | 114,188 | 307,375 |

* Includes slaves over the age of 60, and invalids between 12 and 60.
Source: AHN, Ultramar, Esclavitud, leg. 3553.

problem that the Cuban proprietors found it more expedient to be lenient with the malady, equating it to no worse an offense than simple malingering.[64] But it was not merely that the masters feared losing forever the slave who might have intended to desert only temporarily in the initial stages. Rather it was more significant that the master could not afford to lose a slave who might be required for the harvest time. Part of the idea of leniency, therefore, stemmed from the acute shortage of laborers on the island. Masters could have been motivated by kindness and economic considerations with equal validity. But lenience did not seem to reduce the desire for freedom. This desire could be frustrated; it could never be extinguished.

Desertion, temporary or permanent, was as common among urban slaves as it was among plantation slaves. Slaves with ideas of perma-

64. Klein, *Slavery in the Americas*, p. 155.

nent escape created their abodes in the most inaccessible parts of the mountains. Called *cimarrones,* or maroons, these runaways in their villages or *palenques* often defied the concerted attacks of the whites for extremely long periods. Not only did they carry on their own regular social and political organization independent of the white society, but they practiced cultivation to supplement foraging and stealing from the plantations. Their weapons for defense included machetes stolen from the plantations—still one of the most useful devices in Latin America and the Caribbean—poisoned arrows and wooden spears with improvised iron heads.[65] In addition, the maroons also defended their villages with sharpened bamboo poles, fixed firmly in the ground, and covered with dried leaves.

The main Negro palenques were in the mountains of the east, especially the Sierra del Cristal, "where white men hardly dare to go."[66] One famous palenque there was called Moa, or El Frijol. Other outstanding palenques existed in the Cuzco hills of the Vuelta Abajo region, the marshes of Zapata, and the Organos mountains of Pinar del Río.[67] Some runaways, however, did not live in the palenques, but rather led a wandering life in the country, or drifted to the larger towns where they tried to blend in with the free colored population. White response to the *apalencado,* or Negro slave living in the palenque, was considerably less lenient than to the temporary absconder, who, by the intervention of a third party, called a *padriño,* could be pardoned and restored to the farm.[68] Many whites were semiprofessional slavehunters. These *ranchadores,* accompanied by bloodhounds, led expeditions into the mountains, often to eliminate a troublesome palenque, or its diminutive, the *ranchería,* but more often to get the four dollars per head reward each captive brought from the *capitanes de partido* (the district military or judicial commanders). Sometimes large military expeditions went out to destroy the more formidable maroon villages in the mountains.

The most emphatic form of resistance to slavery consisted of open

65. For the life of a runaway slave, see Esteban Montejo, "The Day I Stopped Being a Slave," *Observer Review,* April 14, 1968 (an extract from his book, *The Autobiography of a Runaway Slave,* ed. Miguel Barnet [London: Bodley Head, 1968]). Also Ortiz, *Negros esclavos,* p. 413.

66. Dana, *To Cuba,* p. 127.

67. Ortiz, *Negros esclavos,* p. 412.

68. [J. G. F. Wurdemann], *Notes on Cuba* (Boston: Munroe, 1844), pp. 260–61; Philalethes, *Yankee Travels,* pp. 38–43.

rebellion.[69] In a number of cases, most notably in 1825 and 1843 in Matanzas, the slave revolts revealed widespread planning, and even included whites and free persons of color. Far more frequently, however, all the slaves on a single estate would erupt in violence, destroying property and killing those whites they could get their hands on. Spontaneous uprisings, confined to the slaves of the same owner, were very common throughout the Caribbean region. Proslavery writers tended to explain them as symptomatic of lax supervision and absenteeism.[70] More objective observers realized that servility bred revolt, and that men subordinate to hostile overseers reacted with hostility themselves.[71]

Of the numerous slave disturbances after 1840, two deserve special attention. One occurred in 1844, and the other in 1866.

The supposed slave "revolt" of 1844 had absolutely no foundation in fact.[72] Basing its actions upon the testimony of a female slave that the blacks on a Matanzas plantation were conspiring with many outsiders to foment a rebellion, the government of Leopoldo O'Donnell precipitately moved in and arrested nearly two thousand whites, free colored persons, and slaves. No one knew the exact number of executions, which included the well-known free colored men Andrés Dodge and Gabriel de la Concepción Valdés, otherwise known as "El Plácido." Many innocent free persons suffered imprisonment and exile to Melilla and Ceuta, while the slaves who escaped death were brutally flogged.

In March, 1866, the slaves on the estates of Zulueta, Aldama, and some other prominent proprietors of Matanzas simultaneously withheld their labor, claiming that they had been declared free by the Cortes in Spain. The Negroes demanded that they be paid for their services. Although there was no report of any violence by the slaves, a large number of troops was deployed to force the men to go back to work.[73] The slaves were in all probability misled by the general excitement among

69. See Ely, *Cuando reinaba,* pp. 492–501; Ortiz, *Negros esclavos,* pp. 429–35.
70. For example, [Wurdemann], *Notes,* p. 273.
71. Suárez y Romero, *Francisco,* pp. 22–23.
72. For the complete report of the commission of inquiry, see AHN, Estado, Esclavitud, leg. 8057. The abolition of slavery in the British West Indies, the large number of slave uprisings in 1843, and the general rumors of a race war on the island all contributed to the government's testiness. There can be no doubt that the government used the opportunity to remove some of the Creoles from the island.
73. Ely, *Cuando reinaba,* p. 495.

the whites on the island about the election of representatives to the Cortes in Madrid, scheduled for 1866.

The opinions expressed about slave mortality as about everything else in the island differed considerably. The only general consensus seemed to be that mortality rates were higher in the rural areas than in the towns, and highest of all on the sugar plantations. Both in town and country, infant mortality was extremely high. One infant sickness alone, a convulsive complaint locally called *espasmo,* or *mal de los siete días,* was purported to have been responsible for over fifty per cent of infant slave deaths.[74] Adult mortality, however, was far less uniformly presented.

Antonio Gallenga thought that the mean life of a slave on the plantation was about five years, which would give an overall mortality rate of 20 per cent.[75] Gallenga, of course, wrote in the 1870's, when the trade had ceased and replacements had become impossible. In the 1850's, Cristóbal Madan put the annual plantation loss at 7 per cent, Urbano Feijóo Sotomayor at 10 per cent.[76] J. S. Thrasher thought the loss to be nearer to 8 per cent on sugar estates.[77] Vicente Vásquez Queipo, writing in 1845, thought that the average life span of a plantation slave was twenty years and the mortality rate 5 per cent per annum.[78] The most reasonable figure seems to be about 4 per cent—a mortality rate comparable with that of other West Indian islands during their plantation era.

The prevalence of diseases certainly played a part in the high mortality figures. Nevertheless, conditions of labor for the Cuban slaves in the nineteenth century were also responsible. Moreno Fraginals asserts that between the last years of the eighteenth century and the decade beginning in 1840, the slave numbers on the sugar estates were maintained exclusively by new purchases.[79] Nor could the slaves be expected to reproduce or resist diseases when they suffered from sexual imbalance, dietary deficiencies, and consistent overwork. The most telling in-

74. Ortiz, *Negros esclavos,* pp. 284–85.

75. Gallenga, *Pearl of the Antilles,* p. 80.

76. [Madan], *Llamamiento,* p. 14; Urbano Feijóo de Sotomayor, *Isla de Cuba* . . . (Madrid: J. Peña, 1855), pp. 44–45.

77. Humboldt, *Cuba,* pp. 206–7.

78. [Vicente Vásquez Quiepo], *Informe fiscal* . . . (Madrid: Alegría, 1845), pp. 18–19.

79. Moreno Fraginals, *El ingenio,* p. 155.

dictment of the severity of Cuban slavery came from the dramatic decline of the black population after the abolition of the slave trade.

The number of slaves fell from 363,288 in 1869 to 227,902 in 1878, a decline of 135,386, of which at least 50 per cent were freed by the Moret Law of 1870.[80] The entire Negroid population decreased from 596,396, or 43.7 per cent of the total population of the island in 1860, to 528,798, or 32.5 per cent of the same total in 1887.[81] The decline was relative as well as absolute, and it is further accentuated if one accepts the general view that the slave census of 1860 underestimated the numbers (some think by the unlikely proportion of 30 per cent) and that the free colored population increased by 70 per cent between 1840 and 1860. Such startling decline in this sector of the population in the island sharply exposes the myth that the Cubans were humane to their slaves, or that the society was less racist than slave societies which lacked an Iberian heritage and Roman Catholic religious tradition. Writing in 1902, Rafael María de Labra laconically remarked on the earlier proslavery propagandists whom he had fought for nearly a generation in the Spanish Cortes:

> One has to admire, Señores, the nerve by which they propagated the belief that the slaves in the Antilles lived happily and contentedly . . . without even mentioning the dungeons, the stocks and the irons, or the awful mortality rates among the slaves.[82]

Unfortunately, the perspicacity of the heroic Spanish liberal has not been shared by many writers of slavery. For what is abundantly clear from any study of Cuban slavery during the nineteenth century is not merely that it was significantly different from slavery in the southern United States. That was almost self-evident. Instead, what emerges, somewhat surprisingly, is that slavery on the sugar plantations of Cuba and slavery on the sugar plantations of the other West Indian islands bore a strong resemblance and were comparable. Plantation slavery—and particularly of the sugar plantation type—was a distinctive system

80. Arthur F. Corwin, *Spain and the Abolition of Slavery in Cuba, 1817–1886* (Austin: University of Texas Press, 1967), p. 294.

81. Spain, Instituto Geográfico y Estadístico, *Censo . . . 1860* (Madrid: Impr. Nacional, 1863), and ibid., *Censo . . . 1887* (Madrid: Inst. Geog. y Estadístico, 1891).

82. Rafael M. de Labra y Cadrana, *La reforma política de Ultramar 1868–1900* (Madrid: Alonso, 1902), p. 22.

which lent itself to systadial comparisons throughout history. Sugar and slavery had a markedly similar development and course from Barbados in the sixteenth century, through Jamaica and St. Domingue in the seventeenth century, and ended up being not very different in Cuba and Brazil in the nineteenth century. Everywhere, slavery was extremely wasteful in human terms. Everywhere its differences were in degrees of wretchedness, not in variations of humanity. One does not have to catalogue the evils of the system to support that assertion—at least not any more. In Cuba the plantation society challenged the traditions of humanitarianism and protectiveness of the Catholic Church and the royal bureaucracy. To find out how well they withstood the challenge we must look more closely at the social structure of the island during the nineteenth century.

# 5

# Structure of a Slave Society

*Two unmixed races exist in Cuba, under a social organization in which the inferior is subject to the superior race.*

J. S. Thrasher, 1856, in Humboldt, *Island of Cuba*, p. 53.

CUBA IN THE NINETEENTH CENTURY had more than two races, and more than two racial mixtures. But the real key to the social situation was not so much the racial background as the caste-like group to which one belonged. The society was structured along caste-like lines which roughly corresponded to racial lines. At the top of the society was a group of whites. Below in the social order came a group of free people who were not white. They were principally slaves and the offspring of slaves who in some way had gained their freedom. After 1847 this group also contained the Asian laborers brought in under contractual obligations to replace slave labor on the sugar plantations. At the bottom of the structure were the slaves—and, after the abolition of slavery, the indentured Asian laborers. The social and economic relationships of the groups followed the pattern established by color and law.

The Cuban situation was not peculiar, but represented the common pattern for all areas in the Caribbean where the plantation economy had taken hold. In the other sugar-producing islands of the region at the same time, for example, the nonwhite subordinate groups consistently outnumbered the white upper caste by ratios varying from 4:1 in the newly acquired British colony of Trinidad to 15:1 in the small island of

St. Kitts.[1] Such a demographic composition gave the appearance of a pyramidal structure with a very broad colored base, and a small, sharp white peak.[2] Because Cuban society had had a relatively long existence as a settlement colony, the unbalanced racial ratios did not reach the schematic pattern of the other islands. Instead, in Cuba the number of white members of the society was almost always equal to that of the

TABLE 8

Cuban Population, 1840–87

| Group | 1841 | | 1860 | | 1887 | |
|-------|------|------|------|------|------|------|
| White | | | | | | |
| Male | 227,144 | | 468,107 | | 607,187 | |
| Female | 191,147 | | 325,377 | | 495,702 | |
| Total | 418,291 | | 793,484 | | 1,102,889 | |
| % of all groups* | | 41.4 | | 56.3 | | 67.5 |
| Free colored | | | | | | |
| Male | 75,703 | | 109,027 | | 275,413 | |
| Female | 77,135 | | 116,816 | | 253,385 | |
| Total | 152,838 | | 225,843 | | 528,798 | |
| % of all groups | | 15.2 | | 16.2 | | 32.5 |
| Slave | | | | | | |
| Male | 281,250 | | 218,722 | | Slavery abolished; | |
| Female | 155,245 | | 151,831 | | slaves joined free | |
| Total | 436,495 | | 370,553 | | colored group | |
| % of all groups | | 43.4 | | 27.5 | | |

* Percentages have been rounded.

Sources: 1841: Cuba, Census. *Resumen del censo . . . 1841* (Havana: Impr. del Gobierno, 1842); 1860 and 1883: Spain, Instítuto Geográfico y Estadístico. *Censo . . . 1860* (Madrid: Impr. Nacional, 1863); ibid., *Censo . . . 1887* (Madrid: Inst. Geog. y Estadística, 1891). All percentages are my own calculation.

nonwhites. And, unlike in the other West Indian islands, the proportion of free colored persons was always relatively large. (See Table 8.)

The uppermost stratum of Cuban society consisted of the whites. Between 1841 and 1887, their number had grown from 227,144 to

1. This does not apply, of course, to the small Antillean islands which never went through the plantation experience, such as the Caymans, etc. Eric Williams, *History of the People of Trinidad and Tobago* (Trinidad: PNM Pub. Co., 1962), p. 79, and Elsa V. Goveia, *Slave Society in the British Leeward Islands at the End of the Eighteenth Century* (New Haven: Yale University Press, 1965), p. 65, support the plantation figures.

2. For a description of conditions in the British colonies, see J. H. Parry and P. M. Sherlock, *A Short History of the West Indies* (London: Macmillan, 1956), chapters V and VII.

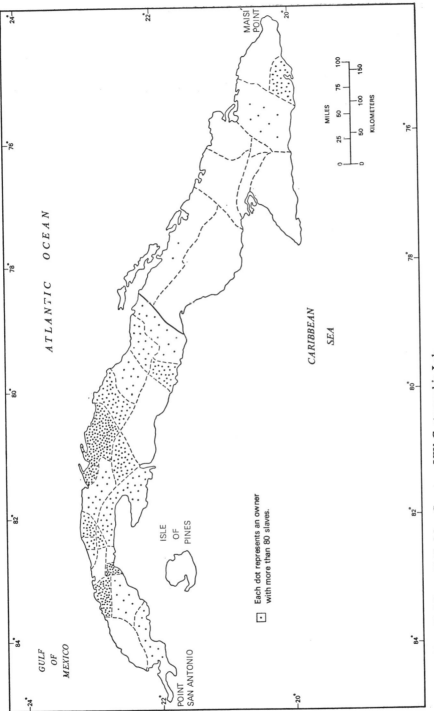

ATLANTIC OCEAN

GULF OF MEXICO

ISLE OF PINES

POINT SAN ANTONIO

MAISI POINT

CARIBBEAN SEA

Each dot represents an owner with more than 80 slaves.

MILES
0    25    50    75    100

KILOMETERS
0    50    100    150

Map 3. Slave Holdings, 1857. Map Courtesy UW Cartographic Lab.

607,187, from 41.4% to 67.5% of the total island population, according to official figures. Not all this increase, however, resulted from internal, insular reproduction. Perhaps the whites derived their most substantial boost from a continuous stream of immigrants from Spain and the Canary Islands, from Spanish-speaking American countries, neighboring Caribbean islands, the United States, and most European countries. And despite the religious disabilities they suffered, a great many foreign residents were non-Catholic.[3]

All members of the white group, regardless of the degree of their "whiteness," had certain things in common. They enjoyed equal political privileges, though not necessarily equal political influence; and they were at liberty to own as many slaves as they could afford, and to get rich in whatever manner they pleased. They owed no duty to anyone, although they exercised a condescending patriarchal obligation to their slaves. The color of their skin was the badge of their elevated social position, and in the realm of economic pursuit they suffered no overt individual handicap. Nevertheless, any apparent homogeneity was entirely superficial. Schism existed within the white stratum. Their apparent cooperation, or felicitous association, was artificially imposed by the cultural heritage and political domination of Spain, and by their collective fear of the large, subordinate nonwhite group.[4] In this way a mutual dependence mitigated their profound mutual hostility.

In the local Cuban idiom, the whites were either "Criollos," or "Peninsulares." Both were derogatory terms, the products of social snobbery. On the one hand, were the Creoles, descended from the American colonists, and born in the New World. In some cases, they were of hybrid stock, with infusions of Indian or African blood somewhere along the ancestral line. On the other hand were the Peninsular Spaniards, who in a common ethnocentric way regarded their own Spanish birth as the symbol of stability and purity, and denigrated those born in the New World.[5] The tension between Creoles and Peninsular Spaniards charac-

3. Non-Catholics could not practice their religion in public in Cuba. See, AHN, Estado, Esclavitud, leg. 8047(14), fol. 17: Howden to Corbin, Nov., 1854. Also, [Cristóbal Madan], *El trabajo libre y el libre cambio en Cuba* (Paris: n.p., 1864). To be classified as a settler, however, a foreigner had to adopt the Catholic religion.

4. A. F. Smith, "Spain and the Problem of Slavery in Cuba, 1817–1873" (Unpublished Ph.D. dissertation, University of Chicago, 1958), pp. 50–52.

5. A Spaniard wrote, "Cubans are generally frail, but especially in Havana, the race reveals marked symptoms of degeneration." Antonio de las Barras y Prado,

teristic of the history of mainland Latin America was less marked in Cuba, owing to the relatively smaller number of bureaucrats and clergy there. But the number of Spaniards rapidly increased after 1762, when the crown decided to station a permanent garrison on the island, and even more so in the nineteenth century, when loyalist refugees of the Latin American wars took up residence there. Official royal policy accentuated the difference between the two categories. For while not entirely legally debarred from the colonial bureaucracy, the Creoles found these positions almost totally reserved for the Peninsulares.[6]

Apart from holding an apparently complete monopoly of the bureaucratic positions, the Peninsular Spaniards dominated the commercial sector.[7] This arose partly because they lacked the original land grants that would have made them a part of the landholding group, and partly because this aspect of trade was greatly neglected in the earlier days of restricted, mercantilistic commerce. The Peninsular Spaniards had the necessary contacts in Spain, and the determination to persevere in a socially deprecated enterprise. In the course of time, a number of them made great fortunes from their humble origins, and either joined the prestigious landholding group, or retired to Spain to participate in social life and politics.[8] Their affiliation was more to the bureaucracy, dominated by their own kind, and to the crown than it was to the large group of Creole planters.

Creoles were principally landholders. But they were not only the cattle raisers and planters of tobacco, sugar, and cotton. They spanned a very wide range from highly professional people such as lawyers, journalists, and educators in Havana to simple, solitary workers wringing a difficult living from a small mountainous plot in the eastern provinces.[9]

In the earlier colonial days, there was not much open conflict be-

---

*Memorias, La Habana a mediados del siglo xix* (Madrid: Ciudad Lineal, 1925), p. 92; and an American observed, "There can be no doubt about it that Creoles and Spaniards live here as dogs and cats locked up in the same cage." Demoticus Philalethes [pseud.], *Yankee Travels Through the Island of Cuba* . . . (New York: Appleton, 1856), p. 22.

6. Salvador de Madariaga, *The Fall of the Spanish American Empire* (London: Hollis & Carter, 1947), pp. 34–46.

7. Philip S. Foner, *A History of Cuba and Its Relations with the United States* (2 vols.; New York: Int. Pub., 1962), 1:52.

8. Barras y Prado, *Memorias.*

9. Foner, *Cuba,* 1:52–55.

tween the two white groups, and even a degree of interdependence. The merchants provided credit, supervised the disposal of the planters' products, and supplied the landholders with their ever increasing list of luxuries and necessities. This pattern of relationship in Cuba was in marked contrast with the rest of the empire, especially Mexico and Peru. The crisis came with the rapid accumulation of wealth in the nineteenth century, and the greater political awareness of the Creoles.

The real crux of the matter rested in their different economic roles. Peninsular Spaniards were ultra-Spanish in their politics for two sound economic reasons. They preferred the mercantilistic channels of Spanish colonial trade insisted on by the crown, since they thereby easily secured the marketing of the planters' products without outside competition; a Spanish domination of the island was their best guarantee for prosperity. Spanish merchants and Spanish bureaucrats firmly supported each other against the aspirations of the Creole planters.

The Creole planters, for their part, resented the loss of much profit by the limitation of their products to the small Spanish market. As they yearned for free trade with other countries, they gradually came to detest their subordination socially and economically to the Peninsular class. And because very many of them had been educated abroad, or at least had traveled to England and the United States, their political ideas ran counter to Spanish colonial policy.[10] By the middle of the nineteenth century, the situation on the island had become extremely critical. Robert R. Madden noted rather sadly, in 1849, that "Cuba, ever since I knew it, has been slowly but steadily becoming Americanized."[11]

In a strange way, however, the economic revolution of the nineteenth century came to forge an uneasy, but basically firm, alliance between Creoles and Peninsulares. Sugar and slavery linked the rival elements. The planters relied heavily on the merchants for plantation supplies, credit, and the marketing of their products, and the merchants soon found that their future economic well-being depended upon the planters.[12] In time the planters became heavily indebted to the merchants.

10. Barras y Prado, *Memorias,* pp. 78–80; also Medardo Vitier, *Las ideas en Cuba* . . . (2 vols.; Havana: Ed. Trópico, 1938), esp. chapters V–VII.

11. Robert R. Madden, *The Island of Cuba* (London: Gilpin, 1849), p. 84. Madden would naturally have preferred that the island be anglicized.

12. For a detailed and extremely informative account of the interrelation between merchants and planters, see Edwin F. Atkins, *Sixty Years in Cuba* (Cambridge: Riverside Press, 1926). Roland T. Ely, *Cuando reinaba su majestad el azúcar* (Buenos Aires: Ed. Sudamericana, 1963) has much useful information.

And the curious system of Spanish law before 1880 forced the merchants to continue subsidizing a bankrupt planter with the expectation that a bumper crop would cut short their losses. Even though some merchants, such as Julian Zulueta and the Torriente brothers, had originally owned large estates, many acquired them as a result of their having lent large sums to the previous owners, who were unable to repay them.

Since the prosperity of Cuba depended on Negro slavery, both groups were unequivocally opposed to any attempts from Spain or elsewhere to alter or abolish the institution. Despite their bitter feud over social and political affairs, Cuban white planters and merchants tended to be unanimous on the question of slavery. The political instability in Spain and the insistence by Britain on an end to the slave trade afforded the opportunity to usurp power. Regardless of how sincere the Spanish official attitude may have been toward the eventual abolition of slavery—and I am convinced that it was sincere after the 1850's—every practical effort was frustrated by local Cuban intransigence.[13] The corruption and inefficiency of the bureaucracy in Cuba was cause as well as result of the strength and determination of the local whites in politics. It was highly ridiculous, therefore, to have expected such a bureaucracy to implement the orders of the central authority in Madrid to abolish slavery. So united could the whites in Cuba become over the issue of slavery, that in 1855, the Spanish Cortes publicly declared that "slavery is a special form of property on the island of Cuba; it is considered essential, and ought to be respected."[14]

As long as the rich sugar planters of the western division wanted slave labor and knew that they could depend on Spanish support for this, they maintained their pro-Spanish attitude. But in the Cuba of the nineteenth century, Spanish hegemony was closely tied to the future of slavery. In fact, any rumors circulating in the island concerning official attempts in Spain to interfere with the institution of slavery on the is-

13. My own research in the archives of Madrid led me to the same conclusions reached by Arthur F. Corwin in *Spain and the Abolition of Slavery in Cuba, 1817–1886* (Austin: University of Texas Press, 1967) on the supremacy of the local planters in political affairs. I have made references to Professor Corwin's book wherever our interpretation of the data coincided. On this topic, see chapters 4–7, 14, and esp. pp. 47–67, 255–59. See also AHN, Ultramar, Esclavitud, 3552(2), ind. 6: Confidential report of the captain-general of Cuba, Sept. 30, 1844.

14. Quoted in Rafael Soto Paz, *La falsa cubanidad de Saco, Luz, y Del Monte* (Havana: Ed. Alfa, 1941), p. 10.

land, brought immediate, strong, white cohesion in Cuba, and threats of secession from Spain.[15] So great did the anti-Spanish threats become, that in 1854, the governor and captain-general, the Marquis of Pezuela, had to issue a public edict which stated, *inter alia,* that any rumor that Spain was about to alter slavery in Cuba, was: "a detestable invention, thoroughly false, highly offensive, against the honor and glory of Spain, and farthest removed from the sentiments of the queen [Isabel II]."[16] Even if the Cuban Creoles were ambivalent, there was little doubt that, until the middle of the nineteenth century, they consistently preferred sugar and slavery to any idea of political change. Profit, not politics, was apparently their major goal.[17]

In the long run, however, economics dictated that an independent Cuba held more potential appeal to this class. The Creoles, through the years, came to regard Spanish political control as increasingly unnecessary. They had acceded to abolition only when they realized the political and economic impracticability of continuing to operate their estates with African slaves. (Even then, as I have mentioned, they tried to import indentured Asians in large numbers to supplement the locally available free labor. And they were confident that the free colored population had little choice but to work on the sugar estates if they wanted to participate in the money economy.[18]) But after abolition in Cuba the same situation prevailed as with the monarchy in Brazil after abolition there. It was unimportant whether or not the planters actively supported those who rebelled against Spanish authority. Once they withdrew their wholehearted support from that authority, it fell, and its fall in Cuba was hastened by the weakening in the political position of the Peninsulares, who might have continued to offer it support, even though much of the support they had given was dictated by a self-interest no longer operative after the abolition of slavery.

15. Spain, Ministerio de Ultramar, *Documentos* [pamphlet] (Madrid: Impr. Nacional, 1879), especially pp. 2–3.

16. Quoted in Soto Paz, *La falsa cubanidad,* p. 10. Pezuela was undoubtedly correct about the queen's sentiments, for at the time she was still collecting tax on every bozal who entered Cuba.

17. José Antonio Saco, *Historia de la esclavitud de la raza africana en el nuevo mundo . . .* (4 vols.; Havana: Cultural, 1938), 4:45.

18. See the responses to the queries in Robert P. Porter, *Industrial Cuba* (New York: G. P. Putnam's Sons, 1899), pp. 78–89. Once Cuba had become wholly a cash economy, and the abolition of slavery had ended the conuco privileges, those nonwhite and other workers who lacked land to continue their private cultivation were forced to seek employment on the sugar estates. They rapidly became debt-peons, a situation probably encouraged by the estates.

Below the whites in the social and economic stratification was an expanding group of free persons of color. Initially, they were the illegitimate offspring of white masters and black slaves, a commonplace occurrence in every slave society. Since miscegenation ran afoul of the mores of the planter oligarchy, those children so produced rarely inherited any substantial property from their fathers, for Roman and common law forbade such legacies. In some cases they became slaves. But often, depending on the individual circumstances, a father gave his half-caste son his freedom.

According to the official estimates of 1791, there were 54,154 free persons of color in the island of Cuba.[19] Of that number, 33,886 had some white ancestor. At the same time, however, the mulatto slaves in the island numbered 12,135. By 1841 the total colored population had grown to 152,838, of which 88,054 were mulattoes (see Table 8). While the number of mulatto slaves stood at 10,974, it would be impossible to ascertain whether the manumission of halfcastes had increased or declined, as the census information for the period was far too limited. In the census of 1860 the authorities removed the former classification of the free colored persons—previously divided into *pardo* (mulatto), and *moreno* (black)—and created the homogenous group called the *gente de color* (colored people). This act, taken by itself, might have been a significant index of deteriorating social and racial relations.

However generous earlier white patrons had been towards their slaves, the practice of manumission declined as the demand for labor increased.[20] And regardless of the enlightened stipulations of the unimplemented slave code of 1789, the political, social, and economic position of the free colored people steadily worsened.[21] A new series of laws sharpened the ostracism practiced against nonwhites.[22] In 1853 a traveler to Cuba even noted that "emancipation of slaves very seldom occurs in Cuba, where they publicly shout that abolitionists are those who have no slaves."[23]

19. Ramiro Guerra y Sánchez et al. eds., *Historia de la nación cubana* (10 vols.; Havana: Ed. Hist. de la Nación Cubana, 1952), 3:334.
20. The optimistic pictures drawn in Alexander von Humboldt, *The Island of Cuba,* trans. J. S. Thrasher (New York: Derby & Jackson, 1856), p. 185; and Herbert S. Klein, *Slavery in the Americas* (Chicago: University of Chicago Press, 1967), pp. 194–95, are not supported by statistical evidence.
21. Foner, *Cuba,* 1:50–51. It became difficult for the free colored man to become a tenant farmer, for example.
22. José M. Zamora y Coronado, comp., *Biblioteca de legislación ultramarina* (7 vols.; Madrid: Alegría y Charlain, 1844–49), 4:461–68.
23. Philalethes, *Yankee Travels,* p. 393.

Nevertheless, as the total population of the island increased the economic role of the free colored sector broadened. Their contribution to the economy had always been quite substantial;[24] as the labor shortage grew more acute, the demand for wage-paid labor steadily rose higher, and was filled more and more by the free persons of color. Despite the pejorations of most whites in Cuba on the abilities of that group, Antonio de las Barras y Prado observed in the mid-nineteenth century that, "the people of color serve the whites in every domestic, agricultural, and industrial job."[25]

Freedmen appeared in every occupation throughout the island. They were most prominent in the urban services, which were either grossly neglected or undersupplied by white labor. And while free persons of color virtually dominated such occupations as cab-driving, cooking, washing, and music, and competed with slaves in domestic service, they seldom featured among the professions, or among the slaveholding and landholding groups.[26]

By virtue of their activities, and from their distaste for the state of slavery (from which many had narrowly escaped), the free colored people concentrated in the large towns or in the eastern provinces. Ramiro Guerra y Sanchez noted that the population trend of mestizos and free persons of color ran almost diagonally opposite to that of the rich whites and the slaves.[27] The twenty-two western provinces of the island in 1870 counted 600,840 white persons, 141,677 free persons of color, and 300,989 slaves.[28] The province of Havana alone had 131,404 whites, 45,366 free colored people, and 29,919 slaves. The great sugar-producing province of Matanzas had 41,027 whites, 7,998 free colored people, and 31,629 slaves. At the same time, the seven eastern provinces of Baracoa, Bayamo, Santiago de Cuba, Guantánamo, Holguín, Jiguaní, and Manzanillo had representative total figures of 113,702 whites, 83,189 free colored, and 47,410 slaves.

Broken down, these figures showed that of every 100 white persons in Cuba, there were approximately 5 in Havana, 5 in Matanzas, and 12 in the seven easternmost provinces. Of every 100 slaves, there would

24. Klein, *Slavery*, pp. 194–227.
25. Barras y Prado, *Memorias*, p. 107.
26. See Jacobo de la Pezuela y Lobo, *Diccionario geográfico, estadístico, histórico de la isla de Cuba* (4 vols.; Madrid: Mellado, 1863–66), 3:350–72.
27. Ramiro Guerra y Sánchez, *Guerra de los diez años, 1868–1878* (Havana: Cultural, 1950), pp. 4–5.
28. These figures, as well as those immediately following, are taken from *Cuba desde 1850 á 1870* (Madrid: Impr. Nacional, 1873), pp. 152–53.

be 10 in both Havana and Matanzas, and 15 scattered throughout the east. On the other hand, of every 100 free colored people, the distribution was 16 in Havana, 3 in Matanzas, and 33 in the east.

In the segmented Spanish colonial society, with its ingrained inequality, the relations between the free colored community and the white upper group were extremely delicate. Before the nineteenth century, there had been evidence of a felicitous affiliation between the two uppermost sectors. And the slave code of 1789 even stipulated some political and social provisions for the intermediate group. This evidence of juridicial benevolent paternalism has misled many authors into the belief that the relationship between the white and free colored people was a model of open social acceptance on both sides.[29] Nothing could be further from the truth.

Both free colored and whites assisted in large organized slave revolts, which were rather rare in Cuba.[30] Although by so doing both groups (as well as the slaves) expressed their caustic disapproval of the institution of slavery, yet it was the free colored people who, as a group, suffered the most severe aftereffects of slave revolts. After the famous but wholly fictitious "revolt" of 1844, Captain-General Leopoldo O'Donnell exacted harsh penalties from the free colored. Thousands were shot or expelled from the island without the slightest material evidence of a plot. A decade later, another captain-general, José de la Concha, decried the travesty of justice, and remarked:

> The findings of the military commission produced the execution, confiscation of property, and explusion from the island of a great many persons of color, but it did not find arms, munitions, documents, or any other incriminating object which proved that there was such a conspiracy, much less on such a vast scale.[31]

José de la Concha further expressed the view that there was no need to suspect the fidelity of the free colored people in Cuba, unless they were aroused by outside agitators.

It was, curiously enough, the problem of slavery which eroded the

29. Most notably, Frank Tannenbaum, whose *Slave and Citizen* (New York: Knopf, 1946) has produced a host of disciples.

30. While small, spontaneous uprisings were commonplace throughout the history of slavery anywhere, large organized revolts, involving slaves from many estates, or covering a wide area, were rare throughout the entire West Indies as well as Cuba. See Orlando Patterson, *The Sociology of Slavery* (London: Macgibbon & Kee, 1967) and Goveia, *Slave Society in the Leeward Islands.*

31. José Gutiérrez de la Concha, *Memorias . . .* (Madrid: Trujillo, 1853), p. 15.

former relatively amicable relationship existing between whites and free coloreds on the island. The spiraling black population led to a sharpening fear of a recurrence of the events in St. Domingue during the last decade of the eighteenth century. The agonizing debates in the British Parliament leading to the abolition of slavery in the British West Indies made the situation of the Cuban white planters even more acute.[32]

For a long time there had been warnings of a social menace (for this was the prevailing view of the transformation of Cuba into a racially mixed society). Nevertheless, the planters, with amazing ambivalence, seemed too busy to take the necessary heed. To them it was better to get rich first, then think about the consequences of slavery later. José Antonio Saco, a wealthy planter himself, but racist enough to advocate strongly a white Cuba, aptly described the dilemma of the other plantation owners in the early nineteenth century:

> The Cubans, lured by the extraordinary prices of sugar and coffee in the markets of Europe multiplied their plantations. And although they should have been restrained, or more circumspect in view of the bloody catastrophe in the neighboring island, the prosperity of the moment blinded them to the dangers of the future. What a misfortune that the good fathers of that epoch did not ask for the abolition of the slave trade and clamor vigorously for the importation of white colonists! Had they promoted so great a benefit, the present generation would bless their names, and adore them as the saviors of their country. But even in the midst of the terrors instilled in them by the destruction of St. Domingue, they still longed for Negroes, believing that, without them, there could be no prosperity for Cuba.[33]

The enormous increase in the number of Negroes and especially the rapid expansion in plantation agriculture led to more frequent local slave uprisings. Between 1820 and 1844, there were over half a dozen small slave disturbances and rumors of many more. This state of affairs further adversely affected the presumed harmony between whites and non-whites, and heightened the specter of a violent racial confrontation. In that atmosphere of fear and suspicion, the police protection measures gradually increased and laws that had long laid dormant on the books began to be implemented against the nonwhite sector.[34] A royal order issued on the March 12, 1837, prohibited the landing of any free person

32. [Cristóbal Madan], *Llamamiento de la isla de Cuba a la nación española* (New York: Hallet, 1854).

33. Saco, *Historia,* 3:29.

34. [Madan], *Llamamiento,* pp. 84–85,

of color in any port in the island of Cuba. David Turnbull reported that in one instance all the colored crew members of a ship were promptly arrested for the entire period that their ship remained in Havana, and were only released and compelled to leave the island a short time before their ship sailed.[35] In the *Bando de gobernación y policía de la isla de Cuba* of 1842, issued by Captain-General Gerónimo Valdés, the government required free colored persons to obtain a license from their local town councils before they could seek employment.[36] The same declaration also forbade the free colored people the "carrying of arms permitted to white persons."[37] Indeed, most white persons began to express very poor opinions of the free colored people. The strongest indictment of this substantial element of the Cuban society was made by Cristóbal Madan, writing in 1864:

> The colored people scarcely contribute to the effective working class on the island, in proportion to their numbers. They do not dwell on their plots of land, but congregate in the towns and villages, where they degenerate more each day into a lazy and vicious bunch. Their women possess the most depraved habits, and it can be said that the race is almost of no use, either to itself or the country in which it lives; a significant portion is mulatto.[38]

Madan's severe criticism of the free colored people was not only a great exaggeration, but also a clear reflection of the growth of a rabid racism among the white persons in the island. It was not so much that the free colored people were unwilling to work, as that they were not encouraged to work. Lacking the capital for the establishment of ingenios, and being more adept at the urban skills—coachmen, seamstresses, tailors, carpenters, masons, and shoemakers—they naturally flocked to the cities. The free colored people gravitated to areas of opportunity. And in some regions in the east, especially in Santiago de Cuba, the free colored landowners and farmers exceeded the number of urban workers. Cristóbal Madan was incensed primarily because the free colored persons refused (with some justification) to work on the sugar estates.

Within their permitted vocations, the free persons of color exhibited

35. David Turnbull, *Travels in the West. Cuba* (London: Longman, Orme, Brown, Green, and Longmans, 1840), p. 70.

36. *Bando de gobernación y policía de la isla de Cuba* . . . (Havana: Impr. del Gobierno, 1842), Art. 17.

37. Ibid., Art. 143.

38. [Madan], *El trabajo libre*, p. 3.

every degree of ambition, energetic application, and success.[39] They were, however, struggling within a system which was not very encouraging. The closed-caste nature of Cuban society relegated all nonwhites to the lower social and economic positions; and persons with black skins found the situation exceptionally difficult. Attempts to elevate themselves—to take advantage of the loudly vaunted Spanish "color blindness"—could be cruelly frustrated by the insuperable handicap of a colored skin. This does not necessarily deny the existence of the avenues of mobility, but merely asserts that the greatest mobility accrued to those in the society who could "pass as white." It is easy to find ample statistics for those who applied (with or without success) for royal permission to breach the color gap and enter the universities, or to practice law or medicine, or even to enter the all-white royal bureaucracy. Yet there must have been tens of thousands whose obvious handicap of skin color or lack of the socially valuable *limpieza de sangre* completely deterred from any attempt to break out of their artificially narrowed world.

It seems reasonable to assume that there could not have been much socioeconomic mobility during the nineteenth century, when one observer in the mid-twentieth century in Cuba noted that there was almost a uniformly rigid exclusion of colored persons from the upper reaches of the structure.[40] By the twentieth century, segregation and discrimination —though not on the scale of the United States—had become customary. By and large, therefore, mobility was restricted within the class divisions of the racial castes. And social distinction rested with the fortuitous nature of birth and skin color. The white persons, regardless of their economic positions or their personal characters, remained forever in the upper caste. One might be of a lower class in that caste, but even there one still enjoyed a status superior to all nonwhites. It is not too great a distortion of the reality to claim that the degree of skin color usually determined the position in the lower sector held by any individual. At the bottom of the society (at least until 1886) were the slaves—almost

39. Klein, *Slavery,* pp. 194–227.

40. See Charles E. Chapman, *A History of the Cuban Republic* (New York: Macmillan, 1927), pp. 311–12; and Lowry Nelson, *Rural Cuba* (Minneapolis: University of Minnesota Press, 1950), pp. 155–58. Nelson's observation (pp. 156–57) that "while there is a distribution of colored workers among all the occupations, it is clear that they are predominantly the hewers of wood and drawers of water," is an accurate description of the Afro-Cubans from the sixteenth into the twentieth century.

all black. And indeed, for some time before 1866, the possession of
too black a skin color could jeopardize the chances of remaining a free
person in the island.[41] Such stratification according to skin color was
sanctioned by Spanish bureaucratic practice—the reflection of the
built-in inequality of Spanish society—and upheld by all whites in the
Spanish overseas colonies. A longtime resident of Havana described the
situation there in the middle of the nineteenth century:

> In no form of public spectacle can the colored people mix with the
> whites; it is forbidden even at dances. At the theatre, the circus and
> other forms of public entertainment the coloreds have their isolated
> section. Besides, they are allowed to hold their own public dances,
> where only their own colored folk are found. But there is no segregation
> in the churches, to show the whites that all are equal before God.[42]

José Antonio Saco, the most intelligent and articulate of the Cuban
racists, upheld the increasingly apartheid policies of the Cuban government. Saco might have been influenced by the then prevailing ideas of
social engineering, a theory fast becoming fashionable among the positivist-inclined of the Latin American intelligentsia. But he could have
arrived at the same position by his experience in a plantation society
which had the historical example of the surrounding Caribbean islands,
particularly the old French colony of St. Domingue, to serve as a guide.
Saco insisted from the early 1830's that white immigration was the
only hope for the future success of the island:

> Upon white immigration depend agricultural improvement, the per-
> fection of the arts, in one word, the prosperity of Cuba in every sphere;
> and the steadfast hope that the crumbling edifice which now threatens
> us, will be restored confidently on a solid and indestructible base.
>
> The colonization of Cuba is necessary and urgently required to give to
> the white population of Cuba a moral and numerical preponderance
> over its black inhabitants . . . it is necessary to counter the ambitions
> of one million two hundred thousand Haitians and Jamaicans who seek
> her lonely beaches and unused lands; it is necessary to neutralize as far
> as possible the terrible influence of the three million blacks who sur-

41. AHN, Estado, Esclavitud, leg. 8043(10), fol. 6.
42. Barras y Prado, *Memorias,* p. 112. When Fredrika Bremer visited Cuba in
1850, she had great difficulty in getting permission to attend a ball for free persons
of color in Matanzas. But the fact that she was admitted along with her white
escort shows that exceptions could be made under unusual circumstances. See,
Fredrika Bremer, *The Homes of the New World, Impressions of America,* trans.
Mary Howitt (2 vols.; New York: Harper & Bros., 1853), 2:306–8, 379.

round us, the millions to come by natural increase, and who will drag us down in the near future in a bitter, bloody holocaust.[43]

Even in the words of Saco, the intellect could be subdued by the emotional response of deep-seated fear.

The racism born of fear and insecurity on the island was not greatly alleviated by the policies of the metropolitan power. During the earlier part of the century there was a deliberate attempt on the part of the Spanish government to maintain a balance of the races in Cuba. Marcelino Oraa confessed to the council of ministers that such a delicate situation enabled the metropolitan military forces to assume the role of "honest broker" between white and nonwhite sectors.[44] In the long run the Spanish attempt to hold an equilibrium became untenable in the light of an ever increasing demand for African slaves to work on the sugar estates. Yet, for the short time that it was attempted, it emphasized the declining moral strength of the Spanish crown, and its colonial bureaucracy. Legitimacy and the ancient mystique of the monarchy had given way to duplicity, political blackmail, and the reckless exploitation of the prevailing racist fear in Cuba.

Probably owing to its moral and physical decadence, but certainly because it suffered from the vicissitudes of Spanish internal politics, the colonial bureaucracy in Cuba was corrupt, inefficient, and sometimes repressive. If the character of the government usually reflected the personality of the captain-general in Havana, then perhaps it could be said that the personality of the captain-general reflected the mood of Spanish court politics.

Spain in the nineteenth century was continually in politically turmoil.[45] The Napoleonic invasion had not only replaced Ferdinand VII, *pro tempore,* by the cautious Joseph Bonaparte, but had given strong impetus to the latent divisions between the liberal groups which favored monarchical reform, and the conservative groups which desperately sought to stifle the dynamism of the society. Although the Spaniards

43. Quoted in Fernando Ortiz Fernandez, *José Antonio Saco y sus ideas cubanas* (Havana: Universo, 1929), pp. 73–74.

44. AHN, Ultramar, Esclavitud, leg. 3552(2), ind. 6, 1846: Marcelino Oraa al Consejo de Ministros, Dec. 22, 1846; also ibid., fol. 3: Confidential dispatch of Captain-General O'Donnell to the Sección de Ultramar del Consejo Real, Sept. 30, 1844.

45. For Spanish history in the nineteenth century, see Raymond Carr, *Spain: 1808–1939* (Oxford: Clarendon, 1966), and Rhea Smith, *Spain: A Modern History* (Ann Arbor: University of Michigan Press, 1965).

threw out the French, the constitution of 1812 clearly revealed how strong was the French intellectual impact on Spanish ideas. The reaction against absolutism that began in the early years of the century continued throughout. Neither liberal nor conservative factions could win a clearcut military or political ascendancy, even though the country underwent a three-year civil war which began in 1820.

While both factions in Spain held widely disparate views, yet they were, internally, merely loosely affiliated groups. Attempts to categorize them as simply liberal or conservative must be fraught with hazards, yet these are convenient terms, bearing in mind the political connotations of that age. Liberals advocated social equality, democratic institutions, and improved administrative organizations. In short, Spanish liberals wanted to bring their country ideologically nearer to France and Britain. Conservatives, on the other hand, wanted a restoration of the situation that had existed before Napoleon Bonaparte.

It is probably accurate to say that the conservative elements were slowly gaining the upper hand when Ferdinand VII died in 1833. The ensuing civil war that was known to history as the Carlist Wars far transcended a simple internal dynastic struggle. The Carlists, the supporters of Don Carlos, Ferdinand's brother, drew their strength principally from the reactionary members of the clergy, the conservative elements in the country, particularly the peasants of Vizcaya and Navarre, and at least officially, the powers of the Holy Alliance. For his part, Don Carlos maintained that the Salic Law of Bourbon tradition upheld his claim to the throne, since his brother had died without a male heir.

Maria Cristina, the regent for the infant Isabel, insisted that the claim of her daughter was valid both by ancient Spanish custom, which preceded the Salic Law, and by the express proclamation of Ferdinand VII, issued a few months before his death. Moreover, with Don Carlos living in exile in Lisbon, Isabel was the *de facto* monarch. The royal ladies had the sympathy and active support of most royalist and Catholic moderates, liberals, revolutionaries, and freemasons throughout Europe, as well as the governments of Britain and France.

The Carlist Wars further depleted the Spanish treasury and disrupted Spanish relations with the Roman Catholic Church, Britain, and France. The wars accentuated the rise and fall of politicians in Madrid, and afforded an opportunity for the inordinate rise of the military in political affairs. For a full generation the country was torn by political factions frantically vying with each other for ascendancy and the favor of the queen. Between 1845 and 1868, the government witnessed a bewildering change of leadership between the Progressives and the Moderates at first, followed by Liberal Unionists, Moderates, Progressives, and Democrats. Generals who had made their fame, and often their fortunes, in the colonies came to power in Madrid. Four of them—Leopoldo O'Donnell, Domingo Dulce, José de la Concha, and Francisco Serrano— had recently served in Cuba. Along with all the other factors, a strong catalyst of discontent and disintegration throughout the period lay in the dissipated and shrewish character of Isabel II. But even after the overthrow of the queen in 1868, political instability ended only with the accession of Alfonso XII in 1874.

As a result of the unstable politics in Spain and the pregnant revolutionary ideas of the post-Napoleonic period, many subversive organizations developed among the white sector of the Cuban population. Most of those conspiracies were quickly discovered and easily suppressed. Many of the conspirators, drawn largely from the Creole intelligentsia and including such eminent future abolitionists as José Antonio Saco and Rafael María de Labra, were exiled for their views. And since the Peninsular Spaniards favored any type of Spanish rule to an independent Cuba, while the Creoles were the most articulate critics of Spanish rule, the traditional divisions between the two subgroups deepened.

Most captains-general, beginning with Miguel Tacón y Rosique in 1834 and ending with Cañedo in 1853, tended to perpetuate the system of favoring the Peninsulares and excluding the Creoles from office, thus further alienating the powerful Creole interests from the regime. Still, that was not the only grievance of the Creoles. For not only was Spanish colonial policy in Cuba highly partisan, but the colonial administration was notoriously corrupt. Bribery was part and parcel of the system. Most high officials, as has been pointed out, actually connived in the illegal slave trade.[46] In 1846 Lord Palmerston, the British foreign secretary, wrote to Sir Henry Lytton Bulwer, the pro-abolitionist ambassador in Madrid, that he had evidence of the longstanding practice of selling emancipados declared free by the court of Mixed Commission at Havana. He told of fifty emancipados being "sold" for five years to the Havana Gas Company, to serve as lamplighters; the com-

46. AHN, Ultramar, Esclavitud, leg. 3547, fol. 1333: Serrano al M. de Guerra y Ultramar, July 2, 1861 (confidential). Almost every visitor to Cuba commented on the venality of the local officials.

pany paid a price of five ounces of gold for each. Another five hundred were sold at prices averaging nine ounces of gold each, while the profits of about 600,000 pesos had been distributed between government officials, and

> 400 had been transferred to the Marquis de las Delicias, Chief Judge of the Mixed Court, and one of the greatest slave proprietors in the island, to be held by him for the benefits of the Countess Gueraga, wife of General O'Donnell [then captain-general], in order that she might receive from their labour, an income of 4,000 dollars per month.[47]

*The Times* of London, deploring the enormous expenditure by the British to end the slave trade, bitterly criticized the collusion in Havana between slave traders and high officials, and noted that "The interests involved in this trade are mainly those of high and mighty personages at Madrid, who have power to obtain the recall of any honest official. . . . But the root of the evil still remains in the corrupt administration of the island."[48]

Most travelers to Cuba during the nineteenth century commented on the venality of officials, whether or not their general impressions of the island were favorable. John Glanville Taylor, a sailor, wrote after a few years' residence in the island, "Whenever it becomes of sufficient importance to evade the law, *any* law, it can be done; and with money enough, you might make all the officials of Cuba (when I was there at least), simultaneously *blind, deaf,* and *lame.*"[49] British consul David Turnbull, noting the improbable returns of the customs officials, and the apparently declining total flour importations in the early 1830's, claimed that:

> The only possible way in which this extraordinary diminution can be reasonably accounted for is, by supposing the existence of smuggling to a large extent from North America—a supposition which is fully borne out by the opinions of the best informed merchants at the Havana.[50]

Since flour was a vital part of the diet of the slaves, and since the slave population during the period steadily increased, Turnbull's hypothesis seemed very reasonable indeed.

47. AHN, Estado, Esclavitud, leg. 8040: Palmerston to Bulwer, Aug. 3, 1846.
48. *The Times,* Aug. 19, 1853. Copy in AHN, Estado, Esclavitud, leg. 8047(14), fol. 2.
49. John Glanville Taylor, *The United States and Cuba: Eight Years of Change and Travel* (London: Bentley, 1851), p. 304.
50. Turnbull, *Travels in the West,* pp. 122–23.

Dr. Wurdemann related the anecdote of an attempt by Turnbull to expose a landing of one thousand bozales, illegally introduced. The captain-general sent a commanding officer to accompany the consul and effect the capture and arrest of the slaves and the sellers. Along the way the Spanish officer to all appearances suddenly fell ill. By the time he had received medical attention and recovered, only a few slaves of Cuban origin were still on the market. The next day, however, the owners of the slaves received a bill of two thousand doubloons, which was equally divided between the captain-general and the Spanish officer who feigned illness and thus afforded the opportunity to clear the bozales from the market place.[51]

William H. Hurlbert had personal experiences of official peculation in the mid-1850's:

> More irreconcilably hostile than the merchants to the Creole population, are the old Spanish officials. It is really hard to exaggerate the extent to which bribery and corruption are carried among these persons, or the annoyances to which the unprotected natives are subjected at the hands of Dogberrys clothed with more or less authority. At Havana, it is notoriously impossible to procure any paper of importance at the government house, without employing an *agente* or general broker, a limited number of whom are licensed by the government. I tried the experiment myself of applying personally for a certain document, but after dancing attendance for nearly a week in the large and little rooms of the Palace, I gave it up and put the matter into the hands of an *agente*, who within the day brought me the required parchment stamped conspicuously with the word *gratis,* and demanded seven dollars as the price thereof! These fees are of course divided with the subordinates at the Palace. The whole thing is in the purest oriental taste, but one must be very immoral to enjoy it.[52]

Edwin F. Atkins, who had extensive dealings with all aspects of Cuban life, not only supports some of the contentions against the officials, but suggested a possible reason:

> Spanish officials, from the lowest to the highest, encouraged this illegitimate trade and shared in its profits; for salaries were small, terms were short, and they were expected to live off the collections during their terms of office. Many honorable Spanish merchants, exact in all other dealings, considered it quite legitimate to evade payment of duties

51. [J. G. F. Wurdemann], *Notes on Cuba* (Boston: Munroe, 1844), pp. 254–55.

52. [William H. Hurlbert], *Gan-Eden: or, Pictures of Cuba* (Boston: Jewett, 1854), pp. 158–59.

wherever possible; in fact, otherwise they could not compete with others in selling, and moreover would have been persecuted by the officials who would have felt themselves defrauded by their share of the profit. It was always claimed by these officials that they had to share the spoils with those higher up, back to their patrons in Spain who had secured them their berths.[53]

It was the corruption of Spanish officials that afforded the slave traders (*negreros*) and the slaveholding group in Cuba the opportunity to attain effective political control of the island. By the 1850's, there was very little action on the treaties of 1817 and 1835 with Britain to end the trade, precisely because the power to do so rested in Havana, not Madrid.[54] But the influence of the negrero group extended as far as Madrid. So cognizant of their economic and political power were the Cuban slaveowners that one boasted to a foreigner:

> There is not a man likely to come to power in Madrid, but has his price. When Prim contemplated the sale of Cuba in 1869, 100,000 dollars opportunely administered, induced him to reconsider the proposal, and even previous to the King's abdication and Zorilla's retirement, the obnoxious bill respecting abolition in Porto Rico had, on consideration, been withdrawn. If Spain proposes, Cuba disposes.[55]

The corruption of the local bureaucracy in Cuba weakened the control of the central authorities, and further inhibited effective interference to eliminate infringement of the laws. Given this inefficiency and corruption, therefore, it was not surprising that the bureaucracy should have been overpowered by the local planters. Every decision vital to planter interest, particularly in the vexing problem of slavery, had to be carefully weighed and shrewdly tested, before it could be acted on in Madrid, at the highest level of government.[56] The colonial bureaucrats, regardless of the laws and the intention of the crown, were in no position in Cuba to intervene on behalf of slaves with any amount of efficacy. They found themselves dominated by the Casino Español, the club of wealthy planters and merchants whose riches came from slaves and

53. Atkins, *Sixty Years,* pp. 62–64. For further bribery and corruption in the judiciary, see also ibid., pp. 68–73.

54. AHN, Estado, Esclavitud, leg. 8048.

55. Antonio C. Gallenga, *The Pearl of the Antilles* (London: Chapman & Hall, 1873), p. 73.

56. See AHN, Ultramar, Esclavitud, leg. 3548, fol. 9: Cañedo al Consejo de Ministros, June 21, 1853; and ibid., leg. 3552(2), ind. 7: Confidential report of secretary of government and development.

slavery.[57] Those callous men never allowed sentiment to interfere with their business interests, and even forcefully expelled their captain-general, Domingo Dulce, on the night of June 1, 1869. To hold, there-fore, that Spanish bureaucracy "softened" Cuban slavery in the nine-teenth century, is an exercise in wishful thinking.

The Roman Catholic Church, in addition to the colonial bureaucracy, was the other all-pervasive organization in Cuba. It affected to some degree the life of every Cuban, regardless of color or social position. In Spanish colonial expansion, church and state often went hand in hand, and to be hispanicized was equivalent to being catholicized. It was not surprising, therefore, that the early colonial Church should have addressed itself to the position of its non-European converts, the Indians and the Negroes.[58] And in an age of strong religious convic-tions, and in a colonial situation pervaded by the influence of the Church, Negroes as well as whites became theoretically equal in the sight of God. Any other position taken by the Church would have denied the hu-manity of the Indians and Negroes and severely undermined the su-premacy of the Church. So once the debate had been settled in the middle of the sixteenth century, a plethora of legislation stipulated that within the organization of the Church there could be no overt racial segregation. Religious instruction for Indian and Negro slaves became a legal requirement.[59]

In the relative simplicity of the socioeconomic structure of Cuba be-fore the arrival of the plantation society, it was not difficult for the Church to exert its influence. Certainly, the Church did support the lower sector of the population, and may have been the arbiter of social con-duct. It is, nevertheless, extremely easy to overestimate its influence in its relations with whites and nonwhites. The Church was a part of the system of slavery. It supported, reinforced, and reflected the status quo.

57. For accounts of the power and influence of the Casino Español, see *Cuba desde 1850*, pp. 273–77; Gallenga, *Pearl of the Antilles*, pp. 32–37; José J. Ribó, *Historia de los voluntarios cubanos* . . . (2 vols.; Madrid: González, 1872); Antonio Pirala y Criado, *Anales de la guerra de Cuba* (4 vols.; Madrid: F. González Rojas, 1895–98); and Justo Zaragoza, *Las insurrecciones en Cuba* (2 vols.; Madrid: Hernández, 1872–73), esp. 2:415–26.

58. See Robert Ricard, *The Spiritual Conquest of Mexico*, trans. Lesley Byrd Simpson (Berkeley: University of California Press, 1966); and Klein, *Slavery*, pp. 87–105.

59. *Recopilación de las leyes de los reynos de las Indias* (3 vols.; Madrid, 1791), lib. I, tit. I, ley XII; and lib. I, tit. I, ley XIII. See also Klein, *Slavery*, pp. 90–95.

It preached obedience to the white master among the slaves, and propagandized the then present inequality and suffering as preparation for an equitable afterlife. Even though the Church may have treated its own slaves with some measure of paternal gentleness, no one could ever precisely assess how great was its moral suasion among the slaveholding laymen.

Where the Spanish colonial bureaucracy had proved itself powerless in the nineteenth century, it was hardly feasible for the Church to succeed. Above all, the Church itself was having its own internal problems. For the clergy was bitterly divided between Spanish priests and Cuban priests, each group preaching the same religious doctrine, but hopelessly separated on matters of secular opinion. The Spanish priests, like the Peninsulares, actively identified themselves with Spain and supported Spanish power on the island.[60] This did not necessarily weaken the organization of the Church, but made the insistence of the priests in delicate matters such as slavery less likely, or merely perfunctory.

It is, nevertheless, highly probable that in the urban areas, and especially among domestic slaves, religious practice and clerical intercession had some influence on the relationship between masters and slaves.[61] This might have been particularly true of the older slaveholding families which did not change over to plantation agriculture—but even here the habitual observations may have had some effect. In looking at the effect of the clergy on the practice of slavery, therefore, the situation of the slaves must be taken into account. Urban and domestic slaves had certain advantages over rural field slaves. The distribution of the clergy was also a factor which may have inadvertently contributed to the apparent neglect of the rural slaves. The location of the parishes was made to accommodate the white members of the society, and since most of these lived in the towns, more priests were assigned to the towns. It may be also that the Catholic Church in Cuba did not fully adjust to the rapid demographic changes of the society. In 1860, of the 779 clergymen ministering to a population of 1,396,530 (a ratio of 1:2,000) more than 50 per cent (401) lived in Havana. Meanwhile, areas of dense slave populations had comparably fewer priests, and there seemed no

---

60. Francisco González del Valle y Ramírez, "El clero en la revolución cubana," *Cuba Contemporánea,* 18 (1918), 140–205, esp. 146–47, 191.
61. See R. R. Madden, *Poems of a Slave in the Island of Cuba* (London: Thos. Ward, 1840).

TABLE 9

Slaves and Clergy: Distribution in Cuba About 1860

| Department | Clergy in 1860 | Slaves in 1857 | Approx. ratio |
|---|---|---|---|
| *Western* | | | |
| Bahía Honda | 3 | 6,912 | 1:2300 |
| Bejucal | 10 | 7,228 | 1:720 |
| Cárdenas | 8 | 59,843 | 1:7480 |
| Cienfuegos | 7 | 15,084 | 1:2150 |
| Colón* | 8 | ? | — |
| Guanabacoa | 39 | 4,871 | 1:120 |
| Guanajay | 9 | 20,562 | 1:2280 |
| Güines | 11 | 16,530 | 1:1500 |
| Habana | 401 | 32,808 | 1:80 |
| Jaruco | 12 | 8,183 | 1:680 |
| Matanzas | 20 | 44,676 | 1:2230 |
| Nuevitas | 2 | 1,374 | 1:690 |
| Pinar del Río | 11 | 14,034 | 1:1280 |
| Puerto Príncipe | 46 | 12,947 | 1:280 |
| Remedios | 16 | 5,654 | 1:350 |
| Sagua la Grande | 6 | 15,156 | 1:2530 |
| San Antonio | 6 | 11,694 | 1:1950 |
| San Cristóbal | 6 | 6,727 | 1:1120 |
| Sancti-Spíritus | 17 | 8,443 | 1:500 |
| Santa Clara | 7 | 6,267 | 1:900 |
| Santa María del Rosario | 3 | 5,329 | 1:1780 |
| Santiago | 8 | 5,429 | 1:680 |
| Trinidad | 14 | 11,121 | 1:790 |
| Total | 670 | 320,858 | 1:480 |
| *Eastern* | | | |
| Baracoa | 6 | 1,719 | 1:290 |
| Bayamo | 13 | 2,709 | 1:210 |
| Cuba | 63 | 34,728 | 1:550 |
| Guantánamo | 3 | 6,872 | 1:2290 |
| Holguín | 14 | 3,393 | 1:240 |
| Jiguaní | 3 | 663 | 1:220 |
| Manzanillo | 5 | 1,208 | 1:240 |
| Las Tunas | 2 | 781 | 1:390 |
| Total | 109 | 52,073 | 1:480 |

* Colon was later created from some of the interior western territories.

Source: Slave totals taken from *cédula de capitación* for 1857, found in AHN, Ultramar, Esclauitud, leg. *3553;* those of the clergy taken from Spain, Instituto Geográfico y Estadístico, *Censo . . . 1860.*

attempt to correlate the number of clergy with the number of slaves. (See Table 9.)

Domestic slaves in an urban setting had, of course, the legal resources mentioned in chapter 4. In extreme cases they could obtain the services of the síndico and petition their masters to sell them.[62] In such a setting the entire structure, regardless of the Church, lent itself to easier relations between the two groups. And as may be expected anywhere, on some estates where there was a resident chaplain, and where the religious convictions of the proprietor overcame both his desire for profits, and diluted his sense of racial superiority, there may have been the opportunity for the intervening balm of Roman Catholicism. Richard Madden, visiting the ingenio Santa Ana, which had a resident chaplain, noted that the slaves were unusually well fed and strong. The ingenio was, too, one of the better managed estates in the area, and even had steam engines. As on most other sugar estates, however, the slaves averaged only three hours of sleep in a twenty-four hour day during the three and a half months of crop-time.[63] The case of Santa Ana supported, to some degree, the belief in the effect of religion on the organization and exploitation of the Cuban slaves. But in general, on the plantations of the interior, the life and condition of masters and slaves brooked little or no interference from state or Church.

But if the resistance of the planters was the main obstacle to religious benefits for the slaves, the condition of the clergy left much to be desired. Many travelers to Cuba during the nineteenth century told of the profligate living of the ordained clergy. While some may have been biased, there certainly must have been some element of truth in their reports.

Dr. J. G. F. Wurdemann of Charleston, South Carolina, visited Cuba in the early 1840s and paid extensive attention to the behavior of clergymen. He frequently noted that priests, although not legally married, were not often supporters of their vows of celibacy. About the priest of Limonar, in the center of the island, he wrote:

> Although he could not be said to have the spiritual welfare of his flock at heart, he was foremost in the ranks of those who strove by schools to improve their mental culture. He owned a fine coffee-estate, which, with his income from the parish, yielded about 5,000 dollars annually. With this he supported his family, for he joined in the custom observed by his brother priests in Cuba; but he was not the less respected as a man, while his house was visited by all the neighboring gentry.[64]

62. Fernando Ortiz Fernández, *Hampa afro-cubana, los negros esclavos* (Havana: Revista Bimestre Cubana, 1916), pp. 307–13; Madden, *Cuba*, pp. 118–24; Richard H. Dana, *To Cuba and Back: A Vacation Voyage*, new ed. (Carbondale: Southern Illinois University Press, 1960), pp. 122–23.
63. Madden, *Cuba*, p. 164.
64. [Wurdemann], *Notes*, p. 130.

The Church insisted on dispensing the sacraments to all its members regardless of race or color.[65] But the practice was another matter. For the sacraments which offered pecuniary gain—at baptism, marriage, and death—there was evidence of a suspiciously high interest on the part of the Church, with differential rates according to the color of the individual, services for the blacks being a little cheaper and considerably less formal.[66] Yet there seemed to be an acute shortage of interested priests. On some estates, if the master was "a policeman as well as an economist and judge," he also had to be the spiritual father. Richard Dana noted:

> The rule respecting religion so far observed is this, that infants are baptized, and all receive Christian burial. But there is no enforcement of the obligation to give the slaves religious instruction or to allow them to attend public religious service. Most of those in the rural districts see no church and no priest, from baptism to burial. If they do receive religious instruction, or have religious services provided for them, it is the free gift of the master.
>
> Marriage by the Church is seldom celebrated. As in the Roman Church marriage is a sacrament and indissoluble, it entails great inconvenience on the master, as regards sales or mortgages, and it is a restraint on the Negroes themselves, to which it is not always easy to reconcile them. Consequently, marriages are performed by the master only, and of course, carry with them no legal rights or duties.[67]

In fact, sometimes marriage was encouraged only as a way to reduce the risk of the slaves running away, and had no religious motivation whatsoever.[68] It was simply a supplementary mechanism of the master to keep his slaves effectively on his estate.

The apparent deterioration of the Cuban clergy was not unique, but was symptomatic of a far wider religious malaise. For by the middle of the nineteenth century religion in general and the Roman Catholic Church in particular were being challenged everywhere. The religious skepticism and vague Deism of the eighteenth-century Enlightenment had been deepened and reinforced by the tremendous strides in the pure and applied sciences, with their concomitant intellectual and philosophical implications. Socially and politically, the power of the Church was in decline. The events of the Revolutionary and Napoleonic eras

65. Dana, *To Cuba*, p. 86; Klein, *Slavery*, pp. 94–98.
66. [Wurdemann], *Notes*, pp. 167–70, and pp. 260–61.
67. Dana, *To Cuba*, pp. 73, 124 (quote).
68. Suárez y Romero, *Francisco*.

had shaken the roots of its power. Anticlericalism was on the rise, and secret societies such as the Masonic lodges, formerly confined to Protestant nations, could be found in wholly Catholic countries like Belgium, Italy, the South German states, and even Cuba itself. After 1815 the Church was almost everywhere on the defensive, identified by liberals and radicals alike with the forces of reaction.[69] Leo XII had congratulated Ferdinand VII of Spain on his "victory" over the liberals in 1814, thus widening the breach between Rome and Madrid. Gregory XVI openly sympathized with Don Carlos during the Carlist Wars, and refused to recognize the government of Maria Cristina. Gregory's attitude so sharpened Spanish anticlericalism that the Cortes passed a bill placing certain proportions of the property of the Spanish Church at the disposal of the state. When the Pope refused to sanction the appointment of bishops, the Cortes threatened to enact a "civil constitution" of the clergy. The impasse between Rome and the Spanish crown was settled when Pius IX recognized Isabel II in 1851, and signed a concordat with her government.[70]

In the Spanish overseas territories, the Church had lost the enthusiasm and dynamic spirit it had in the earlier centuries. The powerful spirit that had searchingly helped to formulate the New Laws of 1542 had by 1842 become a pale ghost. One poignant measure of the political and social decline of the Church in Cuba may be gathered from the queries sent out by the captains-general, in the name of the monarch. In 1841, for example, Governor Valdés, on receipt of a dispatch from Madrid on the proposed meeting with England to discuss the possibility of emancipating all slaves brought into Cuba since 1820, sent out a circular to all the interested parties in the island, "so that the reply may be reasonable and just . . . touching every legal and economic aspect, and consistent with the national dignity and true interests of the country."[71] Although the circular went to every leading planter, and every government department, the clergy was significantly excluded. Such an exclusion would have been highly unlikely in the sixteenth century, and further emphasized the inability of the Church to intercede meaningfully in political matters in the nineteenth century. As far as slavery

69. For a full discussion of this period, see Henri Daniel-Rops, *The Church in an Age of Revolution 1789–1870,* trans. John Warrington (2 vols.; New York: Doubleday, 1967).

70. Ibid., 2:285–87.

71. AHN, Estado, Esclavitud, leg. 8052(7), fol. 1.

was concerned, a slave could expect more compassionate treatment owing to the personality of his master than from the fact that his priest interceded on his behalf. The Church could—and probably did—have some influence on the ethical outlook of some slaveowners. But far more important was that the Church was losing its political authority at just the time when a new class of slaveowners had arisen, with less respect for the customary role of the Church in society. The traditional relations between masters and slaves had little place in the new Cuban society, because so few of the slaveowners knew what those traditional relations were. The Church's loss of political influence gave an impression of religious indifference to the conditions of the slaves in the island —an impression widely propagated by H. H. Johnston, who wrote that the new Church in Cuba had lost the zeal of its counterparts in Haiti and Brazil, and appeared to be "utterly indifferent to the condition of the Negro slaves."[72]

Official circles in Madrid also noted the ineffectual role of the Church. Some members of the advisory council in the Ministerio de Ultramar summarized the waning influence of the Church in the internal relations of the Cuban slave society and linked that directly to the spirit of Antichrist born in Europe:

> There was a time, not so long ago, since some can yet remember, when the residents of that island were distinguished, as were those of the other provinces in Spain, by the depth of their religious sentiments; in those days they saw to it that their slaves received religious instruction. They themselves practised the creed which Christianity imposed on them. There were chapels in the ingenios, the cafetales, and haciendas. They buried (and perhaps their remains are still found there) their dead on some of those estates, and on them they celebrated the divine offices by clergymen supported by the owners themselves. In those days it was correct to speak of the planters as the true heads of a patriarchal family of which the slaves formed a part; and peace and virtue flourished throughout the land, as a general rule. As time passed, there came to Cuba the anti-Christian doctrines, the product of the school of Voltaire and the encyclopedists of the eighteenth century. Unfortunately the clergy and the highest stratum of the society accepted them, and propagated them among the people, fostering religious indifference. The chapels were abandoned; religious zeal disappeared; and the relations

72. Sir Harry H. Johnston, *The Negro in the New World* (London: Methuen, 1910), p. 47.

between master and slave lacked any other motivation than that of material interest, somewhat modified still by the acquired habits and customs.[73]

As Cuban society became increasingly more occupied with agricultural expansion during the early nineteenth century, the planters found themselves in a harsh dilemma. On the one hand they wanted more and more workers, particularly on the sugar cane and coffee plantations. European laborers were thought to be most unsatisfactory for those kinds of activities, and therefore were not an answer to the acute labor shortage.[74] It is irrelevant that the scientific basis for this attitude was shallow even then; most white persons in Europe and the tropical world believed it and acted accordingly. In any case, white workers were not coming to Cuba in the required numbers. For their own economic welfare, therefore, the planters had to secure Africans as the most assured source of labor. Slavery was only the means of organizing and tying that labor supply to the land. "The producer [of sugar]" wrote Manuel Moreno Fraginals, "was a slaveowner out of necessity, not from utility."[75] Slavery was cheap, reliable, and most important, available. The choice seemed to be slavery or no workers on the estates; the planters did not find it difficult.

On the other hand, however, the slaveowners were perpetually haunted by the fear that at any moment their slaves might break out in open rebellion, destroying their properties, taking their lives, and converting the island into another "Negro Republic" such as Haiti. While such fears were common in all slave societies, the remarkable events in Haiti had dramatically converted what had once been remotely probable into something distinctly possible. British public opinion and official attitudes sharpened the discomfort of the Cuban whites, and the British abolition of slavery in 1838 brought things to a fever pitch.[76]

For different reasons, both Cubans and Spanish officials finally at-

73. *Informe presentado a la junta informativa de ultramar . . .* (Madrid: J. Peña, 1869), pp. 11–12.

74. AHN, Ultramar, Esclavitud, leg. 3552(2), ind. 6; [Madan], *Llamamiento,* pp. 27–33.

75. Manuel Moreno Fraginals, *El ingenio* (Havana: Unesco, 1964), p. 144.

76. AHN, Estado, Esclavitud, leg. 8052, 1850–51; leg. 8053–54 (reports on black and white population; protests against Br. Consul Turnbull, and insistence on the recall of Turnbull, 1841–43).

tempted a solution suitable to both sides. The solution consisted of a major concerted attempt to foster white immigration to Cuba, and a complete reversal of the idea that white people could not work on the sugar plantations.

For the Cuban planters, such white immigration heightened the prospects of a larger working class to relieve the growing scarcity of agricultural laborers. Besides, as strong advocates like Saco pointed out, the more white persons were in Cuba, the less would be the fear of a black revolt ever being successful.[77] The Spanish government hoped that by a policy of white immigration it would export some of its displaced and restless population, increase the supply of free laborers in Cuba, and finally, do something positive about the persistent and embarrassing demands by Great Britain that it end the slave trade.[78]

As early as 1817, a cedula dealing with colonization had attempted to liberalize the prevailing restrictions on the movement of whites to Cuba and their permanent settlement there.[79] Initially, attempts were made to attract settlers from Spain and the Canary Islands, Ireland, and Italy. But when not enough Catholic Europeans were forthcoming, the area of origin was broadened. Non-Catholics from different countries, including the United States and Germany, went to Cuba as contract laborers.[80] Those who converted to Catholicism were then able to settle permanently and own property.

Between 1835 and 1839, there seemed to have been encouraging signs of a stream of white immigrants to the island. Over 35,000 white passengers, mostly from the Canary Islands, disembarked in the port of Havana.[81] This influx was still disappointing. The numbers were too small to warrant the high expenditure of the Junta de Fomento. The estimated annual figure of manpower importations was put at "20,000 to 30,000 *colonos.*"[82] While the early white immigrants were coming at

77. José Antonio Saco, *Replica a la contestación* . . . (Madrid: La Publicidad, 1847). Also *Informe fiscal sobre fomento de la población blanca en la isla de Cuba* (Madrid: Alegría, 1845).

78. AHN, Ultramar, Fomento, leg. 93, fols. 16–36: "Expedientes sobre introducción de colonos blancos . . . ," 1844–45.

79. Ibid., leg. 38: José de la Concha al M. de Guerra y Ultramar, Nov. 12, 1858.

80. Ibid., leg. 39, fol. 46: "Estado de trabajadores blancos."

81. Saco, *La esclavitud,* 4:33.

82. AHN, Ultramar, Esclavitud, leg. 3552(2), ind. 6, fol. 3. A "colono" was an agricultural laborer, usually a white contract or tenant farmer.

an annual average of about 7,000, the annual importation of African slaves exceeded 12,000 during the same period.[83]

| Year | Slaves | Free white persons |
|------|--------|--------------------|
| 1835 | 15,242 | 5,708 |
| 1836 | 14,082 | 8,061 |
| 1837 | 12,240 | 7,797 |
| 1838 | 10,494 | 6,319 |
| 1839 | 10,995 | 7,318 |
| Total | 63,053 | 35,203 |

And the high cost of white labor made slave labor more attractive.

European white immigration, however, rapidly declined. Not only were internal European political and economic conditions not yet favorable toward a large-scale exodus, but the Europeans were carefully avoiding areas of slave labor and depressed wages.[84] To obtain white hands, the search extended further afield.[85] Asians, particularly from China, India, and Annam, entered Cuba as contract laborers, especially destined for the sugar industry. These orientals were classified as "white" and were almost entirely males between the ages of sixteen and forty. Indeed, the search for laborers for Cuban plantations en-

83. Saco, *La esclavitud,* 4:33. Saco got these figures from the newspaper, *Diario de la Habana,* and the entry book of the merchants' warehouse in that city. They represent the figures for entry only through Havana, the major entry port, and not for other ports of the island, where there were some entries. Hubert H. S. Aimes, *A History of Slavery in Cuba 1511–1868* (New York: G. P. Putnam's Sons, 1907), p. 26, gives the following slave importations for the same years:

| | |
|------|--------|
| 1835 | 9,500 |
| 1836 | 10,750 |
| 1837 | 12,240 |
| 1838 | 10,495 |
| 1839 | 10,350 |
| Total | 53,335 |

Aimes does not cite the source for his data, which, he claims, were for the entire island. J. S. Thrasher (Humboldt, *Island of Cuba,* pp. 220–21) has figures taken from the reports of the British consul at Havana, and the Foreign Office, London, which are very close to those found in Saco. The British consul claimed that the figures should be augmented by 20% to cover nonascertained importations.

84. William Woodruff, *Impact of Western Man: A Study of Europe's Role in the World Economy, 1750–1960* (New York: St. Martin's 1967) pp. 61–100.

85. The following discussion is based on AHN, Ultramar, Fomento, legs. 94–102.

couraged many fanciful schemes to import adults from such unlikely places as Egypt, Morocco, and Ethiopia.[86]

Once the quest for agricultural laborers for the Cuban planters had shifted from Europe, as it did in the 1840s, the words "white" and "free" underwent an interesting semantic change. To the speculating capitalists involved in the importation schemes, anyone not coming from Africa was regarded as "white." In this way, a vast array of non-Europeans and non-Africans, including brown Mexican Indians, black East Indians, and "yellow" Chinese, became classified for statistical purposes as "white." Nor were those contracted to work "free." They were tied to the sugar estates, and forced to work for periods ranging from four to ten years. In the Cuban context, they became subject to almost the same forms of police measures as the African slaves they were supposed to replace. Asians who thought that the terms of their indentures allowed them to change masters found on their arrival in Cuba that they were virtually sold to the planters.[87] Antonio Gallenga noted during his travels through the island that no Cuban spoke of "hiring" a Chinese coolie. Instead, he bluntly said that he was going to "buy a chino."[88]

The organization of the trade—for such it was—to supply indentured laborers in Cuba took on the appearance of the ancient trade in African slaves, still carried on extensively if somewhat clandestinely in Cuba. In some cases, capitalists after initial hostility readily transferred their interests from slavery to the more secure and equally rewarding trade in Asian coolies.[89] After the traffic was officially authorized in 1847, huge companies became organized to handle the business. And as the future of slavery became increasingly doubtful, the requests for admission to the new trade greatly multiplied. Applications varied considerably. Some were simple requests such as that made by Juan Sechy, in 1876, to import six hundred Indians from Venezuela to work on his own sugar estate.[90] Most applications were to form large companies. Perhaps the wildest scheme came from Juan Carbonell y

---

86. Ibid., leg. 94, 1872, fol. 5.

87. Juan Pérez de la Riva, "Documentos para la historia de las gentes sin Historia. El tráfico de culíes chinos," *Revista de la Biblioteca Nacional José Martí*, 6 (1965), 77–90. Also AHN, Ultramar, Fomento, leg. 102, 1876, fol. 31.

88. Gallenga, *Pearl of the Antilles*, p. 88.

89. See Pérez de la Riva, "El tráfico de culíes chinos."

90. AHN, Ultramar, Fomento, leg. 102, fol. 30.

Martí and José Antonio Carrión, in 1873. They sought to found a company in Havana, to be called the Gran Sociedad Pecuaria y de Colonización, with share capital of between ten and twenty million pesos, to provide "cheap workers" to estate owners. They hoped to import "only 100,000 colonos annually . . . from Nigeria [*Nigricia*] . . . Portuguese East Africa, English India . . . Araucania, Yucatan, and Europe."[91] But the other companies were more modest in financial resources and more limited in their schemes. In each case, the particular company sought royal permission to import a specified number of coolies within a definite period of time.

Usually, the indentured worker signed a contract in the country of his origin.[92] The contracts bound them to seek employment in rural agricultural enterprises in Cuba, for a certain number of years, at wages ranging from four to ten pesos per month. The Asians were expected to repay the cost of their passage from their monthly income. But they received clothes, food, medical treatment, and barrack-type living quarters free of cost. In some cases promises were made to supply a school and priest. But as the imported coolies were all adult males, subjected to the same conditions of labor as the slaves, it is highly unlikely that special attention was given to this aspect. Instead, the plantation chaplain—where there was one—attended the spiritual needs of the coolies, if and when the situation arose. When a coolie's contract expired, he theoretically had the choice of either becoming a tenant farmer, or returning to his native land. Probably very few ever lived to exercise the choice. The rigors of plantation life took a heavy toll on all those involved regardless of racial differences.

The system of indentured labor, as it operated in Cuba, closely approximated the system of slavery. Even the low wages paid to the coolies were extracted from them under a host of pretenses, either as compulsory "savings" or as repayment for advancing their passage.[93] This explains why the system could be so easily grafted to that of slavery, and why estates found the operation of a slave system compatible with that of a free wage system. Regardless of legal technicalities, slav-

91. Ibid., leg. 94, fols. 5, 6.
92. For information on the importation of the Asian coolies, I have drawn material from AHN, Ultramar, Fomento, legs. 94–102, which contain a number of contracts.
93. Ibid., leg. 102, 1876, fol. 31:Cónsul de España en Saigon al M. de Estado, Sept. 4, 1876.

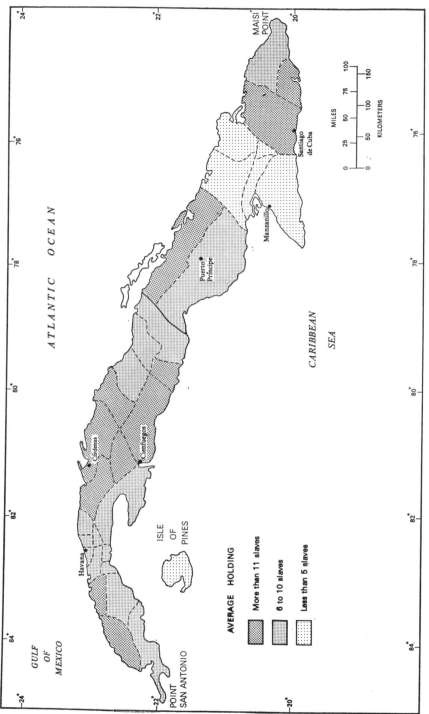

Map 4. Rural Slave Distribution, 1857. Map Courtesy UW Cartographic Lab.

ery and indentured labor were synonymous. Nevertheless, the use of indentured labor in Cuba helped to facilitate the transition from slavery to a wage-paid system. Between 1853 and 1874 Cubans imported 124,835 Chinese coolies, of which 95,631 were loaded at Macao, while, at least until 1866, the others came from Swatow, Amoy, Canton, Hong Kong, Saigon, and Manila.[94] The Chinese came in overcrowded vessels, lodged closely together as the Africans had been. Their long voyage across the Pacific and the Indian Ocean took a heavy toll of lives. Yet they came to satisfy the insatiable labor demand of sugar production in a faraway tropical island. And since the mold of sugar production had already been established, they became coinheritors with the Negroes of the lowliness of caste, the abuse, the ruthless exploitation, and the rigid derogation of all those workers on the ingenio. Chinese labor in Cuba in the nineteenth century was slavery in every social aspect except the name.

Cuban society in the nineteenth century was one in which sugar was king. The sugar planters were selfstyled princes, who dominated the society by virtue of their wealth and political influence. One visitor to Cuba wrote:

> The sugar estate spreads out its solitary but extensive field of cane, with nothing to vary the prospect but the isolated royal palms scattered irregularly over the whole. While the coffee planter's chief care is to unite in his estate beauty with profit, the only object of the sugar planter is money, often regardless if it be attained at the expense of the welfare of his laborers. In society he holds a higher rank than the other. . . . They might well be considered the natural princes of the land. The capital invested in a sugar estate is so large, that it alone gives a certain degree of importance to the planter, if he even be, as is often the case, inextricably involved in debt.[95]

The enormous financial undertaking involved in sugar production enabled the sugar cane plantation owners to live lavishly beyond their means. And as in Jamaica, Barbados, or any other "sugar island," the planters became indebted to the merchants. But in Cuba, the planters soon found themselves heavily indebted not only to the merchants in Havana or Matanzas but also to the large consortiums in New York and Boston. As the debts increased, there was little recourse left to the American interests but to continue subsidizing the planters until an un-

94. Ely, *Cuando reinaba*, p. 608.
95. [Wurdemann], *Notes*, p. 149.

usually large harvest enabled them to recover some of their money. Unfortunately, the only way some United States interests could salvage anything was by taking a personal interest in Cuban estates, and as in the case of the Atkinses foreclose on some of them. Edwin F. Atkins went to Cuba on such a mission of foreclosure for his father in the early 1860's, and wrote one of the best descriptions of the splendor of the debt-burdened planter oligarchy:

> The Estate was very beautiful; the *batey* (section with buildings and factory) occupies about thirty acres and is surrounded by a cement wall. The house and garden are simply princely. The house has twelve sleeping rooms, a dining room with marble floors, two long verandahs with inlaid floors, set basins in some of the rooms and all kinds of fixings. The garden is large and beautiful with many foreign plants and trees, fountains, baths, grottoes, hothouse for ferns, etc. It is easy to see where the six hundred thousand dollars which Juan Antonio owes went to, as he always had his house filled with company.[96]

It was obvious, even to the Cubans then, that their society was something new in their history. It was a plantation society, where the economy depended predominantly on the export crops of sugar and coffee. In economics, politics and social conduct, the new plantation owners determined what was important, and what was best for the entire society. Never before in the history of Cuba had this been so. For Cuban slave society in the nineteenth century was not just a collection of colonial Spaniards with their slaves, closely identified with their metropolis. It was, rather, a dynamic, cosmopolitan society whose umbilical cord transmitted to it the reciprocal influences of the whole world.

96. Atkins, *Sixty Years,* pp. 37–38. Prior to 1880, foreclosure could only be made against the planters' crops, not against their land or slaves. In this way, a heavily indebted planter could still get money from his creditors. By 1880, many Cuban planters were so encumbered by their debts to the United States firms that they willingly surrendered their estates to the American interests. This is how the American sugar holdings developed in Cuba. Only later did United States interests consolidate and monopolize Cuban sugar lands, and the industry.

# 6

# The Legal Framework of
# Cuban Slavery

*Nothing is more illusory than the extolled
effects of those laws which prescribe the model
of whip or the number of lashes to be given in
sequence.*

Alexander von Humboldt, 1827.

AMBIVALENCE AND AMBIGUITY have always characterized the attitudes
of the white elite groups in every society where slavery played a significant role in the social structure. Such characteristics varied from one
place to the other, but they were very pronounced in the American
colonial experience owing to the peculiarities of slavery there, and to
the changing nature of the societies themselves. For the ideals of the
early settlers, either to create the perfect society or to reproduce a
microcosm of the metropolis, rapidly faded against the realities of
their new physical environment. The new situations offered few parallels
with the established patterns of the mother country. And in some cases,
most notably in the Caribbean (though not in Cuba), the successive
changes of European governments left a mosaic of administrative forms
and practices.[1]

Against the realities of frontier conditions, both colonists and central
authorities made compromising responses. The colonists, in general,
created an ideal form of conduct and attitudes which they assumed to be
representative of the metropolis, and to which they paid lip-service.

1. See, J. H. Parry and P. M. Sherlock, *A Short History of the West Indies*
(London: Macmillan, 1956), especially chapters XIV–XV.

Colonial behavior, nevertheless, freely deviated from the ideal in every way, sometimes to such an extent that it bore no resemblance. For their part, the metropolitan powers attempted in a great variety of ways to reconcile the pecularities of frontier existence with a centralized authority and legislation.

In some British colonies, the laws of England automatically applied to the colonists. In the legislatures over which the governor presided as the representative of the crown, however, the colonists could formulate laws for their own local communities. The only open restriction upon such legislation was that it had to conform to the royal will. The crown held the powers of veto, and could exercise it to nullify any piece of legislation it thought damaging to any important interests either in England or in the particular colony, and, indeed, did nullify acts of the local legislatures considered to be contrary to the laws of England.

Spanish colonial practices were far more centralized than those of their other European counterparts in the earlier centuries of overseas colonization.[2] Guided to a certain extent by the great Council of the Indies, the Spanish crown dictated all colonial laws. But regardless of the extent to which such laws reflected reports, recommendations, and complaints from the colonies, they could not be equally applicable to all parts of the farflung Spanish empire. Naturally conflicts developed over goals and standards, making "observance and nonobservance . . . a necessary component of the system."[3] This ambiguous local response by the chief colonial administrators was summarized in the famous and graphic phrase "obedezco pero no cumplo" (I obey but I do not execute).

Since wide variations between ideal and practice were an accepted part of Spanish colonial life, it would be foolhardy to accept the sets of laws and decrees promulgated in Spain as a conclusive description of "real" conditions in the Indies. And while not denying the substantial contribution that an intensive study of such laws might yield to the study of master-slave relations, John L. Phelan has persuasively demonstrated the limitations of central decrees in some local conditions, even

2. Charles Gibson, *Spain in America* (New York: Harper & Row, 1966), and Clarence Haring, *The Spanish Empire in America* (New York: Oxford University Press, 1947).

3. John Leddy Phelan, "Authority and Flexibility in the Spanish Imperial Bureaucracy," *Administrative Science Quarterly*, 5 (1960), 47–65.

with vigorous and conscientious officials.[4] The appearance of strong centralization within the Spanish empire did not always preclude the operation of local checks and balances.

During the nineteenth century, local planter power often came close to crippling the central authority in Cuba. In 1842 Captain-General Valdés, sensitive to hostile local opposition, refused to publish the law declaring free the slaves who had been introduced illegally since 1820, despite an Anglo-Spanish agreement on that matter.[5] Later, the same problem enveloped the Moret Law of phased abolition which passed the Cortes on July 4, 1870. The Spanish government, under great international pressures to abolish slavery in Cuba and Puerto Rico, greatly desired that the law be implemented with the least possible delay.[6] In Cuba the governor and captain-general, Antonio Caballero de Rodas, acting on his own initiative—at least in the official context—suspended the implementation of the laws for two years, offering the feeble excuse that the government had not issued the *reglamento* outlining the operation of the law, and that a census had to be taken to determine the slaves who fell under its provisions.[7]

The truth of the situation, however, was that Caballero de Rodas sympathized with the planters, who, contrary to Moret's assertion, had not been consulted prior to the formulation of the law. But, of course, at this time the local Havana plantocracy had already usurped effective political power, and, with a civil war already on his hands, the governor might have realized the difficulties in which he could find himself if he obeyed his superior officers.

In spite of the discrepancy between theory and practice, the slave laws were important as an index of changing conditions and attitudes. Although the principles governing slaves in the New World had their basis in the extremely humane thirteenth-century code of laws, the *Siete partidas,* the Spanish crown found it necessary from time to time to reiterate specific laws, or to issue a complete summary of the laws. In 1680, therefore, the *Recopilación de las leyes de los reynos de las Indias*

---

4. John Leddy Phelan, *The Kingdom of Quito in the Seventeenth Century* (Madison: University of Wisconsin Press, 1967).

5. Arthur F. Corwin, *Spain and the Abolition of Slavery in Cuba, 1817–1886* (Austin: University of Texas Press, 1967), pp. 73–74.

6. Ibid., chapter 14.

7. AHN, Ultramar, Esclavitud, legs. 4880–81.

became the most comprehensive attempt to create order out of the chaos of colonial legislation. Later, as the general proliferation of laws seemed to have got out of hand again, further attempts were made to codify the laws, many of which conflicted with one another.

The change in official attitude towards the slave trade in the later years of the eighteenth century made it necessary to repeat in detail the various decrees governing slavery in the Spanish New World. To this end the crown issued the slave code of 1789. Again, the changed milieu of mid-nineteenth century Cuba required a special legal pronouncement on slavery.

Elsa Goveia has argued persuasively that the West Indian slave laws could not exist without a favorable climate of opinion.[8] By examining the changes in emphasis over the years, therefore, it is possible to glean quite a lot of information about changes in attitudes and situations in any particular slave society.

The *Siete partidas* was an extremely liberal slave code, without equal among the other European nations. The legal basis for slavery was acknowledged, and the personality of the slave received recognition. The *Siete partidas* emphatically held aloft the idea of liberty: "It is a rule of law that all judges should aid liberty, for the reason that it is a friend of nature, because not only men, but all animals love it."[9] But the public sentiment in the thirteenth century had not yet experienced plantation slavery. Apart from that, the frontier conditions in the New World constituted a unique experience for the Spanish legislators.

The great code of 1680 reflected the changed conditions.[10] The most important considerations were police regulation measures, and attempts to maintain the stratification and racial separation of the colonial society. The biggest problem had been that of runaways, and the fear of Indian-Negro resistance to public order. Free colored people, too, had their lives supervised, and their social station clearly defined. Laws forbade them to wear gold, silk, cloaks, or other kinds of clothing which would make them indistinguishable—in apparel—from the white elite. Free colored people were required to have a patron, even though they had their freedom. An unsuccessful attempt was made to eliminate racial intermixture

8. Elsa Goveia, "The West Indian Slave Laws of the Eighteenth Century," *Revista de Ciencias Sociales,* 4 (1960), 75–105.

9. Quoted in ibid., p. 77.

10. *Recopilación de las leyes de los reynos de las Indias* (4 vols.; Madrid: I. de Paredes, 1681).

between Spaniards, Negroes, or Indians. From the outset, of course, religious instruction was a requirement of Spanish slave laws.

The slave code of 1789, besides summarizing all the legal precedents, attempted to introduce ameliorative measures for the slaves. Apart from the usual religious requirements of baptism, daily prayers, religious instruction, and mass, the code freed the slaves from work on holidays, except during the harvest when it was customary to grant permission for them to do so.[11] Masters had to feed their slaves and dress them according to the custom of the country, and in a way which conformed to that of the free workers. The corporal punishment meted out to slaves for misdemeanors on the estate was restricted to twenty-five lashes, preferably administered by the master or overseer. One new feature of this code was the legal restrictions put on the master class; if they failed to obey they could be subject to fines, and, depending on the nature of the contravention, they could even lose their slaves. The royal decree further appointed a protector of slaves to safeguard their rights.

The slave code of 1789 would have been a monumental achievement if it could have been implemented. Unfortunately, contrary to the common opinion—especially as expressed by H. H. Johnston in *The Negro in the New World*—the so-called magnificent code of 1789 was never even read in the colonies.[12] When word leaked out of the new provisions, the colonists became so hostile that the measures were quickly shelved. José Antonio Saco described the nonimplementation in his monumental work on slavery:

> When the royal order of May 31, 1789, was sent out, the *vecinos* of Havana, as well as those of Santo Domingo, Caracas, and New Orleans, which then belonged to Spain, on the 19th of January 1790, begged the Governor, through their organ, the town councils, not to publish the decree, lest the slaves, interpreting it in a bad light, might revolt. In fact, the Captains-General did not publish it, and when the Council of the Indies consulted Francisco de Saavedra, Ignacio de Urriza and other persons familiar with affairs in America, they all said that it should be suspended, and that in each capital a body of the leading planters, the Bishop, and the Captain-General should propose the laws which ought to govern in that matter. In this way, then, a royal order

11. A summary of these conditions is found in Fernando Ortiz Fernández, *Hampa afro-cubana, los negros esclavos* (Havana: Revista Bimestre Cubana, 1916), pp. 357–62.

12. Sir Harry H. Johnston, *The Negro in the New World* (London: Methuen, 1910), pp. 42–46.

was nullified, which would have extended the greatest benefit to the slaves of any nation which had them in their colonies.[13]

The 1842 slave code was the result of a series of concurrent pressures on the Spanish government, and came generally as a surprise to the Cuban planters, even though some may have found it convenient.[14] Great Britain, eager that Spain should observe her treaty agreements, was becoming more aggressive about the large-scale illegal traffic in African slaves to Cuba.[15] In Cuba, a state of high tension prevailed. The planters expressed fear that Spain had made a secret deal with Britain to abolish slavery and ruin their property.[16] Minor slave uprisings had led to the belief that a general insurrection was imminent.[17] The slave code was an

---

13. José Antonio Saco, *Historia de la esclavitud de la raza africana en el nuevo mundo . . .* (4 vols.; Havana: Cultural, 1938), 3:16–17. Herbert S. Klein, who dealt extensively with this code in *Slavery in the Americas: A Comparative Study of Virginia and Cuba.* (Chicago: University of Chicago Press, 1967), pp. 78–85, virtually dismisses the nonimplementation of these stipulations: "There is some debate about how much of this famous code was actually implemented, but there is no question that it had a major impact on all nineteenth-century legislation." Obviously there was continuity in all Spanish colonial legislation, and once the 1789 code was written, it became a continual point of reference whether or not it was implemented. The fact that it remained a dead letter, however, is quite damaging to Klein's argument about the humanity of conditions for slavery in Cuban society.

14. See the evidence of David Turnbull before the House of Commons on May 7, 1850, in *Parliamentary Papers, Reports,* vol. 419 (1850), no. 53, Report from the Select Committee on the African Slave Trade:

"711. Would an attempt to supress the importation of slaves meet now with considerable support from a large portion of the inhabitants of Cuba?

I think so; from all the most intelligent and most humane planters, from all those who have their estates in good order.

.   .   .   .   .   .   .   .   .   .   .   .   .

713. Those parties are convinced that a sufficient supply of slaves may be maintained by keeping up the existing provision by breeding?

I believe so. Those that have their estates in good order, believe that their own slaves will increase year by year, and that as the slave trade ceases, their rivals in the labor market having neglected the precautions which humanity and sound policy alike demand, and having relied on fresh importations from Africa through the continuance of the Slave Trade, will be unable to compete with them in the markets of the world to which their produce is sent."

15. Corwin, *Spain and Cuba,* chapter 5.

16. Mariano Torrente, *Cuestion importante sobre la esclavitud* [pamphlet] (Madrid: Viuda de Jordan, 1841). It was also thought that the treaty of 1835 with Great Britain had some secret agreement on abolition in return for British support of Isabel II during the Carlist Wars, but there is no evidence for this supposition.

17. Corwin, *Spain and Cuba,* p. 74.

attempt to diminish the state of suspense. The preamble to the decree declared:

> . . . on dealing with such details, I could not but fix my attention on the fields, interesting in so many aspects, and especially concerning the hands dedicated to the agricultural tasks. To procure the conservation and propagation of such hands through every possible means, to assure the continuation of a humane treatment [*un trato humano*] without ceasing to maintain them under a severe discipline and unalterable subordination, is the object of our legislation, as it is to work in every way consistent with the true interests of this rich and important part of the monarchy.[18]

The slave code of 1842 formed an appendix to a very long government decree—a sort of colonial constitution—issued by the governor and captain-general. Of the more than 260 articles in the main edict, nineteen directly referred to the slaves and free colored population. Some articles, following the familiar Spanish practice, duplicated other articles in the separate slave code. The main body of the decree, however, applied specifically to the whites. Article 5 commanded masters to supply religious instruction to their slaves, or pay a fine of fifty pesos. Article 6 stated that there should be no field work on Sundays and recognized public holidays, adding that its provisions did not apply to personal and domestic slaves. Article 17 claimed that no slave or free colored person should be employed without permission of his master, or, in the case of the free colored people, a license from local authorities.

By the terms of Article 21, any slave found more than three leagues from a cattle farm or a league and a half from any other farm should be detained as a runaway, and his master forced to pay the four-peso recapture tax, unless such a slave had written permission from his master. Article 40 gave any citizen (vecino) the right to detain any suspected runaway slave and turn him over to the authorities. No slave could be transported on a ship without his master's consent, under a fine of fifty pesos (Article 29). In addition, all owners had to make every month a lengthy descriptive report of all slaves deserting their estates (Article 39).

Other articles forbade giving or renting lodgings to slaves without legal permission (Article 27); selling liquor to slaves (Article 98); or

18. *Bando de gobernación y policía de la isla de Cuba* . . . (Havana: Impr. del Gobierno, 1842), p. 4.

carrying on trade with slaves without the permission of their masters and the military commander of the district (Article 101).

Slave dances with drums could be permitted on fiestas during the afternoon hours, provided they were supervised by some white person, and no slaves from any other estate attended (Article 51). The Negro cabildos should only be held on Sundays and on days of "important fiestas," and only along the city walls (Article 87). Meanwhile, Article 88 declared that the Negroes required special permission to have marches with flags and native costumes. Such marches could only be held twice a year, and during the daylight hours. Any march held in defiance of that article would result in a fine of ten pesos, to be paid by the *capataz de cabildo* (club chairman).

Article 42 offered a reward of ten pesos for the return of any escapee from prison or military service. Article 102 insisted that no slave should be issued any firearms, or used on hunting expeditions. Article 143 prohibited any colored person from "carrying arms permitted to white persons," while Article 261 made masters responsible for the fines imposed on their slaves.

The slave code itself, consisting of forty-eight articles, reflected some principles of the unimplemented code of 1789, but more of the code adopted in Puerto Rico in 1826.[19] Its provisions covered five major topics: religion and hispanization; slave welfare and recreation; slaves' rights or benefits; public protection measures; and the administrative procedures for implementing the order.

The first five articles dealt with instruction and moral education of the slaves. The code entreated masters, as a standard practice carried down through the years, to see that their slaves were given religious instruction (even every night after work), baptism, and the sacraments. On Sunday and fiestas, slaves should only work for two hours, except during crop-time, when they should "work as on labor days." Article 5 implied instruction in citizenship—referred to herein as hispanization, since it attempted to create a Spanish social order and propagate Spanish mores:

> The masters will place the greatest possible attention and diligence in making them [the slaves] understand the obedience which they owe to the constituted authorities; the obligation of reverence to the priests,

19. *Reglamento sobre la educación, trato y ocupaciones que deben dar a sus esclavos los dueños ó mayordomos de esta isla* (San Juan, Puerto Rico: Impr. del Gobieno, 1826).

and to respect all white persons; to behave themselves well with the free persons of color; and to live harmoniously with their companions.[20]

The largest portion of the code pertained to the welfare of the slaves, on matters of food, clothes, health, housing, recreation, and work. Article 6 specified what the slaves should be fed: six to eight plantains, "or their equivalent in ground provisions," eight ounces of meat or codfish, four ounces of rice or flour per day for each slave. It further stated that "the master should give two or three meals per day according to what seems best to him, and what he judges is in the slaves' best interest." Small children whose mothers worked in the fields should be fed milk or porridge until they had teeth to chew harder foods (Article 8).

Slaves should be given two changes of clothing per year, in December and May (Article 7); and little children should be well dressed (Article 11). All infants should be kept in a nursery, under the care of an old Negress (Article 9), but in case of illness, such children should be returned to their mothers who ought to be taken in from the fields, and set on domestic tasks (Article 10). Sick slaves ought not to be freed, but should be attended by their masters (Article 15). Each estate was also required to have a sick bay with medicines and adequate facilities (Articles 27 and 18).

According to the code, the day's labor was set at nine to ten hours of work. In crop-time, however, the day was allowed to be "sixteen hours with two for rest in the days, and six at night to sleep" (Article 12). On Sundays and fiestas, slaves could pursue their own occupation (Article 13); and slaves "over sixty and under seventeen" should not be allowed to work (Article 14).

Visiting and slave dances could be held during daylight hours, under white supervision (Articles 19 and 23). Housing of slaves received detailed consideration (Articles 25, 26, 29). Sleeping quarters for married slaves should be separated from those for single slaves, with "a light to burn all night to see that no mixing took place between the unmarried sexes." No slave should be permitted out at night.

Article 29 stipulated that "masters should prevent illicit relations which foment marriages," but they should not impede marriages involving slaves from another estate, and should permit such couples to get together under the same roof. Article 30 advocated that the master of either slave should purchase the other, or both should sell the married

20. The *Reglamento de Esclavos* (slave law) is found on pp. 59–68 of the *Bando de gobernación* (1842).

couple to a third party. If the owner of the husband was the purchaser, he should also buy all children under the age of three who belonged to the married slaves.

The articles aimed at public protection sought to prevent the slaves being in a position to conspire, or arm themselves with the intention of fomenting a riot. Articles 16 and 17 sought to have all work implements locked away securely, the master ensuring that the slaves received their tools only in the mornings, and that they returned them in the afternoons. Under no circumstances should any slave be given the keys to the tool room. Neither should any slave leave a hacienda with a tool in his possession (Article 18). Nevertheless, if such a slave were accompanied by a white person, then he might carry a machete on his person. Articles 20, 21, and 22 governed the escape of slaves from the plantations, with the usual provisions that any free person might detain any slave suspected of running away. Return of such slaves should be a mutually gratuitous service among slaveholders. In other cases, masters should pay a reward of four pesos, plus any costs incurred for food and medicines. Article 24 stipulated that the greatest care should be taken to eliminate excessive drinking by slaves, or intercourse with free colored persons.

One section of the code concerned what may very loosely be termed "slave rights." The most important of these rights was the local custom which had finally been accepted in law, coartación.[21] This practice of coartación was simply the procedure by which a slave and his master definitely fixed the price of the slave so that at no time in the future could the master demand a higher price for the liberty of that slave. It was, in short, a process to remove the value of the slave from the impact of market place considerations or personal whim. It was such a novel legal concept that the word was italicized in the code of 1842. Article 34 established the slaves' right to coartación: "No owner may refuse to coartar his slave, provided he is offered fifty pesos toward the price of purchase." Article 35 emphasized the meaning of the Spanish word, "to cut off, or fix": "A coartado's price remains constant, provided he is not sold without his owner's consent," otherwise the sale price would be

---

21. Coartación was a peculiarly Spanish custom which slowly worked itself into law. See Goveia, "West Indian Slave Laws," pp. 76–79; Ortiz, *Negros esclavos,* pp. 373–74; Hubert H. S. Aimes, "Coartación: A Spanish Institution for the Advancement of Slaves into Freedmen," *Yale Review* 17 (1909), pp. 412–31; and Eugenio Alonso y Sanjurjo, *Apuntes sobre los proyectos de la esclavitud . . .* (Madrid: Bibl. de Instrucción y Recreo, 1874), pp. 6–7.

augmented by various additional taxes and costs. Children of coartado slaves did not enjoy the benefits of their mothers, but could be sold like any other slave (Article 36). Once a coartado had paid fully his agreed price, he could not be denied his liberty (Article 37). Articles 32 and 33 allowed owners to sell any slaves they mistreated, or found continuously difficult. Such owners could determine the price at which they would sell the slave. On the other hand, any slave could petition to have his master sell him.

Besides coartación, the slaves had two other opportunities to get their freedom. Article 38, in a patent reflection of the troubled times, stipulated that any slave reporting any conspiracy, whether of fellow slaves or of free persons, would receive his immediate freedom and a cash reward of five hundred pesos. The money for such rewards was to be obtained from a public fund supported by fines collected from infringement of the slave laws (Article 39). Article 40 allowed slaves to be given their liberty in wills, "or any other legally justified manner, and proceeding from an honest and laudable motive."

Articles 41, 42, and 43 outlined the punishment which could be meted out to slaves in order to discipline them and make them respect white persons. Corporal punishment was limited to twenty-five strokes, to be administered only by the master. Most of the common forms of torture and detention such as "stocks, shackles, chains, clubs, and prisons" were admitted as legal punishment for slaves.

The remaining articles outlined the fines for infringement, and the appointment of the síndico procurador, the official protector of slaves. Slaveowners who were unable to pay the fines imposed on them or their slaves could undergo imprisonment at the rate of one day for each peso of the sum (Article 45). One-third of the fines went to the judges, and the balance to the public fund required by Article 39. The protector of slaves could intercede on the slaves' behalf in any legal action brought by a slave against his master. Apart from that, his duties were not clearly outlined, although his presence was required on commissions investigating matters affecting slaves.

The slave laws of 1842 as represented in the codes were considerably less liberal than the attempted recommendations of 1789. The restrictions on the movements and activities of the slaves, the more detailed regulations for work, and the stronger emphasis upon the obedience of slaves to white persons and the constituted authorities revealed a severe hardening of the attitudes of the master group toward their slaves. Two significant omissions in the code of 1842 were the leniency toward all women, and the equality in the punishment meted out to slaves and persons of color. The general impression conveyed by the slave laws of 1842, then, was one of increased repression.[22] Any further attempt to explain this change would probably have to take into account the increased European racism and ideas of social engineering which manifested themselves in sharper lines of separation between people of European stock and others. These tendencies were most cogently expressed in the positivist ideas that found their way into the thinking of most erudite Latin Americans at this time. Yet in the absence of a detailed study of their effect on the Cuban people at this time we can merely speculate.

But in part the diminishing liberality of the Cuban slave laws can be laid definitely to the sugar revolution, which brought an increased number of Africans to the island as slaves. In the late eighteenth century, more than 60 per cent of the population were white. By 1842 the percentage had declined to a little more than 40 per cent, and events elsewhere in the Caribbean had further increased the uneasiness about the longevity of slavery in the area. Indeed, by 1842 the Cubans were forced to defend slavery in their land, as slaveholding societies became steadily more scarce in the western world. British opposition to the slave trade was powerful and persistent.[23]

British naval interceptions of slave ships bound for Cuba led to serious labor problems.[24] To deny the Cuban planters their slaves at that time was like bleeding their lifeblood.

22. Klein, however, asserts that "throughout its centuries of development the Cuban slave law had shown a remarkable cohesion and a consistent extension of rights to the slaves. Although the law might be more or less enforced in given periods, we can nevertheless assume that by the nineteenth century the attitudes universally expressed in the vast body of canonical and civil law of Spain and Cuba had come to be expected as legitimate and morally operative by the majority of Cuban whites" (*Slavery in the Americas*, p. 85). There is, of course, no way to determine how the majority of whites felt on the question of slavery. It is reasonable to assume from the evidence that the legal stipulations were more conservative than the actual practice; if, then, the laws became increasingly more restrictive toward the slave, the general public opinion was sharper and more hostile. In the light of the contemporary West Indian situation, and the frequent reference to events in Haiti and Jamaica by the more articulate elements in the Cuban society, the latter assumption seems more plausible.

23. See Corwin, *Spain and Cuba*.

24. Jacobo de la Pezuela y Lobo, *Diccionario geográfico, estadístico, histórico de la isla de Cuba* (4 vols.; Madrid: Mellado, 1863–66) 2:285–87.

Yet many Cubans failed to realize that slavery was slowly changing the traditional pattern of their society. The sugar revolution and slavery had brought to the fore of the society a new landowning and slaveholding oligarchy who were keenly interested in making money and running profitable plantations. If they knew about the old patriarchal relationship between masters and slaves, they could no longer accommodate it within the new system of plantation agriculture, which tended to destroy personal relations between masters and slaves. For one thing, the new system changed the ratio of the races on the estates, and demanded a more regimented organization of the labor force than the previous systems. For another thing, the new plantation owners, particularly in the sugar areas, lived in the towns, and used intermediaries recruited from among the lower levels of the white element to assume most of the on-hand, upper managerial tasks of the estates. And as the number of slaves increased, the white supervisors in particular and the white caste in general feared violent, physical retaliation by their slaves, as well as the loss of their "property" and, of course, their laborers. This increasing fear of a body of oppressed men did not permit a more lenient attitude toward the slaves, and the slave laws of 1842 reflected this change.

Slavery was an institution which affected the entire Cuban society. While the majority of white persons were by no means large landholders requiring a great number of African workers, almost every family desired or possessed slaves of some sort. Owning a slave was a significant social index: the more slaves any person had, the more social prestige accrued to him. José de la Concha claimed that even the poor whites (guajiros) who worked in the fields along with the slaves strongly aspired to be slaveowners themselves some day. They were the most overtly racist group in the island and in the minor positions of responsibility which they attained they often sharpened racial tensions by their attitudes.[25]

A very wide difference existed between the numbers of slaves owned by urban white people, under better conditions, and those held by rural planters. According to the census data, the slaves of the towns were either domestics or hired hands. But more important than occupation was the pattern of slaveholding: in the towns, the individual master held far fewer slaves than in the plantation areas.

25. José de la Concha, "Memoria remitida al Excmo. Sr. Ministro de Gobernación, en 21 de diciembre de 1850," in *Cuba desde 1850 á 1873* . . . (Madrid: Impr. Nacional, 1873), p. 21.

In 1857, there were 372,943 slaves in the island and 49,111 owners
—a mean holding of 7.59 per owner.[26] Broken down further, however,
the figures of Cuban slaveholding emphatically expose the imbalance between the number of slaves in the towns and those of the rural plantation zones of the island. The census of 1857 gave 22,753 persons owning 65,568 urban slaves, a mean holding of nearly 3 slaves per
owner. Havana, the capital city, had 29,420 slaves, owned by 9,421
persons—a mean holding of 3.1, not significantly different from the urban pattern throughout the island. The median holding was close to the
mean, for the only owner to have an unusually large number was the
firm of Irias and Company, Successors, which had 155 slaves, of which
only 6 were registered as urban slaves.[27]

The total of 307,375 registered slaves in the rural areas had 26,358
owners, an island-wide average holding of 11.6 slaves per owner. But
the picture was very different in the plantation areas: 483 rural owners
had more than 80 slaves each, yielding a total of 95,523 slaves for a
mean holding of 197 slaves each. In other words, less than 1 per cent of
the slaveowners of Cuba held more than 25 per cent of all the slaves in
the island.

These slaveowners in the middle of the nineteenth century were very
influential men in political affairs, and owned the largest sugar estates.
Some of these tycoons included Nicolás Martínez de Campos y González del Alamo, Conde de Santovenia, the Diago and Torriente families,
the Aldamas, Poeys, and Canteros, and many more who were to become
outstanding in the later history of Cuba.[28] Julian Zulueta, the acknowledged political boss of Cuba and certainly one of the richest men in the
island, owned more than 1,475 slaves in Cárdenas.[29]

While it would quite obviously be a gross distortion to say that the

26. These and the subsequent figures are taken from the capitation census in
AHN, Ultramar, Esclavitud, leg. 3553. The total in the official returns contains an
error of more than 6,000 slaves.
27. The difference in the tax levied on urban slaves might have prompted some
persons to register their slaves as rural, when in fact they were used in the towns
as hired hands. This could clearly not have been done in Havana, where only
the firm of Irias had rural registrants. In smaller urban areas with a less pronounced difference between town and country, the ruse may have succeeded. I
do not believe that many persons resorted to this method of tax evasion; it is more
likely that they did not register all their slaves.
28. See the capitation census returns in AHN, Ultramar, Esclavitud, leg. 3553.
29. On Zulueta, see Antonio C. Gallenga, The Pearl of the Antilles (London:
Chapman & Hall, 1873), pp. 100–102.

## TABLE 10
### Slaves and Slaveowners in Cuba, 1857

| Territory | Urban | | Rural | | Owners holding over 80 slaves | |
|---|---|---|---|---|---|---|
| | Slaves | Owners | Slaves | Owners | No. | Slaves held |
| Bahia Honda | 93 | 55 | 6,819 | 345 | — | — |
| Baracoa | 462 | 121 | 1,257 | 205 | — | — |
| Bayamo | 934 | 351 | 1,775 | 463 | — | — |
| Bejucal | 526 | 280 | 6,762 | 841 | — | — |
| Cárdenas | 2,137 | 731 | 57,706 | 2,812 | 173 | 37,106 |
| Cienfuegos | 1,344 | 478 | 13,740 | 1,092 | — | — |
| Cuba | 7,462 | 2,318 | 27,266 | 1,864 | — | — |
| Guanabacoa | 1,551 | 527 | 3,314 | 623 | 6 | 1,114 |
| Guanajay | 527 | 181 | 20,035 | 947 | 56 | 12,912 |
| Guantanamo | 233 | 64 | 6,639 | 257 | 26 | 3,685 |
| Güines | 645 | 398 | 15,885 | 1,638 | 29 | 5,711 |
| Habana | 29,420 | 9,421 | 3,388 | 398 | 1 | 155 |
| Holgüin | 1,102 | 500 | 2,291 | 516 | — | — |
| Jaruco | 171 | 81 | 8,012 | 851 | 22 | 3,864 |
| Jiguaní | 204 | 84 | 469 | 154 | — | — |
| Manzanillo | 444 | 164 | 762 | 220 | — | — |
| Matanzas | 6,208 | 2,036 | 38,468 | 1,996 | 13 | 2,465 |
| Nuevitas | 205 | 79 | 1,169 | 74 | 2 | 261 |
| Pinar del Río | 347 | 148 | 13,687 | 2,122 | 9 | 1,064 |
| Puerto Príncipe | 4,248 | 1,480 | 8,663 | 1,360 | — | — |
| Remedios | 775 | 308 | 4,879 | 618 | 13 | 1,738 |
| Sagua la Grande | 527 | 191 | 14,599 | 892 | 42 | 8,740 |
| San Antonio | 725 | 271 | 10,969 | 1,171 | 24 | 3,460 |
| Santa Clara | 1,106 | 572 | 5,161 | 874 | 9 | 1,034 |
| San Cristóbal | 193 | 88 | 6,534 | 896 | 8 | 1,291 |
| Santa María del Rosario | 147 | 108 | 5,182 | 848 | 8 | 1,091 |
| Santiago | 616 | 493 | 4,813 | 548 | 8 | 1,113 |
| Sancti-Spíritus | 1,334 | 518 | 7,109 | 938 | 12 | 2,689 |
| Trinidad | 1,760 | 658 | 9,361 | 588 | 22 | 6,030 |
| Las Tunas | 120 | 49 | 661 | 207 | — | — |
| Total | 65,568 | 22,753 | 307,375 | 26,358 | 483 | 95,523 |

Source: Figures compiled from the census return contained in AHN, Ultramar, Esclavitud, leg. 3553.

planters in Cuba made the slave laws of 1842, yet the laws clearly could not ignore them. The facts speak for themselves. Slave population and plantation production formed corresponding patterns. The nine largest provinces in terms of slave population—Cárdenas, Cienfuegos, Guanajay, Güines, Matanzas, Pinar del Río, Sagua la Grande, San Antonio, and Santiago de Cuba—held 62 per cent of all the slaves in the island, accounted for 80 per cent of all agricultural products, and produced 80 per cent of the total sugar crop. Moreover, a very small number of slaveowners held a disproportionately large number of slaves.

Cuban society and economy in the middle of the nineteenth century were, it is clear, heavily dependent on, indeed dominated by, the plantation, and by extension, the plantation owners. In trying to deduce the relation of the masters and the slaves from the slave laws, therefore, one must consider this aspect. For it was not the efficiency or laxity of the administrative bureaucracy (or, as some writers would have it, the Roman Catholic Church) which most weightily affected the conditions of the slaves. Rather, these conditions were determined by whether or not the slave found himself on the plantation or in the city, and by the unwritten laws of the individual, often very powerful, owner. Clearly the laws did have some humanitarian elements acquired from the earlier days and more relaxed atmosphere of slavery in the island. Yet bearing in mind the strains placed upon laws and tradition by changes in the economic basis of the society, we must consider the laws themselves as a very misleading index of the relations between masters and slaves.

# 7

# Political Milestones Along the Road to Abolition, 1835–1868

*Far be it from us to encourage American schemes*
*of unjust agression, or of lawles outrage.*
*But of evils in this world, there may be a*
*choice: and the question as to what power shall*
*ultimately possess Cuba is rapidly becoming a*
*choice of evils.*

*London Daily News*, November 15, 1853.

DURING THE NINETEENTH CENTURY Great Britain exerted relentless diplomatic pressure on Spain to put an end to the slave trade as the first step toward the abolition of slavery in the Spanish empire, and particularly in Cuba. But after 1835 the British relied less on the cash incentives it had tried since 1817 than on the strength of its naval forces and on slightly veiled threats of a possible loss of the island which was proudly called the "jewel in the Spanish crown." The British government possibly thought that Spain could act as easily against slavery in her empire as the British Parliament had in affairs in the British empire. But the Spanish government did not have similar facility. Spanish official response to the British demands took the form of delaying tactics and token reforms. Part of the Spanish problem was of course, the difficulty of getting its orders executed in Cuba, but part of the problem was definitely the ancient exaltation of Spanish pride, which usually impeded acceptance of external advice about internal affairs. Yet slavery in the nineteenth century was hardly an internal affair any longer. And, indeed, international politics affected Spanish decisions about slavery, and promoted the growth of a Spanish abolitionist society in the 1860s. The long-term effect of a series of official "concessions" to the changing conditions surrounding slavery throughout the world had by themselves undermined considerably the position of Cuban slavery.

The first significant advance came with the Anglo-Spanish treaty of 1835, which greatly alarmed the Cuban planters and slave traders, although it did not, by itself, seriously affect the number of Africans imported annually. The British reiterated their demand of 1817, that the Spanish government adopt more stringent measures to put an end to the Cuban slave trade. Both governments reconfirmed the organization and the powers of the courts of Mixed Commission established by the treaty of 1817. Both governments also agreed to the mutual search of ships suspected of being slavers. Spain agreed to enact legislation to punish all Spanish subjects who engaged in the trade, and to give liberty to all Africans found on captured Spanish slave ships. Such legislation was to be published within two months after the ratification of the treaty.

Even before the two governments ratified the treaty, however, rumors concerning the details led to frenzied activity by Cuban traders. The increase in the trade produced a sharp rise in the number of vessels captured by the British cruisers around the island. Between 1830 and 1834, the British captured nine vessels and 2,760 Africans off the Cuban coast. During 1835 they captured eight vessels and 2,146 Africans.[1]

Yet by British estimates, the overall effect of the treaty of 1835 was disappointing. The emancipados did not gain their liberty. Local Cuban officials did not show greater enthusiasm to curb the trade. And ten years passed before the Spanish government enacted the promised legislation to punish its citizens for dealing in African slaves.

The "Law for the Abolition and Repression of the Slave Trade," passed on March 2, 1845, was a major event.[2] The law outlined the detection, confiscation, and destruction of any Spanish ship engaged in the slave trade, and imposed punisment of fines, imprisment, or exile on the organizers and crews of any slaving expedition. For the first time a Spanish law stipulated that any official who directly or indirectly connived in the disembarkation and distribution of the bozales faced suspension from his duties, and the possible loss of his job.

1. See Appendix I, and AHN, Ultramar, Esclavitud, leg. 3554: "Estado de las expediciones de Negros Bozales capturados en las costas de la isla de Cuba."

2. Ibid., leg. 8040: "La Ley penal contra los traficantes en esclavos del 28 de Febrero de 1845."

Nevertheless, the requirement stated in the ninth article practically nullified the law. At the same time that the government demanded instant action from its officials when they heard of the preparation or landing of an expedition, it limited the exercise of the authority vested in the officials by prohibiting their entry on the estates to ascertain the origin of any slave. The explanation offered in the law for the very strong wording of the clause was the government's desire to maintain the tranquility on the estates, and its respect for the masters' rights to their property. Such an explanation concealed the desire to placate both sides in the dispute over slavery.

The official preamble to the law pointed out the disturbances during the previous years among the Cuban slaves, and the growing fears of a serious racial problem that they had always sought to avoid.[3] Notwithstanding this consideration, other factors also contributed significantly to the timing of the legislative measures. For even at the peak of the disorders in Cuba, the Spanish government had stubbornly insisted that any further concessions made to Great Britain concerning the slave trade would be a national indignity, illegal and impractical to implement.[4]

In Cuba and Spain, the opinion about slavery was sharply, though unevenly, divided between planters and merchants on one side, and men who were predomiantly intellectuals on the other. For a short time in 1842 and 1843, the general fear of insurrections had popularized the call to end the trade, but a state of normality had returned by 1845. It was almost "business as usual" for the planters and merchants. From the middle 1830s, however, the intellectual community had consistently and unanimously deprecated the continued tolerance towards the slave trade. The Creole, José Antonio Saco, and the Peninsular Spaniard, Ramón de la Sagra, strongly argued for the complete cessation of the trade.[5] As usual, their reasons differed. To Saco, slavery was a social menace which would wither away when the trade ended. Sagra stressed that it was an uneconomic system of labor organization which should be replaced by a free, wage-paid labor system.

3. Fernando Ortiz, Fernández, *Hampa afro-cubana, los negros esclavos* (Havana: Revista Bimestre Cubana, 1916), p. 95; Arthur F. Corwin, *Spain and the Abolition of Slavery in Cuba, 1817–1886* (Austin: University of Texas Press, 1967), pp. 84–86.

4. AHN, Estado, Esclavitud, leg. 8052(1), fol. 7.

5. Corwin, *Spain and Cuba*, p. 83.

By early 1845, the Spanish government faced two unpleasant choices. It had refused to fulfill the agreement of 1835, on the basis of injury to national pride. While deeply concerned about the slave trade, it was not willing to appear to be taking orders from the British government. But the British were exceeding the limits of polite diplomacy. Toward both Spain and Brazil, the other major "delinquent" nation in the slave trade, the British threatened the use of unilateral action not only to end the trade but also to liberate the emancipados.[6] To forestall such a final indignity, the Cortes passed the law of March, 1845. The ninth article was the sop to the affected interest groups, providing the loophole for the Cubans to "obey but not execute" the law.

The immediate impact of the law—the ninth article notwithstanding—was to create a general panic among the planters on the island. Some sold their estates, and many persons thought that total abolition of slavery was imminent.[7] The volume of the trade plunged from more than 10,000 Africans imported in 1844 to a negligible number in 1848.[8] No one expected the law to stop the trade, but rather to provide more powerful weapons for the officers of the government. And actualy the new law changed the procedure of litigation. Formerly, judicial action on the illegal trade depended on a legal suit initiated by the captain-general's office, after it had collected all the pertinent evidence. But after 1845 any official could complain directly to the courts. Despite a hesitant start, the courts, encouraged by the examples of the more forthright governors such as José de la Concha and the Marquis of Pezuela, began to assert themselves. They declared that the introduction of bozal Africans constituted a legal violation, an infraction of treaties, and a threat to peace. But they placed heavy emphasis upon their reputation, and "bright honor," which would probably suffer from a continuation of the trade.[9]

The sharp decline in the trade after 1845, and the urgent need to replace the diminishing African manpower supply, led to vigorous protests against the law of 1845, as well as the treaty of 1835 which had engen-

6. Ibid., pp. 89–91.

7. John Glanville Taylor, *The United States and Cuba: Eight Years of Change and Travel* (London: Bentley, 1851), p. 194.

8. Christopher Lloyd, *The Navy and the Slave Trade* (London: Longmans, Green, 1949), pp. 275–76.

9. Quoted in Ortiz, *Negros esclavos*, pp. 95–96.

dered it.[10] The protests were also calculated to deter any immediate act of emancipation of the slaves. The planters and proslavery advocates pointed to the parlous condition of the British Antilles after the slaves gained their freedom, and the extreme difficulty in getting the ex-slaves back to work. They further argued that to avoid a total economic collapse the British government had to implement a system of contract labor for its colonies which was merely a disguised form of slavery (*servidumbre disfrazada*).[11] Cuban appeals did not go unnoticed.

Between 1846 and late 1847, the captain-general wrote to Madrid of the rising dissatisfaction among the white people. He mentioned that the total failure to attract sufficient white immigrants for agricultural jobs, coupled with the sudden cessation of the trade, had resulted in a spiralling price for laborers, and a rising daily wage for hired hands. He mentioned also the concern over the proposal to abolish slavery in the Danish colonies, and said that while he did not think any serious repercussion would be felt among the slaves in Cuba, the government was fully equipped to deal with such an eventuality.

On the immediate problem of maintaining the slave population, the captain-general suggested that Negroes should be imported from Brazil and other places where slavery still existed, since that would not contravene the treaty of 1835. He further strongly urged that the slaves should not be emancipated, nor should the administrative structure of the island be altered, as either measure could result in civil disturbances.[12] For a short time, the Spanish government permitted the importation of slaves from Brazil and Puerto Rico but discontinued the practice in 1854 after sustained British objections.

The penal law of 1845 and the concern about the slave trade did not obscure the need to find laborers for the Cuban plantations. In fact, it seemed that the Spanish government was extremely interested in finding an escape for the Cuban slave traders. A letter written by the Spanish consul-general at Sierra Leone on October 3, 1848, offered an interesting method of subverting the law. He proposed that in the future all Spanish slave traders should register their boats and personnel as Brazilian, and in the event of capture, they should throw their proper docu-

---

10. AHN, Ultramar, Esclavitud, leg. 3552(2), ind. 5: "Tráfico de esclavos."

11. Ibid., ind. 5, fol. 5: Duque de Sotomayor al M. de la Gobernación, Nov. 29, 1847.

12. Ibid., ind. 6, esp. cartas 550 (July 4, 1846) and 854 (Nov. 10, 1847).

ments overboard. Such a gesture, he insisted, would not only save the Spanish government the £480 sterling which was the daily cost of maintaining the Spanish marine off the African coast, but would also save the Spanish government the necessity of punishing, according to the penal law of 1845, those participating in the traffic, "thereby improving the fortunes of the culprits."[13]

The Spanish minister of state wrote to the captains-general of Cuba and Puerto Rico, asking what would be local reaction to a system of compulsory contract labor based on the English apprenticeship system. The idea, of course, was to contract Africans and transport them to the islands, subjecting them to work in the indicated form, and under the same conditions which were "applied in Jamaica to those Negroes called free."[14] The reply from Puerto Rico stated bluntly that the island did not want more slaves, nor did it need an increased population, and that the government was already organizing the class of free, daily-paid laborers.[15] The Cuban captain-general repeated that the time was most inopportune for any new measure affecting slavery there.[16]

By 1850, the initial panic had worn off and Cuban slave trading steadily increased. The British renewed their attacks on the trade. A British Foreign Office directive informed Spain that all Spaniards caught off the African coast would be sent to Sierra Leone for trial, regardless of the flag under which they were trading.[17] Another curt note to the Spanish government on August 14, 1851, stated that Great Britain was reinforcing the cruisers around the island of Cuba, and would be willing to employ any means to extinguish the trade, since the government of Madrid was unable to cause its subordinate officers in Cuba to execute the treaty engagements of the Spanish crown for the suppression of the slave trade.[18] British public opinion, as reflected in the leading newspapers, or collected by the Quakers, strongly supported a harder line against Spain, and the use of even more drastic measures against the Cuban branch of the slave trade.[19]

13. AHN, Estado Esclavitud, leg. 8042.
14. AHN, Ultramar, Esclavitud, leg. 3552(2), ind. 6, fol. 8.
15. Ibid., fol. 12. The situation in Puerto Rico is more fully described in chapter 9.
16. Ibid., fol. 9.
17. AHN, Estado, Esclavitud, leg. 8044(11), fol. 3, 1851.
18. Ibid., leg. 8045: Howden to Miraflores.
19. See various examples in ibid., leg. 8042(10), fol. 4, and leg. 8045(12), fol. 11.

During the course of the Crimean War the British began to assert themselves even more strongly. In late 1854, the British demanded that Spain join the eleven other countries that had equated the naval aspects of the trade to piracy.[20] At the same time, Britain protested to Spain over every proved, or alleged, landing of African slaves along the Cuban coast. The British government made three specific demands, which, it claimed, would prove the Spanish sincerity about ending the trade. The first demand was repeal of Article 9 of the penal law of 1845, forbidding entry on estates to search for bozales. The second was for new laws empowering the officers of the crown in Cuba and Puerto Rico to capture all Africans illegally imported. The third demand was for the registration of all slaves.[21]

The Spanish government refused at first to yield to these demands. Since any of the three measures would ultimately involve entry on the estates, the council of ministers declared them to be "illegal and impolitic," and clearly opposed to the government's desire not to molest the masters in possession of their slaves.[22]

The government's thinking reflected the prevalence of the various filibuster expeditions at this time alarming the Spanish government. But by the mid-1850's sentiment favoring Cuban annexation to the United States was on the decline—witness the defection of José Antonio Saco from the ranks of the annexationists—and this created a new perspective on the internal situation in Cuba.[23] While it gave the Spanish government less uneasiness about the loss of the island, it removed the principal excuse for rejecting the British demands to end the trade, or to declare it tantamount to piracy. In a confidential despatch of January 8, 1855, the government told José de la Concha, the captain-general, that it was becoming impossible to resist English insistence on declaring that slave trade piracy. The despatch stated that it was time to re-examine every aspect of such a declaration in terms of the social structure of the island, its labor demands, the Africanization scare, the annexationist elements, and the filibuster expeditions from the United

---

20. Ibid., leg. 8047(14), fol. 17. The eleven countries: England, the United States, Mexico, Brazil, Portugal, New Granada, Ecuador, Russia, the Germanic Confederation, Argentina, and Venezuela.

21. Ibid., leg. 8046(13), fol. 10.

22. Ibid., leg. 8060.

23. Philip S. Foner, *A History of Cuba and Its Relations with the United States* (2 vols.; New York: International Publishers, 1963), 2:14–19.

States. It emphasized, however, that no action would be taken without "consulting the interests of Cuba."[24]

José de la Concha, who was honest, efficient, and an opponent of the slave trade, increased his unpopularity by proposing that a civil register be made of all slaves in the island, and that the basis of taxation on the slaves should be revised. His proposals gained acceptance in Madrid, and the first register of slaves took place in 1855.

The new register required every slave to have a separate cedula, renewable semiannually, and bearing a full description of the slave. The cedulas for all rural slaves, and those in the towns who were either under the age of twelve, invalid, or over the age of sixty, cost one-eighth of a peso. In the towns, the constables and the commissaries of police issued cedulas, while the capitanes de partido issued those for rural slaves and supervised the general bookkeeping. The governors and lieutenant-governors of the territorial divisions periodically inspected the books and made semiannual reports to the captain-general.

The great number of officials, the tremendous amount of bookkeeping and the indifference of the majority of the slaveholding white population defeated the purpose of the registration, which was to eliminate the slave trade entirely.[25] Abuses were prevalent in the form of fraudulent cedulas, substitution of newly imported slaves for dead ones, and the notorious corruption of lesser officials. Despite the most eloquent pleas to all the people by Captain-General Concha, and a plethora of decrees and circulars to his subordinate officers, the registration system failed after four years. The failure of Spain to revoke Article 9 had also played a part in undermining the effect of the registration, since the captain-general complained that the newly imported Africans were quickly put on the estates, where, though easily distinguishable, they could not be removed.[26]

The end of the registration did not reflect a diminished Spanish interest in ending the slave trade. In fact, it became a matter of "national honor." And the captains-general who succeeded Concha in Cuba displayed great zeal in bringing the trade to an effective end. In 1861 Francisco Serrano issued a circular to his subordinates throughout the

24. AHN, Estado, Esclavitud, leg. 8047(14), fol. 17.
25. AHN, Ultramar, Esclavitud, leg. 3551, 1855, fol. 99.
26. Ibid., leg. 3547, Capitan-General de Cuba al M. de Guerra y Ultramar, Nov. 7, 1859 (confidential).

island ordering them to supply him with detailed information about any person known or suspected, to be in any way associated with the clandestine landing of Africans. He promised that regardless of the social position of the individuals concerned he would banish them to Spain.[27] The Spanish government encouraged him to use every legal means available to end the trade, and at the same time, it asked the minister of the navy to exercise greater vigilance along the coasts of Cuba.[28]

The vigorous efforts of Spanish and Cuban officials to end the slave trade to Cuba received unexpected support from events in the United States. The Civil War involved the future of slavery in the whole New World. Cuba and the United States had been closely linked by the common institution of slavery, which consistently played a role in their relations, and by the economics of plantation agriculture. By 1860, events in the United States were bound to affect the destiny of slavery in Cuba.

Before 1848, the Cubans, fearful of unfounded Spanish schemes to abolish slavery in the island, had eagerly supported the idea of annexation to the United States. Such support waned as the Cubans observed the americanization of the areas in Texas, northern Mexico, and California where Manifest Destiny had drawn the United States. Although José Antonio Saco, Domingo del Monte, and other eminent polemicists had some influence on the changes of opinion in Cuba, they did more to articulate and exemplify such changes, rather than actually to initiate them. The vigorous economic growth of Cuba gave the people a new awareness of themselves—an incipient nationalism—which they became loath to lose in any incorporation into the United States. Annexation, therefore, drew its strength from the fears about the abolition of slavery, and subsided when those fears disappeared.[29] By 1850, annexation had lost its broad appeal, and the initiative shifted from the Cubans to the predominantly proslavery groups in the United States.

Between 1845 and 1848, the United States government unsuccess-

27. Ibid., leg. 3547.
28. Ibid.: M. de Guerra y Ultramar al Gobernador Capitan-General de la Isla de Cuba, con traslado al Sr. M. de Marina, Aug. 6, 1861 (confidential).
29. Raul Cepero Bonilla, *Obras históricas* (Havana: Inst. de Historia, 1963), pp. 51–56; also [Cristóbal Madan], *Llamamiento de la isla de Cuba a la nación española* . . . (New York: Hallet, 1854), pp. 186–233.

fully tried to purchase Cuba from Spain. The policy of acquiring Cuba had the support of the adherents of Manifest Destiny who favored the expansion of the United States anywhere, and the Southerners who sought political advantages by the addition of another slave state. Nevertheless, significant opposition, especially in the industrial North, existed to schemes either of purchasing or of capturing Cuba.

Spain's blunt refusal to sell the island did not deter the Southerners. Until 1850, they saw the addition of Cuba to the United States as essential in counteracting the effect of the Missouri Compromise and the Compromise of 1850. Disregarding the official stand of the government, that it would not reconsider the purchase of Cuba without overtures from Spain, and notwithstanding the waning support from the local planters in Cuba, the rich Southern planters and politicians supported filibuster expeditions to the island. Narciso Lopez, after some abortive attempts, led an expedition to the island in 1851. It had considerable Southern support, but it failed completely to achieve popular sympathy in Cuba, or to overthrow the government. In 1853 and 1854, General John Quitman organized an impressive expedition drawn from the Gulf states, and partially supported in the initial stages by the Cuban junta in New York. But the Cuban government heard of the plans. A preliminary expedition in 1855 ended in disaster, and José de la Concha, the Cuban captain-general, promised a similar fate for Quitman. The Quitman expedition dissolved before it left New Orleans, and brought to an end the active plans to acquire Cuba by force. The failure of the filibuster expeditions in general emphasized the decline of Cuban support for annexation to the United States.[30]

The outbreak of the United States Civil War divided planter opinion in Cuba. Ideologically, the Creole intellectuals and abolitionists easily identified themselves with the aspirations of the North. Many Creoles, such as José Morales Lemus, Miguel Aldama, and the Count of Pozos Dulces had earlier supported the annexationists, and considered the North to be the epitome of progress and "civilization." Although they owned slaves, they realized that slavery was passing away as an economical system of agriculture. The Count of Pozos Dulces was strongly influenced by the positivist ideas circulating in France at that time, and was both a racist and an ardent supporter of technological progress.

30. Foner, *History of Cuba*, vol. 2, chapters 1–10.

Cuban agriculture, he contended, needed the intelligence and the machines of white people, not the "dangerous brute force of the Negro and Chinese."[31] The industrial North, with its large centers of consumption, also offered more favorable trade for the Cubans. And Cuban Creoles had always thought that trade with the United States was more "natural" than trade with Spain.[32]

Cuban Peninsular Spaniards tended to support the South. The Peninsulares had, in general, deplored the annexationist tendencies in the island, and thought that Creole admiration for the North was subversive and treasonable. A Southern victory, in their eyes, would weaken the United States, and enable Spain to assert her dominance in Cuba even more positively.[33]

Economic interests, however, greatly fashioned the direction of support of many white Cubans. Nothing had been more deeply desired by the sugar planters than a larger share of the United States sugar market, and a lowering of tariffs on Cuban sugar. Louisiana sugar production, assisted by protective tariffs, had been making tremendous strides in the decades before 1860. In hoping that the North would win the war, the Cuban planters were expecting only a greater measure of free trade. In fact, the Civil War almost completely destroyed the sugar industry in the South, where production fell from 459,410 hogsheads in 1861 to 10,000 hogsheads in 1864, and the 1,200 plantations fell to 175. The abolition of slavery alone in 1863 had destroyed nearly 50 per cent of the capital investment in the Louisiana sugar industry.[34]

The proclamation of the emancipation of slaves in the United States and the success of the North in the Civil War meant that slavery in Cuba became more difficult to defend. The moral complacency of the planters who had used the United States as an example of the "compatibility of Negro slavery and civilization" disappeared.[35] To Cristóbal Madan, 1864 signalled the beginning of a new era. The Count of Pozos

31. Francisco de Frías y Jacott, conde de Pozos Dulces, *La isla de Cuba: Colección de escritos sobre agricultura, industria, ciencias* . . . (Paris: Kugelman, 1860), pp. 22–23 (quote), 84–89, 348–53.

32. Cepero Bonilla, *Obras*, pp. 93–100.

33. Foner, *History of Cuba*, 2:131–34

34. J. Carlyle Sitterson, *Sugar Country: The Sugar Cane Industry in the South, 1753–1950* (Lexington: University of Kentucky Press, 1953), p. 226.

35. Compare, for example, [Madan], *Llamamiento*, pp. 179–80, and *El trabajo libre y el libre cambio en Cuba* (Paris: n. p., 1864), p. 1

Dulces thought that it "would be madness and a crime" not to change the system for one of free labor.[36] Abolition sentiment received substantial stimulus both in Cuba and in Spain. The planters, however, were not prepared to release their slaves without compensation. And although abolition finally became acceptable to all groups in Cuba, great differences existed over methods and over compensation to the owners.

Cuban slaves themselves were affected by the war—many, indeed, thought that the forces of Lincoln would ultimately give them their freedom. Local chants declared that Lincoln was their hope: his assassination created such a great shock among the slaves that the slaveowners tried to suppress all public expressions of grief.[37] Both for the slaves and the slaveowners in Cuba, the Civil War clearly signified the beginning of the final phase of slavery.

When Captain-General Francisco Serrano arrived in Cuba in 1859, his policy was not only to suppress the slave trade as vigorously as he could, but also to integrate the Creoles into the mainstream of local politics. Called a *política de atracción* ("policy of attraction"), this new plan of action removed censorship of the press, relaxed political restrictions, and opened the way for Creole participation in the island's administrative affairs. Although political parties were illegal, the Creoles formed a club, which they quickly converted into a political party called the Partido Reformista.

Both Seranno and his successor, Domingo Dulce, permitted the operation of the party, which included Cubans outstanding in wealth and intellect, owners of large estates: José Morales Lemus, Francisco Calderón Kessel, José Manuel Mestre, Miguel Aldama, José Valdes Fauli, Pedro Martín Rivero, José Silverio Jorrín, Antonio Fernández Bramosio, José Antonio Echeverría, and the Count of Pozos Dulces. Miguel Aldama alone owned five of the most valuable estates, shares in some railroad companies, and what was reputedly the most splendid private residence in Havana. He later lost all his possessions in the Ten Years War.

The Reformist Party was not cohesive in political outlook. Some members favored representation for the island in the Cortes. Others halfheartedly flirted with the idea of annexation to the United States,

36. Frías y Jacott, *Cuba*, p. 23.

37. Herminio Portell Vilá, *Historia de Cuba en sus relaciones con los Estados Unidos y España* (4 vols.; Havana: Montero, 1939), 2:171.

while a few supported some form of political autonomy approximating the relationship of Canada in the British empire. In principle the party advocated a reduction in the absolute powers of the captain-general, greater political freedom for individuals, equal political rights for Cubans and Spaniards, representation in the Cortes, and the application of peninsular laws to Cuba. In short, the program of the party represented the sum total of the desires of the incorporated groups. The Reformists also declared themselves in favor of the liberalization of commerce, the total prohibition of the slave trade, and every form of collective, nonwhite immigration, while at the same time, demanding the elimination of every obstacle to white immigration.[38] To propagate their ideas, the Reformists in May, 1863, took over *El Siglo,* a newspaper founded in 1862 by José Quintra Suzarte. The party at first offered the editorship of the paper to José Antonio Saco, who rejected it, and then to the very able Count of Pozos Dulces.

Politics and economics mixed freely in Cuba. Discussions about political reform involved an examination of the economic system, of which slavery formed an integral part. Every reform movement had expressed some view on slavery, and invariably such views reflected the dominant social and economic interests. In the early years of the nineteenth century, the reformers led by Arango y Parreño had vigorously defended both slavery and the slave trade, on the ground that the Cubans needed slaves to boost sugar production in order to establish economic stability.

The reformers of the 1830's, led by Saco, defended slavery but insisted on the abolition of the slave trade. In part, the desire to end the trade resulted from selfish motives—the larger estate owners had enough slaves, and felt that with mechanization and free labor they were secure against the new farmers of Cárdenas and Matanzas. But the clamor to end the trade also came from racially conscious white Cubans who felt that a larger black population in Cuba, in addition to the large black population in the neighboring West Indian islands, presented a serious social threat.

The third reform movement, in the 1860's, advocated the total cessation of the slave trade, and the gradual abolition of slavery. For the first time wealthy Cuban planters openly sought such abolition. *El Siglo* and the Reformists did not speak for the majority of Cuban

38. Cepero Bonilla, *Obras,* pp. 251–71.

planters, yet opinion was clearly tending toward acceptance of the gradual abolition of slavery, if combined with some form of compensation to the owners of slaves.

British insistence on abolition, the American Civil War, and especially the economic disadvantages of slavery helped create this new sympathy towards eventual emancipation. The example of Louisiana had clearly exposed the disasters that would result from any unorganized, unindemnified emancipation should a revolution break out. Economic vulnerability, therefore, was a cardinal consideration in the reevaluation of the role of slavery in the labor system of Cuba, while concern for continued production led to the demand for gradual emancipation.

In 1865, the Cubans formed an anti-slave-trade association. Organized by a wealthy Havana lawyer, Antonio González de Mendoza, the association included both Creoles and Peninsulares. Many members of the Reformist Party, including Juan Poey, the Count of Pozos Dulces, and José Manuel Mestre, also joined the association, which not only concerned itself with the trade, but also with the eventual demise of the entire system of slavery. But the most practical plan of the association came from a Spaniard, Fermín Figuera, who claimed that a bloody civil war was not necessary and that emancipation over a period of twenty-five years was both possible and rational.[39]

Other groups took up the demand for abolition. An editorial of *El Siglo,* written by Pozos Dulces on April 7, 1865, declared that the paper would never support any program for abolition which jeopardized property guaranteed by law—an explicit reference to compensation as an integral part of emancipation, and one expressing disapproval of any revolutionary or immediate change in the slave system.[40] For the Civil War in the United States had left all Cuban slaveowners in a state of nervous tension, as Echeverría described to his exiled friend, Saco, in June, 1865:

> The end of the war leaves everyone in Cuba excited, although there is no revolutionary tendency . . . . Everyone is expectant, but no one knows why. The alarmed Peninsulares are beginning to send their cash to Spain, and some timid Creoles are following their example. But the conduct of the Creoles reveals a strong confidence and enthusiasm over

39. Fermín Figuera, *Estudios sobre la isla de Cuba: La cuestión social* (Madrid: Colegio de sordos-mudos y de ciegos, 1866).
40. Cepero Bonilla, *Obras,* p. 77.

the awaited new day and the end of the present conditions. What is amazing is that no one considers early abolition of domestic slavery. Nevertheless all accept it without the previous fear that a mere mention of it evoked earlier. Nor is the destruction of the island feared if we adopt adequate protective measures. What scares us is the thought that the metropolis, after making us suffer from her mistakes in this affair, will, in a fit of generosity, abandon us as she did Santo Domingo.[41]

Cuban political exiles in the United States, however, actively clamored for the immediate abolition of slavery. They were less concerned with its economic and social aspects, however, than with the political handicap it represented to the cooperation of all whites in an organization to liberate Cuba and Puerto Rico. The Republican Society of Cuba and Puerto Rico, founded in New York on April 7, 1866, demanded independence for the Spanish Antilles, and the absolute liberty for all its inhabitants without distinction of race or color.[42]

Within Cuba, the Reformists were strongly opposed by a group of Peninsulares, who formed a *Partido Incondicional Español* ("unconditional Spanish party"), bent on maintaining the status quo. The Peninsulares had their own newspaper, *El Diario de la Marina,* in which they consistently decried any alteration in the political position of the island and the social and economic conditions that supported their own personal positions and privileges. They warned every captain-general that concessions to the Creoles prejudiced the continuation of Spanish government in the island. It was this party which later formed the nucleus of that destructive, reactionary group of Volunteers who expelled Domingo Dulce in 1869, and took over effective control of the government.

In 1865, Spain was suffering from internal dissension, and political and economic difficulties—difficulties aggravated by the loss of prestige after the failure to subduc Santo Domingo and the support for the ill-fated Maximilian of Hapsburg in Mexico. Nevertheless, the government decided to extend its policy of conciliation towards Cuba. A royal decree of November 25, 1865, established a colonial reform commission to discuss proposals for reforms on the basis of the Creole demand. Despite strong conservative opposition in Madrid, the Spanish Antilles elected twenty commissioners, sixteen of whom came from Cuba, and the remaining four from Puerto Rico. Twelve Cuban representatives

41. Quoted ibid., pp. 95–96.
42. Ibid., p. 90.

came from the Reform Party while three Puerto Ricans also supported liberal reform.[43]

Before the representatives reached Madrid, however, their optimism received a severe reversal. The Conservatives, led by Ramón María Narváez, replaced the Liberal Union government of Leopoldo O'Donnell, which had been sympathetic to Creole demands. Antonio Cánovas del Castillo, the reform-inclined colonial secretary, fled from Madrid. But the most stunning blow came when the new government appointed twenty-one persons to the commission, thereby ensuring a clear majority for itself in any decision.

The abolition of slavery presented the most difficult matter on the agenda of the commission. The Puerto Ricans supported immediate, total abolition. But slavery was not a primary economic interest in Puerto Rico, where only about 7 per cent of the population were slaves. The colony depended more on contraband trade than on the large plantation for the main source of income. Besides, relative poverty had reduced the gap between the rich and the poor, and had facilitated the social mixing of Creoles and Peninsulares.[44]

The Cuban representatives, also morally condemning slavery, found it difficult it accept the position of the Puerto Ricans, and offered a number of plans of their own. They proposed seven bases they deemed indispensable for successful abolition: the total suppression of the slave trade; declaration of freedom for all those born after September 29, 1866; registration of all slaves, and the absolute prohibition of all unregistered persons of color from being made slaves; no emancipation without compensation; no legislation on slavery without consulting the slaveowners; the establishment in Havana of a development bank especially to assist agriculture; and, finally, the application in the Antilles of a modified version of the Spanish mortgage law.[45]

The government accepted the proposals of all the participants, but claimed that the matter required more consideration. Nevertheless, it ordered the registration of all the slaves in the island, and outlined

43. Foner, *History of Cuba*, 2:153–61.

44. See, Luis M. Díaz Soler, *La historia de la esclavitud negra en Puerto Rico* (Rio Piedras: University of Puerto Rico Press, 1965), pp. 265–88; and Arturo Morales Carrión, *Puerto Rico and the Non-Hispanic Caribbean: A Study in the Decline of Spanish Exclusivism* (Rio Piedras: University of Puerto Rico Press, 1959), pp. 133–43. Puerto Rico did, nevertheless, have some large plantations.

45. Eugenio Alsono y Sanjurjo, *Apuntes sobre los proyectos de abolición de la esclavitud en las islas de Cuba y Puerto Rico* (Madrid: Bibl. de Inst. y Recreo, 1874), pp. 12–18.

more severe punishment for the slave traders; however, it still refused to equate the trade to piracy.[46] The commissioners returned to their homes thinking that they had the reforms they desired. But Alejandro de Castro, the new Spanish colonial secretary, could pursue his abolitionist convictions no further than the ordering of the new registration and the declarations that the trade must end. Spain was too poor to afford compensation to the planters who would lose their slaves, and the Conservatives were too afraid that the question of abolition would ruin the colonies.[47] The government was prepared to bide its time over abolition. But in 1868 the "Glorious Revolution" drove Isabel II from the Spanish throne, and the Ten Years War began in Cuba.

46. AHN, Estado, Esclavitud, leg. 8049(16), fol. 1.
47. Corwin, *Spain and Cuba,* pp. 189–214; also AHN, Ultramar, Hacienda, leg. 4517(104).

# 8

# The Ten Years War and the Abolition of Slavery

*The causes of the insurrection
in Cuba lie in the tragic colonial
tradition which began in 1823, and
continued in the deceptions of 1837
and 1854, but especially following
the Reform Commission of 1866, and
the rigorous and unrealistic administration
of General Lersundi between
1867 and 1868.*

Rafael María de Labra, to the Cortes,
1871.

NOTHING COULD BE MORE MISLEADING than to think that slavery was an important factor contributing to the outbreak of the civil war in Cuba that lasted from 1868 to 1878. Instead, as Rafael María de Labra correctly pointed out to the Spanish Cortes, the causes were basically political and economic. The Cuban civil wars of the later nineteenth century were essentially a manifestation of the universal struggle between metropolis and frontier, and a belated continuation of the struggle which had plagued the earlier colonies of Spain at the beginning of the century. Cuba and Spain had developed varied interests during the nineteenth century, and the relations of colony and mother country were to be marred by continual conflict. The presence of this conflict did not mean that an outbreak of hostilities was imminent in 1868, yet, given the particular conditions of both metropolis and frontier colony, war would come eventually. Nor did this war necessarily have to lead to separation of the colonies, as the history of the continual strife in the Portuguese empire has shown. Imperial metropolises can demonstrate stubborn persistence.

Some of the underlying causes of the outbreak of war in 1868 could be found in the nature of Spanish colonial policy, which fluctuated between indecision and repression. The unstable political situation at home throughout the nineteenth century undermined any attempt at a flexible colonial policy that would satisfy the demands of the colonists in Cuba without undermining metropolitan power there. The rapid turnover of political chiefs in Madrid was followed by the equally rapid succession of governors in Cuba. These governors, sometimes alienated both from the people they ruled and from the people for whom they ruled, were in difficult situations. Balancing official policy and local reality, they adopted the pragmatic approach, and tried their best to restrain separatist tendencies in Cuba. Such a policy appeared to be in the longterm interest of the Spanish government. Colonies existed for the benefit of the mother country and the national honor demanded that they remain in that subordinate condition. And Spanish national honor was not a hollow thing.

Good government, however, suffered because the highest officials in Cuba were vulnerable to their superiors in Madrid, and to the rich merchants and planters in Havana. Above all, Cuban taxes contributed significantly to the administration and supported the nearly bankrupt Spanish treasury. The local planter oligarchy, therefore, used their wealth to exert great political influence in Madrid. And, indeed, after the middle of the nineteenth century effective political power came not from the crown's representative but from this local elite. Political decisions were often made not after any consideration of the island as a whole, but merely by consulting the narrow, often selfish, interests of the few rich men who came to embody the general will, and ruthlessly expelled any who challenged their claims or their system.

The sugar plantocracy of Creoles and Peninsulares, temporarily united by Serrano's liberal "policy of attraction" between 1858 and 1862, completely overlooked the economic and ecological gap which corresponded to the political divisions of east and west. Although continuous common threads of dissatisfaction and dissent with Spanish rule had characterized the entire Creole group irrespective of location, the war emphasized the mutually reinforcing separatist tendencies of economy, geography, population composition, and topography.[1]

Vast differences existed between the two departments of Cuba. The eastern department was the more mountainous section of the island, with rugged peaks and dissected valleys dominating the topography from Manzanillo to Baracoa. Northwesterly, however, the provinces of Puerto Príncipe and Las Tunas presented an aspect of rolling hills, swamps, and well-drained plains almost indistinguishable from the western department. The luxuriant forests of the eastern region have proved an excellent base for guerrilla warfare from the days of the unfortunate Indian chief Hatuey to the success of Fidel Castro. In its hills the Cuban insurgents of the Ten Years War found refuge from the Spanish cavalry, while they were able to inflict random disruptive attacks on the Spanish columns. The failure to wage any sustained effort in the western department resulted partly from the lack of topographical facilities for guerrilla warfare. The rolling hills and cultivated plains facilitated the type of orderly, organized battles with horses and cannon against which the Cubans were extremely vulnerable.

In economy and manpower, the western department exerted a tremendous preponderance. It contributed more than 90 per cent of the island's total agricultural production, and had more than 77 per cent of the total population. A further examination of those statistics emphasizes still more its supremacy over the eastern department in the ability to sustain war. In 1862, the western department had 78 per cent of all cattle in the island, as well as 80 per cent of the horses, and 66 per cent of all the mules and donkeys. Railroads and highways were also considerably more developed in this part of the island, since they were constructed principally to serve the sugar estates. In 1869, moreover, 78 per cent of all unmarried males of military potential lived in the western department.[2]

The location of the capital city of Havana and the assistance of the military and naval resources of the Spanish government afforded extensive facilities for the coordination and deployment of resources within the west, further bolstering its military potential. Nevertheless, the Ten

1. Ramiro Guerra y Sánchez, *Guerra de los diez años 1868–1878* (Havana: Cultural, 1950), pp. 4–25.

2. *Cuba desde 1850 á 1873* (Madrid: Impr. Nacional, 1873), pp. 152–53. Also Jacobo de la Pezuela y Lobo, *Diccionario geográfico, estadístico, histórico de la isla de Cuba* (4 vols.; Madrid: Mellado, 1863–66), 1:38–39.

Years War was not a mere sectional dispute. The ability of the rebels to prolong their activities revealed important cleavages cutting across the society as a whole.

The economic vitality of the western sector of the island rested on the large, partially slave-operated sugar estates. Sugar and slavery not only gave political importance to the Creole planters, but also established a community of interest between rich Creoles and Peninsulares which superseded the differences of class. Both groups interpreted the abolition of slavery as the forerunner of economic ruin, and therefore tried to forestall any attempt to grant immediate emancipation to their slaves.[3]

But economics were not the only major concern of the white people living in the western region and owning slaves there. Obviously the economic value of the slave was higher in this region, since freed slaves and impoverished whites were not present in the numbers required for the successful operation of the estates. But the absence of this semifree, low-status group left the division between free and nonfree rather sharp. The coincidence of slave uprisings and slave concentrations created a climate of fear throughout the western department which made the region more vulnerable to the rumors that spread from time to time suggesting that any precipitate end to slavery would engulf the island in a racial war like that in St. Domingue. The difficulty of the western department, therefore, was that class lines followed racial lines, and the white classes were tied together by a community of interest.

Class, interest, and race did not synchronize in the eastern department—or if they did, the fact was not of enormous significance. The relative poverty of the area combined with the relative absence of Spanish merchants and bureaucrats removed the economic and social friction which assumed so much importance in the western department. Of course, here and there existed enclaves almost identical in social structure and economic base to the sugar areas of the western department. The fertile valleys around Santiago de Cuba and Guantánamo were not really typical of the eastern department, for in general, its population was predominantly free, rural, and white—in that order. The relatively larger number of free colored persons and smaller proportion of slaves did not make slavery the outstanding social and economic issue

3. Philip S. Foner, *A History of Cuba and Its Relations with the United States* (2 vols.: New York: International Publishers, 1963), 2:149–58.

that it was in the rest of Cuba. Moreover, since the white population outnumbered the nonwhite population in most areas of the east, emancipation did not engender fearful visions of racial violence among easterners, as it did in the west. Racial hostility existed, but was far less evident than in the full plantation zones.

In the western department approximately 11 per cent of the population were free colored persons, and fully 30 per cent were slaves. But the city of Havana tended to throw off the balance of the races, so that

TABLE 11

Population of the Eastern Department, 1869

| Division | Total no. of inhabitants | White | Free colored | Slave |
| --- | --- | --- | --- | --- |
| Baracoa | 12,065 | 42.0% | 41.0% | 17.0% |
| Bayamo | 24,612 | 40.0 | 48.0 | 12.0 |
| Guantánamo | 19,314 | 32.0 | 26.0 | 42.0 |
| Holguín | 54,169 | 80.0 | 15.0 | 5.0 |
| Jiguaní | 17,623 | 72.0 | 22.0 | 6.0 |
| Manzanillo | 27,758 | 52.0 | 41.0 | 7.0 |
| Nuevitas | 6,011 | 67.0 | 2.0 | 31.0 |
| Puerto Príncipe | 65,663 | 64.0 | 18.0 | 18.0 |
| Santiago de Cuba | 89,593 | 26.0 | 41.0 | 33.0 |
| Las Tunas | 6,250 | 51.0 | 41.0 | 8.0 |
| Total & Averages | 323,058 | 50.0 | 30.0 | 20.0 |

Source: *Cuba desde 1850 á 1873*, pp. 152–53.

in the plantation zones the proportion of slaves was much greater. Only three jurisdictional divisions in the eastern department, however, had more than 30 per cent of their total population registered as slaves. These three divisions were Guantánamo (42 per cent), Nuevitas (31 per cent), and Santiago de Cuba (33 per cent); four of the remaining seven divisions had less than 10 per cent registered as slaves. Figures for the whole eastern department gave a population of 50 per cent white persons, 30 per cent free colored persons, and 20 per cent slaves (see Table 11).

As the Ten Years War developed, slavery became an increasingly important factor. But initially, the war was essentially a nationalist revolt against Spain, fought by individuals who were predominantly free, white, and rural in residence. It grew out of the accumulated colonial resentment against the Spanish political and economic policies of the decades of prosperity before the 1860's, and it was exacerbated by the dismal failure of the reform commission of 1866–67. Indeed, the failure of the reform commission created a crisis of confidence between the politicians in Madrid and the rich planters in Havana. It provided the spark of Creole revolution in the eastern department; for the "Grito de Yara" which set off the first sign of war began after the reform commission had failed to achieve anything satisfactory to the Cubans.

The election of Cuban commissioners to the Cortes in Madrid, and the lengthy debates which took place there, had created a great climate of optimism, especially about political reorganization, which would benefit all the Creoles, and the reduction of customs duties, which the richer planters and merchants had proposed in return for a new income tax. The failure to implement the suggestions made by the colonial representatives in Madrid led to spirited protests in the island which were ignored by the government in Madrid. Instead, in early 1867, the Spanish government, without consulting the colonies, imposed a new tax ranging from 6–12 per cent on real estate, incomes, and all types of business.

Contrary to local expectations, the new tax did not replace the onerous customs duties against which the Cubans had continuously complained since the early part of the century. And the timing of the imposition was particularly bad. The tax coincided with a period of economic depression. The price of sugar fell to its lowest point in thirteen years. All the leading banks except the government-operated Banco Español suspended payments, exciting fears of an imminent economic catastrophe. Economic depression resulting from the wider international situation had been no novelty to the Cubans, since it came, with varying degrees of intensity (though a consistently high level of alarm), in cycles of ten-year intervals.[4] Although the situation of 1866 was not desperate, the richer planters and merchants complained loudly that they could not afford the added taxation. And if the wealthier members of the society found the increased levy burdensome, it was even worse for the poorer subsistence farmers of the eastern department, who existed almost outside the export economy. The new income tax failed to provide more money for the administration, and added an economic grievance to the simmering cauldron of political discontent. While the yield was only 25 per cent of the estimated amount, the opposition to the tax was wide-

4. Ramiro Guerra y Sánchez, et al., *Historia de la nación cubana* (10 vols., Havana: Ed. Hist. de la Nación Cubana, 1952), 4:169.

spread, and sometimes quite bitter. In the eastern department, angry farmers caught and hanged an unfortunate tax collector. The political opposition which had found its cells of strength in the Masonic lodges became more organized and more militant.

The spirit of rebellion which had reared its menacing head at irregular intervals gained strength during 1867 and 1868. Although some revolutionary leaders, including Carlos Manuel de Céspedes, had always been skeptical of the efficacy of the reform commission, the real kindling spark of revolt came from the coincidences of international politics. The "Glorious Revolution" in Spain and the presidential elections in the United States provided the catalysts.

The September revolution of Serrano, Prim, and Topete which drove the Spanish queen, Isabel II, into exile reawakened the aspirations of the Carlists, and ushered in a new period of intense political restlessness. Repercussions were felt in the Antilles. In Puerto Rico a small group declared the independence of that island, and made an abortive attempt to defend it. The Cuban rebels hoped that Spain would never be able to defend her rule in the Antilles, and that if they could hold out until the new and presumably sympathetic administration of Ulysses S. Grant took over in the United States, victory was probable. But the optimism of September 1868 had been fermenting during a year of watching and waiting.

The revolutionary organization in eastern Cuba began in 1867. Built around the Masonic lodges, it drew its strength from the Creole middle sector, from small slaveholders, and from the free, urban black population in Bayamo, Holguín, Manzanillo, Las Tunas, and Santiago de Cuba. The leaders were Céspedes, the Masó family, and Salvador Cisneros Betancourt. All those men had personal as well as ideological grievances against the Spanish colonial government. Céspedes, had a long history of involvement in revolutionary activity both in Spain— from where he was once exiled to France—and in Cuba, where he was openly known for his subversive activity.[5] Antonio Maceo, who distinguished himself in the Ten Years War, was a member of the Masonic lodge at Santiago de Cuba, and had also been drawn into the revolutionary deliberations long before the outbreak of hostilities.

In August 1868 the Bayamo branch of the conspirators sent Pedro

5. Antonio Pirala y Criado, *Anales de la guerra de Cuba* (4 vols.; Madrid: F. González Rojas, 1895–98), 1:255.

Figueredo to Havana to contact Morales Lemus, and to find out what support the reform movement would give to an organized revolution. Lemus and the Havana reformers showed little enthusiasm for violence. Being basically moderates and wealthy Creoles, they considered revolution too inimical to their social aspirations and their economic and political interests.[6]

The failure to gain the cooperation of the "respectable" Creoles did not dismay the men of the cast. In Bayamo, Céspedes, leader of the loosely coordinated rebels of the whole department, declared that the time was opportune for revolt, and that no help could be expected from the western sector of the island, at least in the beginning. In a highly emotional speech, Céspedes urged his followers to disregard the apparent grandeur of Spain, for its power was in reality decrepit and wormeaten. He cited the long-standing grievances of the Cuban Creoles: arbitrary government, oppressive taxation, corruption in the administration, the exclusion of Cubans from the Cortes, and the limitation of political and civil rights; and he declared that Cuba should be an independent nation.

In Bayamo, as in Havana, however, economic interest prevailed over liberal thought. The other members of the junta, although impressed by the oratory of their leader and the cause of a free Cuba, decided that any outbreak should come at the end of the planting season. But by agreeing to accept December 24, 1868, as the day to begin the war, they were alienating the big sugar planters, whose harvests would be about to start. It was also a clear indication of the exclusion of the slaves from the arena. The expected war was to be fought by the Creoles for the whites, many of whom would never join.

While the rebels were awaiting the arrival of arms, the plot was revealed, allegedly by the wife of one of the conspirators, who told her priest about it during confession. The priest informed the governor of Bayamo, Colonel Julian de Udaeta. The captain-general of Cuba, Francisco Lersundi, already disturbed by reports of the liberal revolution in Spain, and fearing the spread of liberal ideas to Cuba and Puerto Rico, immediately ordered Udaeta to arrest all the conspirators, since Cuba should belong to Spain no matter what happened in Madrid. On October 4, 1868, Isabel II had sent a telegram from exile at Pau,

6. Raul Cepero Bonilla, *Obras históricas* (Havana: Inst. de Historia, 1963), p. 120.

across the French border, beseeching Lersundi to protect "at any cost, the overseas provinces from the Revolution." Lersundi, faithful royalist though he was, replied that he would accept the de facto situation in Spain, but as long as he commanded in Cuba peace would prevail.[7] But the contents of Lersundi's telegram to Udaeta were released by the telegraphist, Ishmael Céspedes, to Carlos Manuel Céspedes, who hastily convened the junta. Thirty-seven members supported his pronunciamiento of October 10, 1868, the "Grito de Yara."

The declaration at Yara reflected the vast differences of opinion within the revolutionary council, and was designed to attract all shades of opinions and all groups and interests in Cuba. Indecision and a lack of coordination were rampant. No platform was broad enough to accommodate the differences in ideology and military strategy which prevailed. Nevertheless, the rebels, ill-armed, ill-fed, and often exhausted, won a series of small skirmishes with the Spanish troops at Yara, Baire, Jiguaní, and Bayamo in a few days, and before the end of the year had gained considerable support throughout the eastern section of the island.[8] In a short time, the hopes that the revolt would be quickly and easily crushed began to fade away among the loyalists in Havana.

Slavery was not among the issues considered at first by the rebels. Once the war broke out, however, it assumed greater importance. The revolt began under conservative leadership, but did not remain conservative for very long. Céspedes was no egalitarian, and some writers even thought that he betrayed a cardinal weakness in his pretences toward aristocracy.[9] In any event, Céspedes immediately freed his own slaves, while insisting that the revolution supported the gradual indemnified abolition of slavery. Céspedes' early plans in general, seemed to be merely to bring an end to Spanish rule and taxation, substituting Creole domination of the same political structure and bureaucracy. To this extent the revolt was simply nationalist in origin. No evidence supports the assertion that the rebels were united "without distinction of race, in a common quest for freedom," since "freedom" had differing significance for both Creoles and slaves.[10]

The outbreak of war brought the upper sector—the wealthy, pro-

7. Pirala, *Anales,* 1:245.

8. Guerra y Sánchez, *Guerra de los diez años,* pp. 109–20.

9. Pirala, *Anales,* 1:254.

10. Emilio Roig de Leuchsenring, *La guerra libertadora cubana de los treinta años 1868–1898* (Havana: Historiador de la ciudad de la Habana, 1952), p. 44.

Spanish elements—closer together. Lersundi immediately mobilized all the available troops and naval units to crush the revolt. Besides the army, groups of citizen volunteers were formed in all the larger towns, primarily to defend the property of the wealthy and other supporters of the government. Within a year, these Volunteers had successfully usurped the powers of the captain-general, and dictated the direction of the war. They led a relentless attack on the rebels and all persons suspected of supporting rebel activity in an effort to crush thoroughly the threat to Spanish rule.[11]

The Volunteers executed the most deplorable atrocities and destroyed much valuable property during the first two years of the campaign. And if their action helped preserve Spanish dominion at a crucial period, their violence drove the rebels to a greater and more determined resistence, and forced the moderate elements to flee abroad or choose sides. Liberal reformist Creoles such as Morales Lemus, José Manuel Mestre, José Antonio Echeverría and Antonio Fernández Bramosio only decided to support Céspedes after they despaired of any compromise between the Creoles and the Peninsulares.[12] And much despair arose from the angry accusations of Lersundi that local criticism of the government of the island not only undermined his authority but also gave moral support to the rebels.[13]

As the division in the island began to polarize sharply between Creoles and Peninsulares, the government in Madrid replaced the intransigent conservative Lersundi by the liberal Domingo Dulce, who had gained considerable popularity among the Creoles during his previous assignments in Cuba. Dulce arrived on January 4, 1869, only to find that real power was no longer in the hands of the captain-general. The Volunteers not only rejected Dulce's conciliatory schemes, but rudely expelled him from the island in July. The acquiescence of the government in Madrid in this arbitrary action underlined the weakness of the central authority.

The rebel cause drew its support from three types of people, who may have very roughly reflected different political inclinations. One faction was composed of the wealthy Creole planters of the western

11. For a very sympathetic account of the Volunteers' activity during the war, see José J. Ribó, *Historia de los voluntarios cubanos* (2 vols.; Madrid: González, 1872).

12. Guerra y Sánchez, *Guerra de los diez años*, pp. 183–88.

13. Pirala, *Anales*, 1:293–98.

division, typified by the Aldama family, who were drawn into the struggle after the outbreak of hostilities rather than before. Another faction comprised smaller planters, principally from the eastern division—Céspedes was typical—and ideologically oriented toward Cuban nationalism. These men approached the separation of Cuba from Spain in a very legalistic and constitutionally oriented way; they followed the tradition of the early nineteenth-century liberals of Spanish America. Finally, there was a third faction of the rank and file of the revolution—a very heterogenous group of poorer whites, free persons of color, and slaves and indentured Asians. It was to this group that real power quickly moved after the war broke out, and after Céspedes had shown a certain timidity in declaring immediate emancipation for all the slaves, or in burning the estates of the larger planters. Dissatisfaction with the leadership of Céspedes had developed quite early among the rebels: the reinforcements from Spain plus the ferocious offensive of the Volunteers during the early months demanded better organization and resistance if the movement were to have any chance of success.

The first constitutional convention met at Guaímaro on April 10, 1869, with delegates coming from Villa Clara, Sancti-Spíritus, Jiguaní, Holguin and Camaguey. The leaders made an attempt to unite the discordant forces of the revolutionary party, and to formulate some commonly accepted goals and methods of procedure. As a matter of local and international strategy, a republican form of government was accepted. The convention divided the island into four states, reflecting the localism of the delegates: Oriente, Camaguey, Las Villas, and Occidente. Each state should have equal representation in a house of representatives, but further details of the structure of the government had to await the end of the war. Céspedes became the first president of the new republic simply because he was most acceptable to the wealthy Creoles, particularly the wealthy exiles of the Central Republican Junta in New York. Manuel Quesada was elected commander-in-chief of the revolutionary forces. Under the insistence of the less conservative delegates, particularly Ignacio and Eduardo Agramonte and Salvador Cisneros Betancourt, the constitution vaguely expressed a desire for "the liberty and equality of all men regardless of race."[14]

The failure to confront squarely the problem of the nonwhites and slavery was a severe handicap to the Cuban cause. Céspedes realized

14. Cepero Bonilla, *Obras*, p. 136.

very slowly that something had to be done or the war effort would be further weakened, especially after the Spanish government began to discuss new measures on slavery. And although Céspedes reluctantly agreed to the burning of all the cane fields in October 1869, he still adamantly refused the granting of unconditional freedom to all slaves. James O'Kelly, an American journalist travelling through the eastern area in 1870, noted that many discouraged slaves were returning to the estates from which they had previously fled.[15] Prior to the outbreak of the war, the Santa Ana sugar estate had four hundred slaves. Almost all deserted to join the revolution, thinking they would thereby gain their liberty. By 1870, some eighty slaves had been recaptured, or had returned voluntarily.

The rebels also encountered many other difficulties apart from the strife and petty jealousies of their leaders. The chronic shortage of supplies and ammunition, the reluctance of the troops of one area to fight in another area, and the terrible reprisals on the families of the participants by the Spaniards tended to weaken the appeal of the rebel forces.[16] The Spanish cruisers patrolled the seas and restricted the supply of firearms smuggled in from abroad. Meanwhile, the Spanish troops were steadily reinforced by fresh recruits from Spain and the most modern rifles from the United States.[17] The Cubans had no option but to conduct guerrilla warfare, harrassing the Spaniards as much as possible, burning the cane fields whenever they could, and supplementing their meager imports of arms through Jamaica and Haiti by capturing the abundant supplies of the Spanish soldiers.

Cuban attempts to win recognition abroad were largely unsuccessful. The United States was prepared to wait for the Spanish government to straighten itself out and then offer the island for sale, or until the rebels showed the capacity for a decisive blow to Spanish rule. In any event, the American secretary of state, Hamilton Fish, was not prepared to intervene in Cuba when the general feelings of the country were opposed to such a move.[18] Great Britain, realizing that her commercial interests

15. James O'Kelly, *The Mambi Land* (Philadelphia: Lippincott, 1874). I used the version with introduction by Fernando Ortiz Fernández, *La tierra del Mambi* (Havana, 1930), pp. 98–99.

16. AHN, Ultramar, Insurrección, leg. 4360(30).

17. Ibid., Gobierno, leg. 4728, 1869–70.

18. Allan Nevins, *Hamilton Fish: The Inner History of the Grant Administration,* rev. ed. (New York: Frederick Ungar, 1957), pp. 191–200.

were best served not in rivalry with the United States, but rather in association with that country, no longer was interested in whether or not Cuba remained a Spanish possession. Moreover, on the overriding problem of slavery, the British could wait to see whether Spain would abolish slavery or let the rebels do so. Any action by either side would be acceptable to the British.[19] The official position of Great Britain and the United States was very important for Spain, but had deplorable consequences for the rebels. President Grant's reaffirmation of the neutrality laws on October 13, 1869, adversely affected arms shipment to the rebels, and forced the Cuban junta in New York to be more discreet in its propaganda and solicitations. Furthermore, the Spanish consular services in the United States found it easier to glean information on the activities of exiles, and sometimes to bring them to the attention of the government in Washington.[20]

Despite the formidable handicaps, the rebels were able to defy the Spaniards for ten years, largely owing to a number of able leaders. Antonio Maceo was undoubtedly the most successful and the most determined military leader during the war. The son of a free Afro-Cuban, and one from a family with access to revolutionary ideas through membership in a Masonic lodge, Antonio Maceo and his entire family joined the revolution from the beginning. After repeatedly defeating the Spaniards in a number of engagements, he rose rapidly to be brigadier-general of the liberating army, and chief of the second division of the first corps. More than any other leader, Maceo offered inspiration and encouragement to the rebel forces through the darkest moments of the bitter struggle against Spain.[21]

Maceo's outstanding service was never appreciated by the white members of the revolutionary forces. A strong racist element was always present in Cuba, and most rebel leaders were more anti-Negro than they were anti-Spanish. Beginning in 1869, a sinister smear campaign, enthusiastically exploited by the Spaniards, dogged Maceo's efforts. Rumors, widely believed, claimed that Maceo was motivated by the ambition of setting up a Negro republic after the example of Haiti. For a long time, Maceo disregarded the rumors. In 1876 things came to a climax. Revolutionary success was waning, and morale was gradually

19. Christopher J. Bartlett, "British Reaction to the Cuban Insurrection of 1868–1878," *Hispanic American Historical Review*, 37 (1957), 296–312.
20. AHN, Ultramar, Insurrección, leg. 4360(30), exp. 148.
21. See Leopoldo Horrego Estuch, *Maceo, heroe y carácter* (Havana: La Milagrosa, 1952).

ebbing. The Spaniards, having ended the second Carlist War, renewed a vigorous campaign in Cuba under the able general Arsenio Martínez de Campos. The rumors and fears of a Negro republic increased. Maceo strongly protested, and threatened to resign, but no official action was taken by the rebels to end the slanders.[22] Maceo, nevertheless, continued to fight with undiminished zeal in a cause gravely divided by selfish interests.

The internal troubles of the rebel forces could not, and did not, prove disastrous while the military activity remained stalemated between 1873 and 1876. The grandiose plans to invade the sugar-rich western sector which Máximo Gómez had energetically pursued for nearly three years faded from a lack of supplies, and the immobility of the troops. Rebel generals such as Vicente García and Carlos Roloff did not share the devotion and egalitarian spirit of Gómez and Maceo, and probably thought that a successful invasion of the west would release the slaves and increase the potential power of the revolutionary black leaders. On another level, while the poorer cigar-makers and other exiles in Florida and New York were giving as much as they could to aid the Cuban rebels, the richer exiles refused to contribute.[23] This reluctance on the part of the rich to contribute to the revolution to which they paid lip service further crippled the ability of the fighting men to purchase necessary military supplies, although these, as it turned out, encountered monumental difficulties in reaching the insurgents in Cuba.

In reality, the racial fears of the revolutionary Cuban Creoles were unfounded; the revolution had failed to attract black people from outside the zones of conflict. The conservative and often wealthy section of the revolution had strongly resisted any form of immediate abolition. In the early stages of the revolution, this group supported Céspedes, whose official policy served their ends. By 1872, however, Céspedes moved toward a more radical policy involving the burning of estates and unqualified freedom of the slaves. While this action lost him the support of the conservatives, it failed to gain that of the masses or of the military. Matters came to a head in late 1873, and Céspedes was replaced by Salvador Cisneros Betancourt as president of the republic. No one even bothered to inform Céspedes beforehand that he was dismissed.

Repeated assertions that the revolutionary forces were composed

---

22. Foner, *A History of Cuba*, 2:258–62.
23. Cepero Bonilla, *Obras*, pp. 161–65.

principally of Afro-Cubans and Chinese gain no support from an examination of the papers in the archives in Madrid.[24] Despite the energetic appeals made by the Cubans, it does not seem that they were successful in attracting the slaves to their cause.[25] Although I made only a preliminary search, and although the available material is astonishingly deficient, the general impression gained from the documents pertaining to trials, executions, and exiles, is that the vast majority of the rebels were white persons, who were generally small landowners, or guajiros.

One reason for the reluctance of the black people, either slave or free, to join the rebels may have been that they had greater confidence in an ultimate victory of the metropolitan government. In that event, the promise of freedom made by the Cubans could never be fulfilled. Nevertheless, it was quite possible that the severe regimentation of the slaves in the western department prevented them from getting a true picture of the actual situation in the east. And regardless of the impression which most black people had, it seemed that they remained unconvinced that a Creole victory would significantly ameliorate their servile condition. Not only were many Creole leaders in the rebel forces openly racist, but the overtones of division had spread down through the ranks. This did not augur well for future race relations in the island, and the revolutionary propaganda organs tried their best to woo the Afro-Cubans by denying evidences of Creole racism, while picturing the Spaniards as the persistent advocates of slavery.[26]

But, notwithstanding Cuban calumnies, the Spanish government had been making well-publicized legal advances towards the abolition of slavery as an integral part of the program of the revolution of 1868 that overthrew Isabel II. This new, vigorous approach towards the emancipation of the slaves in the colonies was the work of the revolutionary junta in Madrid, which had the influential abolitionists Labra, Julio Vizcarrondo y Coronado, and Nicolás María Rivero among its ranks.[27]

On September 19, 1868, the Madrid junta issued a manifesto in which it strongly condemned slavery, and suggested that the newly

24. See, AHN, Ultramar, Insurrección, esp. legs. 4340–47.
25. Ibid., Gobierno, leg. 4728: Papeles y Periódicos de la Revolución.
26. Ibid.: *La Revolución* for Thursday, Aug. 18, 1870, and Thursday, Nov. 18, 1869.
27. Arthur F. Corwin, *Spain and the Abolition of Slavery in Cuba, 1817–1886* (Austin: University of Texas Press, 1967), pp. 216–21.

formed provisional government of Spain immediately declare all slaves born after that date to be free, as an earnest symbol of the government's desire to help the colonies. The junta further recommended, however, that the peculiar history of slavery made any immediate total abolition unwise and even harmful to the slaves themselves; this should await carefully considered practical measures approved by the new Cortes.[28]

The provisional government under the leadership of Francisco Serrano accepted the suggestion of the junta in Madrid, and issued a decree whereby all slaves born after September 29, 1868, should be given their freedom (*vientre libre*). Such a declaration committed the government to the principles of abolition, and the colonial ministry began to formulate methods for a peaceful and equitable transformation of the labor systems in Cuba and Puerto Rico.

But an acceptance of the principle of abolition by the government in Madrid did not mean that abolition became suddenly more imminent. Serrano's decree was not put into effect overseas, and the proslavery interests immediately formed a *junta cubana* in the larger Spanish cities which renewed the famous and extremely effective cry of "Remember Haiti." José Antonio Saco rushed to the defense of the propertied classes by invoking the euphemistic argument that the emancipation of the Cuban slaves threatened the property, security, and prosperity of the island, and that since Spain was in no position to indemnify the slaveowners, they might be forced to separate themselves from the mother country in order to defend their property.[29]

Saco's arguments did not go unchallenged, especially by the competent Labra. Nevertheless, the government found it more discreet to attempt reforms in the colonies, and to have elections so that the colonists themselves would be able to participate in the Cortes according to the earlier promise that the revolution was "not conducted for the sole benefit of the inhabitants of the Peninsula, but also for our loyal brothers overseas."[30] Before those elections could be held, however, the revolt at Yara completely upset the government's plan.

The revolutionary outbreak led by Carlos Manuel Céspedes in Octo-

---

28. Ibid., p. 218.
29. José Antonio Saco, *La esclavitud en Cuba y la revolución en España* [pamphlet] (Madrid: La Politica, 1868).
30. AHN, Ultramar, Gobierno, leg. 4933, vol. 1: "Circular del M. de Ultramar a los Gobernadores Superiores Civiles de Cuba, Puerto Rico, Filipinas, 27 de Octubre de 1868."

ber 1868 brought the problem of slavery to the forefront of colonial reforms. Despite the conservative approach of their Creole leaders, the
rebels had already accepted the principles of abolition. While this position was similar to that of the Madrid government in many respects, the
rebels made the situation critical by threatening total abolition, and dis-
rupting the conventional basis of labor and production in the island.
Any threat to Cuban economic prosperity could not fail to elicit the immediate response of the Spanish government, which above all valued its
receipts from the island's treasury.

As soon as the fighting broke out, the government sought the most
effective way to combat any precipitate emancipation of the slaves. Abolition became far more imminent than many politicians had ever con-
templated only one year earlier. On September 25, 1869, the captain-
general, Caballero de Rodas, wrote solemnly to the minister for the
colonies that among the many evils brought on by the insurrection had
also come a solitary good, which was the "death of slavery."[31]

The Spanish government, however, confronted its traditional problem
of pride. It steadfastly refused to accept any compromise with the rebels,
or to accept a serious plan of abolition while the colony was in revolt.
Every discussion of colonial reform heard the familiar evocation of the
glory of Spain and the dishonor of yielding to "ungrateful sons." Abolition and reform succumbed to the reactionary element in Spanish politics.[32]

Yet even the most conservative and reactionary factions in Spain were
not immune from the pervasive influences of international politics. The
international situation, therefore, acted as a catalyst to the Spanish government, and hastened some measure of abolition, at least in order to
deny the rebels the active sympathy or recognition of the United States,
Britain, and France. For had any of those three powers recognized the
rebels as belligerents, that action could have abruptly terminated Spanish rule in Cuba.

The most serious threat, of course, came from the United States. On
April 5, 1869, the Congress voiced sympathy for the rebel cause, and
hinted at possible recognition of the rebels.[33] Spain was plainly afraid

31. Ibid., Gobierno 4933, I, IV: "Mando de Rodas."
32. Corwin, *Spain and Cuba*, pp. 239–54.
33. See Jerónimo Becker y González, *La historia política y diplomática de
España desde la independencia de los Estados Unidos hasta nuestros días, 1776–
1895* (Madrid: Romero, 1897), p. 502.

that official recognition by the United States would not only cut off to her the supply of gunboats and Remington rifles so necessary to the war effort, but would open the supply of arms to the Cubans. The Spanish government undertook to mount a propaganda campaign in the United States to the effect that the rebels had been overthrown, and to actively encourage the renewed American attempts to purchase Cuba.[34] Once Americans felt that the Cuban affair could be settled by negotiation and purchase, the likelihood of their recognizing the rebels diminished.

Nevertheless, the delicate problem of slavery, which evoked resentment or indifference to the Spanish cause abroad, demanded redress. Slavery was in fact the strongest connection among the great national powers, which had all officially condemned the practice. It was with this in mind that the colonial minister, Segismundo Moret y Prendergast, wrote to the Cuban captain-general on May 8, 1870: "Not another day must pass without doing something about this. France and England will not help us while we are slaveholders, and this one word gives North America the right to hold a suspended threat over our heads."[35]

The situation in Puerto Rico also influenced the Spanish government towards some definite measure of abolition. By its own declaration in 1868, the government had made itself an advocate of abolition. The reasons proffered for suspending colonial reforms and abolition in Cuba did not apply to Puerto Rico, where slavery was a negligible economic and social factor, and the small revolt had been completely subdued. Moreover, Puerto Rico, unlike its sister island, had elected representatives to the Cortes in accordance with the decree of December 14, 1868.[36] Of the eleven Puerto Rican deputies in the Cortes, three were outspoken abolitionists who joined forces with the small number of Spanish deputies who supported the abolitionist society in the capital city.[37]

The Spanish abolitionists argued that some measure of abolition should be worked out for Puerto Rico suitable to be applied to Cuba when the revolution had been extinguished in that island. And since the Puerto Ricans did not have powerful, organized, proslavery advocates, the Spanish government could produce no valid rebuttal to the argu-

34. James M. Callahan, *Cuba and International Relations* (Baltimore: Johns Hopkins, 1899), pp. 375–82; Allan Nevins, *Hamilton Fish*, pp. 180–87; Corwin, *Spain and Cuba*, pp. 243–44.

35. AHN, Ultramar, Esclavitud, leg. 3554, fol. 8.

36. The Cubans lost their privilege to elect representatives to the Cortes as a result of the revolt of Yara.

37. Corwin, *Spain and Cuba*, pp. 232–33.

ment of the abolitionists. Indeed, the measure which later became the Moret Law of 1870 was an official response to foreign and domestic pressures.

Abolitionist sentiment in the Cortes was not strong enough to permit any measure affecting slavery, however diluted, to pass without substantial opposition. And the entire policy of colonial reform for Puerto Rico ran into such intransigent opposition from the conservatives, led by the ex-colonial minister, Cánovas del Castillo, that Manuel Becerra, the colonial minister appointed by Prim in September 1869, resigned on April 1, 1870. Becerra's successor, Moret, had been a vicepresident of the abolitionist society, and was a shrewd political tactician, possessing great perseverance and patience.[38]

Moret's plan was to adopt a compromise measure which would, nevertheless, be an advance on the inadequate existing system of vientre libre. At the same time, he wanted some scheme that would not cost the Spanish government, which was on the verge of bankruptcy, anything approaching the substantial indemnity paid by the British to their colonial slaveowners in 1838. The best way to avoid the indemnity, therefore, was to institute a patronage system by which the slaves would be tied to the estates as wage-earners for a period ranging from ten to fifteen years.[39]

The measures which Moret introduced to the Cortes were signed by the regent, Francisco Serrano, on July 4, 1870, and were to become effective immediately.[40] Article 1 established the right of free birth to every child born of slave parents after the publication of the law. Article 2 declared that all slaves born between September 17, 1868, and the date of publication of the law became the property of the state; masters were to be paid 125 Spanish pesetas for each such acquisition.

Article 3 extended liberty to all slaves who had served under the Spanish flag, or had helped the metropolitan forces in any way. Slaves could gain their liberty at the discretion of the captain-general of Cuba as a reward for any service he thought deserving of that distinction. To the master of any slave who obtained liberty through meritorious war

38. Ibid., pp. 239–45.

39. AHN, Ultramar, leg. 4481, 1870–72, vol. 1: Sr. M. de Ultramar al Gob. General de Cuba, May 8, 1870.

40. *Ley de cuatro de julio de 1870 sobre abolición de la esclavitud y reglamento para su ejecución en las islas de Cuba y Puerto Rico* (Havana: Impr. del Gobierno, 1873).

service, the state would offer an indemnity equal to the assessed value of the slave, provided that the master remained faithful to the Spanish cause. If the master were sympathetic to the rebels, however, no indemnity would be paid.

Article 4 declared all slaves over the age of sixty years to be free without indemnity to their owners. It also established the automatic, unindemnified freedom for every slave who should attain that age in the future.

Article 5 granted freedom to all slaves belonging to the state, and to all the emancipados who were still under its protection.

The slaves who gained their freedom by Articles 1 and 2 were called *libertos,* and remained attached to their owners under a system of trusteeship (*patronato*) until the age of eighteen (Articles 6, 7). The master was obliged to feed, clothe, protect, and care for them, and to teach them a useful trade. In return, any work done by the slave for his master would not be compensated. Between the ages of eighteen and twenty-one, the libertos should be paid one-half the wage of a free worker in a similar occupation. The trustee, however, should retain 50 per cent of the liberto's daily wage as a sort of compulsory saving for his ward (Article 8). On attaining the age of twenty-two, the liberto gained his complete independence from the master, and was paid the sum saved during the four years (Article 9).

The trusteeship could be immediately revoked if the liberto married, provided the female was more than fourteen years and the male more than eighteen years of age; or if the master physically abused his ward, or prostituted a female liberto (Article 10).

The remaining eleven articles outlined the relationship between the libertos and their patronos, and promised new legislation to terminate the process of total emancipation as soon as the Cuban war was over, and the deputies from that island had taken their seats in the Cortes. Articles 13, 19, and 21 were the most important.

Article 13 promised that any liberto or free black who desired to return to Africa would be given transportation to that continent. In addition, the local authorities were given the responsibility of protecting the rights of that new group, and providing employment for them. Article 19 insisted that any colored person omitted from the census lists made for Puerto Rico in December 1869, and due to be completed in Cuba in 1870, should be declared free. This article removed suspicion that slaves were deliberately left unregistered in order to substitute for others, or to defraud the tax collectors. Article 21 forbade, in vague terms, the continuation of the corporal punishment which was legally sanctioned by the slave codes of both islands. This article also prohibited the separate sale of mothers and children under fourteen years of age, or legally married couples.

The Moret Law satisfied neither the abolitionists, especially the persuasive Emilio Castelar, who wanted a more extensive bill and, possibly, immediate emancipation of all slaves, nor the reactionaries, who cried that the law was already too extreme, and wanted assurance that no further measure would be adopted before the end of the war in Cuba.[41] Yet all its critics accepted the fact that the law was nothing more than a temporary measure, designed, as its author often repeated, to appease all parties, and to initiate the phased abolition of slavery in Cuba.

The Cuban planters, however, did not accept the moderate Moret Law without a struggle. In a series of meetings with Caballero de Rodas, they repeated the impracticability of any partial abolition. Not only did the planters repeat the aging arguments on the social and economic threat to their island, but they also declared that a new census had to be taken in order that "justice" might be done to both the masters and the slaves. The Cuban captain-general, sympathetic to the cause of the planters, employed many excuses for procrastination, despite angry urging from Madrid.[42] Finally, towards the end of 1870 Caballero de Rodas published the law of July 4, 1870, in the official gazette and immediately resigned his post. Moret accepted the resignation with discernible satisfaction, and appointed Blas Villate y de la Hera, Count of Valmaseda, a minor expert on Cuban affairs, to succeed him as captain-general.[43] Nevertheless, without the reglamento to put into effect the Moret Law, it remained in abeyance.

Valmaseda's arrival in December 1870 did not reverse the obstructionist tactics of the local planters. A prior agreement by the colonial ministry in Madrid that the planters could formulate the details of the reglamento considerably weakened the bargaining position of the captain-general. The planters, for their part, determined to use this opportunity to subvert the law by weakening the structure created to administer it. According to Caballero de Rodas, they hoped to gain time, and

41. Corwin, *Spain and Cuba*, pp. 247–51.
42. Ibid., pp. 261–62.
43. Valmaseda had served as civil governor and organized the taking of the census of 1867. See AHN, Ultramar, Esclavitud, leg. 3555, fol. II.

consequently profit, from a delay in abolition.[44] Valmaseda suffered from other handicaps, particularly when the assassination of Prim again threw Spanish domestic politics into a medley of confusion, and colonial problems became temporarily submerged.

The chaos in Madrid provided further opportunities for the Volunteers in Cuba to exert their power. Valmaseda, succumbing to the local realities, arrested and later executed the Cuban poet Juan Clemente Zenea, who had credentials from the regent, Serrano, and a safe-conduct pass from the Spanish minister in Washington, Mauricio Lopéz Roberts, to mediate a possible cease-fire.[45] The war effort greatly intensified on both sides. A mob of Volunteers, out of control, murdered some medical students in Havana, on the frivolous charges of disrespect to a loyalist "martyr," while Valmaseda was away in the central zone coordinating military activity. Meanwhile the attempts to implement the Moret Law were suspended until after Valmaseda resigned in late 1872.[46]

The Republican government which succeeded the short-lived monarchy of Amadeus I of Savoy (1871–73) enacted into law the abolition of slavery in Puerto Rico before itself falling from office the following year. The situation in Cuba forbade the adoption of similar measures there. But if abolition in Puerto Rico in 1873 signified a victory for the Spanish and Puerto Rican abolitionists, the failure to win a similar measure for Cuba was a victory for the reactionaries who argued that only an end to the war qualified Cuba for social and political reform.[47]

A form of gradual abolition, however, was already taking place in Cuba. The Spanish government granted freedom to a relatively small number of slaves who helped the loyalist troops, as well as those who belonged to persons sympathetic to the insurgents. In practice, slaves were confiscated along with other property, a fact which emphasized the chattel character of Spanish slavery.[48] Sometimes such slaves were returned to their owners, but more often their owners had either joined the rebels, or left the island. On July 30, 1870, for example, the government manumitted thirteen slaves. Twelve gained their freedom in return for various services to the Spanish cause. One slave, Federico Céspedes,

44. Quoted in Corwin, *Spain and Cuba*, p. 256.

45. Guerra y Sanchez, et al., *Historia*, 5:131–35.

46. Some authors contend that Valmaseda was removed as a result of the uproar caused by the murder of the medical students. See, for example, Nevins, *Hamilton Fish*, pp. 623–26.

47. AHN, Ultramar, Esclavitud, leg. 3555.

48. Ibid., Insurrección, leg. 4366, fol. 396–487, 1871: "Embargo de Bienes."

got his liberty because his master, Enrique Céspedes of Manzanillo, had purportedly joined the rebels.[49]

Death, either from natural causes or as a result of the war, accelerated the decrease in the number of slaves, especially as new importations had ceased. In the middle of the nineteenth century, the overall rate of decrease was between 3 and 5 per cent. But this general decrease also reflected the small number of manumissions which took place.

After 1870 the application of the Moret Law, particularly to the newborn children of slave parents, became by far the most powerful legal factor diminishing slavery in the Spanish colony. Between 1869 and 1878, the Cuban slave population fell from more than 363,000 to less than 228,000, a decline of 37 per cent in ten years. Between 1870 and 1875, the Moret Law freed 32 of every 50 slaves who received their freedom, while less than 1 per cent—a total of 301 out of 50,046 —received freedom in return for meritorious services.[50] Nevertheless, the Moret Law of 1870 and its reglamento of 1873 were neither bold nor imaginative attempts to abolish slavery. They were indexes of the anachronism of slavery as a form of labor organization or a social system. Spanish abolition derived less from humanitarian convictions than from the desire to catch up with the rest of the world.

The pact of Zanjón, which established a truce in the long duel between Spain and Cuba, created an anomaly by declaring in its third article that all slaves and Asians who fought for the revolution should gain their liberty.[51] At the same time, the vast majority of adult slaves in the western part of the island, who by their loyalty had not only kept the revolution from spreading throughout the island, but had also maintained the high level of sugar production and economic viability so important to the war effort, remained in bondage. Nevertheless, the end of the war accelerated the decline of slavery.

In August 1879, General Martínez Campos, the successful military commander who had negotiated the pact of Zanjón in February 1878, returned to Spain to become prime minister to the young King Alfonso XII (1875–85). He immediately appointed a subcommission to study the social and economic problems of Cuba, including the ques-

49. Ibid., Esclavitud, leg. 3549, 1827–72, fol. 32.
50. Corwin, *Spain and Cuba*, p. 294. The author is incorrect, however, in stating that the Moret Law liberated only about 50%. If by 1875 the Moret Law had freed 50,000 and the slave population fell by 135,000 during the ten years, then the law must have accounted for a greater percentage.
51. Guerra y Sánchez, et al., *Historia*, 5:244–48. Also Pirala, *Anales*, 3:572.

tions of slavery and taxation. By November 1879 the government had prepared a new law of abolition, which the colonial minister explained as a fulfillment of Article 21 of the old Moret Law, which had promised new legislation as soon as Cuban deputies sat in the Cortes.[52]

The new law came into effect on July 29, 1880. It abolished slavery, but extended the patronage system to all the newly freed slaves in lieu of any indemnity to their owners. It was administered with more efficacy, and a large number of unregistered slaves were declared to be free. Meanwhile, the eight-year tutelage established by the law set the terminal date for slavery in 1888.

But as in the case of the earlier attempt by the British government to implement an apprenticeship system in its colonies, as the best form of transition from slavery to freedom, the stipulated time ended prematurely. In Cuba this premature end came from a combination of internal factors and agitation by the abolitionists in the Cortes.

Within the island, fear concerning the consequences of abolition had dissipated. The reduction in the number of slaves had not led to any racial turmoil. The richer planters had accepted the situation and had sold their slaves or freed them. In any case, those planters could afford to pay the wages for their labor and did not suffer any great inconveniences. The poorer whites still raised an outcry, but were politically powerless. The slaves, even when they had the money, appeared to be unenthusiastic about purchasing their freedom, preferring, perhaps, to serve out the eight years. By the end of 1883, only 99,566 registered slaves remained in the island—less than 10 per cent of the total population. Slavery, moreover, was superseded by a rapidly deterioriating economic situation, aggravated in part by a general decline in the price of sugar on the world market.[53]

In Spain the abolitionists joined the Cuban deputies in clamoring for the total abolition of slavery. Together they mounted a concentrated attack on the patronage system, pointing out that abuses were rampant and that physical punishment—especially the cepo and grillete—had not been abolished.[54] In November 1883 a royal decree finally ended the use of the cepo and grillete, and on October 7, 1886, another de-

---

52. Corwin, *Spain and Cuba*, pp. 299–308.

53. Ibid., pp. 308, 310–11; Edwin F. Atkins, *Sixty Years in Cuba* (Cambridge: Riverside Press, 1926), pp. 66–70, 77–90.

54. AHN, Ultramar, Esclavitud, leg. 4815, 1880–82: "Exposiciones abolicionistas a las Cortes." Also ibid., leg. 4814, 1882–83: Exposición de la Sociedad Abolicionista Española al M. de Ultramar, May 3, 1883.

cree formally dissolved the patronage system, thereby releasing the last
30,000 blacks who remained as direct symbols of the former system of
slavery.

The demise of Cuban slavery coincided with the last stage of the
revolution in the manufacture of sugar, with science and technology
finally replacing guesswork. This stage also coincided with the first
phase in the taking over of the Cuban sugar industry by American interests, in an attempt to salvage some of their capital advances to the
Cuban planters and producers. By the beginning of the 1880's, sugar
manufacture had become an enterprise for the very wealthy. The workers included a fulltime engineer, and an expert chemist who, in the
words of Edwin Atkins, "was an innovation in those days."[55] Large
centers with modern machines and railroads replaced the teams of
ox-drawn carts, and the large slave gangs gave way to a racially mixed,
wage-earning labor force. The last shred of the traditional system broke
when the maestro de azúcar, like his earlier counterpart in the Spanish-
American mining industry, the *azoguero,* succumbed to the advance of
technology, and lost his place in the process of sugar manufacture to
the trained chemist. Slavery in Cuba was partly the victim of the steam
engine.

55. See Atkins, *Sixty Years,* pp. 86–99; quote p. 94.

# 9

# Cuban Slavery and Race Relations

*The system of extensive agriculture*
*which has prevailed in our*
*country until now had its origins*
*in the past, when land was cheap,*
*and workers were abundant and*
*cheap. . . . But today it would be*
*criminal folly to persist in the*
*same system, however logical it*
*was for our ancestors. . . . The conditions*
*of labor and production*
*have changed, and will continue*
*to change in the future.*

The Count of Pozos Dulces, 1857.

THE CUBAN PLANTATION SOCIETY based on slave labor reached its apogee between 1840 and 1860. At the beginning of this period, slave labor accounted for 77.8 per cent of the labor force of the entire island, while wage-earners supplied the remainder.[1] After 1860, the abolition of the slave trade and the increasing mechanization of the process of sugar manufacture resulted in a gradual decline in the proportion of slave to free labor being used in Cuba. This decline was accelerated by the political developments in Madrid and the Ten Years War in Cuba, and by 1880, less than 23 per cent of workers were slaves. The brevity of the period of the slave-operated plantation undoubtedly had great impact of the nature of the society. For at the very time when the slave society reached its maturity it began to disintegrate—a factor that

1. Charles Albert Page, "The Development of Organized Labor in Cuba" (Unpublished Ph.D. dissertation, University of California, 1952), p. 3.

helped further to fashion the different pattern of Cuban slavery during the nineteenth century.

In most other West Indian islands, the sugar revolution had occurred not long after the initial settlement. The adjustments that took place were to be repeated in Cuba in the nineteenth century—a virtual exclusion of the small, yeoman farmer, a new pattern of landholding and land use, and a rapid importation of Africans to supply the increased labor demand of the sugar plantations. Cuba, however, was the only Caribbean island (with the exception of Puerto Rico) to begin its agricultural expansion after the Industrial Revolution had begun in Europe. The lateness of the arrival of the large-scale, slave-operated sugar plantation created many new problems for the Cubans both internally as well as in the realm of international politics. For the nineteenth century brought not only significant changes in the general attitudes toward African slave labor, but also significant new concepts about the nature of society. It was, after all, the age of humanitarianism, evolution, positivism, and industrial progress.

The timing of the sugar revolution had advantages and disadvantages for the Cuban planters. The Cuban industry expanded at a time when the production of the neighboring islands was declining from a combination of transferred capital, exhausted soils, and disrupted labor organizations. Borrowing in the way that had characterized the industry for hundreds of years, the Cubans started with the latest and most effective methods of manufacture then known. Farms and mills could be organized without the restrictions of old methods and obsolete machinery that were some of the handicaps of their rivals.

Nevertheless, expansion involved labor, and labor at that time was almost synonymous with African slavery. This demand for African slaves presented the greatest problem to the expansion of the sugar industry in the nineteenth century. For the large-scale importation of Africans was no longer an easy matter in the 1840's. The abolition of the British slave trade in 1807, the abolition of slavery throughout the British empire by 1838, and the persistence of the British navy in putting an end to the trade wherever it existed adversely affected the transfer of slaves from Africa to the Caribbean. And since the trade was principally conducted by foreigners, every additional country which agreed to stop dealing in slaves deprived the Cubans of potential vendors. As a last resort, Spaniards and Cubans conducted the commerce by themselves, under the guise of foreign flags. But British naval activity made the trade hazardous, and so expensive that the price of a bozal increased from 300 pesos in 1845 to 1,500 pesos in 1860. Yet, while the Americans did not join the group of nondealers, and as long as slavery flourished on the great North American continent, the Cubans could get their slaves, and feel reasonably secure of their future as a slaveholding society.

Given the choice, however, the Cubans would probably not have accepted slave labor to operate their estates. The political, moral, and philosophical opposition to slavery was extremely great, even within the island itself. Haiti stood as an example of the sort of tinder-box which every slave system potentially represented. Positivist-inclined speakers, such as Saco, saw a racially mixed society as jeopardizing "progress and civilization," and adopted a racist stand in favor of a white Cuba. But a white Cuba was no longer feasible by 1840.

Despite the fact that Cuba had a far higher proportion of white persons in its population than any other West Indian sugar-producing island, the white population alone was inadequate to supply the labor required on the ingenios. The island tried desperately to increase white immigration. But here the problem was twofold: the scarcity of labor brought on by the internal situation in Europe, and the social attitudes engendered by three centuries of slavery.

The rise of industrialization after 1850 in Europe, accompanied by the series of domestic wars and preparation for wars beginning with the Crimea in 1854 and continuing through Sedan in the Franco-Prussian campaign of 1870, all but dried up the stream of useful would-be emigrants.[2]

Industrialization absorbed a considerable percentage of the "excess" population, and the wars, while not disastrous by themselves, mobilized vast numbers, and inhibited freedom of movement. In any event, the great waves of immigrants did not begin to leave until after 1870. But the Europeans who left for the New World generally tended to avoid the regions where they faced competition from cheap native laborers, or slaves. And where they encountered slavery, as in the southern United States and southern Brazil, they were not competing on the labor market. The majority of the white immigrants who came to Cuba, therefore, were from Spain or the Canary islands.

If the number of white persons fell far short of the desired goal, pre-

2. Herbert Moller, *Population Movements in Modern European History* (New York: Macmillan, 1964).

vailing social attitudes tended to eliminate them from most classes of estate work where they were required. In tropical colonies there prevailed
a myth, based on misunderstood tropical experiences, primitive medical
theories, and European ethnocentricity, that white persons could not
do certain types of work, and could serve only in managerial positions,
because they could not endure prolonged exposure to the enervating
rays of the sun.[3] Throughout the Caribbean, the planting of sugar cane
and production of sugar, or indeed any other type of strenuous physical
exercise, was considered to be work for black people. The new immigrants in Cuba, therefore, went primarily into independent small farming
—particularly tobacco growing—to the despair of the labor-deficient
sugar planters.

Technology, however, was the salvation of the sugar industry. In the
first place, it made possible a substantial reduction in the work force.
The railroads, the use of steam, and more scientific processing enabled
a higher output capacity with a lower ratio of laborers to land. No
longer did more sugar necessarily mean more land and more slaves.
Nor did a larger work gang necessarily mean the acquisition of more
slaves, as Indians, Chinese, and white wage-earners joined the estates.
Technology, therefore, changed the nature of the sugar estates.[4]

Slave labor was, to a great extent, unskilled labor. However adequately it served the older methods of sugar manufacture, slave labor
was woefully incompetent to deal with the scientific advances of the industry. Intricate machines required skilled technicians, who, under the
prevailing circumstances, had to be white. Modernization of the sugar
industry, therefore, gradually undermined the old stigma attached to
plantation labor by bringing more white persons to work alongside the
blacks on the sugar estates. Yet this "mechanical" integration of the
labor force did not automatically mean any amelioration of the conditions of slavery, or a broader general inclination toward abolition by
the planters. For the process of mechanization was gradual.

As long as the greater proportion of the laborers on the island were
slaves, not only did the Negroes represent economic assets, but the institution of slavery generated certain peculiar social attitudes. On the
one hand, the slave was invested capital, and simply giving him his
freedom would result in pecuniary loss. The opposition to abolition on

3. Philip D. Curtin, *The Image of Africa: British Ideas and Action, 1780–1850*
(Madison: University of Wisconsin Press, 1964), p. 58–86.
4. Manuel Moreno Fraginals, *El ingenio* (Havana: Unesco, 1964).

economic grounds frequently linked the loss of a slave with the loss of "property," and the consequent ruin of the planter.[5] On the other hand, however, slavery represented a social order. To emancipate the slaves would be to alter that order, and most Cubans feared that any alteration would result in fearful and bloody consequences. They euphemistically called discussions concerning slavery, "the social problem."

It is fruitless to argue whether or not slave labor was economical in nineteenth-century Cuba. Quite obviously it was not. It was expensive, inflexible, and grudgingly done in the fashion of all coerced labor. Of course, some planters insisted that it was cheaper to buy successive African slaves and work them to death than to pay the wages of free workers. But actually the choice simply did not exist. Slavery was a necessity because it was the only way to get and keep the laborers. It was the practical response of the sugar-producing capitalists in a situation of open resources where accessibility of land far outstripped the availability of workers. Had the population of Cuba been greater in the nineteenth century, it is unlikely that the opposition to abolition would have endured as long as it did. And the defenders of slavery readily surrendered when they could get substitutes—poor whites, Asians, or, after slavery, seasonal immigrants from the other Caribbean islands.

One of the distinctive features of the Cuban planter class was in their method of investment. Diverging from the general practice in the southern United States and the British West Indian islands, the Cubans did not direct their investments exclusively into land and slaves, which, being equivalent to the original investment, would have resulted in quantitative economic progress.[6] Instead, Cuban planters (who in many cases were also merchants) often readily and willingly invested in new machines along with slaves and land. The early gamble on new machines must have been quite unrewarding for some time after the inventions were implemented, but before they were perfected, and would undoubtedly run counter to the desire to maximize profits. But the appeal of the new machines reinforces the fact that the new planter class were slaveholders by necessity rather than mere tradition.

5. Arthur F. Corwin, *Spain and the Abolition of Slavery in Cuba, 1817–1886* (Austin: University of Texas Press, 1967), p. 51.

6. On the United States South, see Eugene D. Genovese, *The Political Economy of Slavery* (New York: Pantheon Books, 1965), pp. 16–17. On the West Indies, see J. H. Parry and P. M. Sherlock, *A Short History of the West Indies* (London: Macmillan, 1967), pp. 143–49.

The sugar plantation created the inordinate need for African slaves. Naturally, the revolution was far more intense in Cuba than in Puerto Rico, and it was the intensity of the changes which formed and extended in Cuba the historical course of the plantation society and slavery. With a larger, landless population as prevailed in Puerto Rico at the time, there would be no need for the Cubans to import such large numbers of Africans. It seems that they would have resorted to the example of forcing the landless to work. Indeed, the parallel with Puerto Rico is interesting and instructive.

Until the end of the eighteenth century, Puerto Rico, to an even greater extent than Cuba, remained outside the manifest interest of the Spanish crown. It was a small, poor island. No acute rivalry between Peninsular bureaucrats or clergy and Creoles took place there. Unlike the case of Cuba which was a sort of testing ground for colonial reforms, the political and economic measures of Charles III were quite modest. No British occupation opened the floodgates of expectation by suddenly inundating the island with slaves. Until the middle of the nineteenth century Puerto Rico existed as a community of small farmers, smugglers, and pockets of plantation agriculture, where a relative equality was enforced by the tenuous position of the colony in the sphere of Spanish imperial politics. Finally, when the sugar revolution arrived, it was able to do so without the dramatic consequences which characterized the changes in Cuba.

The socioeconomic pattern of the transformation which took place in Cuba was repeated in the sister island. There was, however, one significant difference. In Puerto Rico, the divisions between classes and races could not be clearly and precisely distinguished, owing to the increase of the free colored population during the previous centuries. In the nineteenth century, vitally important cross-cutting cleavages made significant variations in the patterns in both islands. In social terms, the upper and lower strata of the Puerto Rican society were not rigidly divided along racial lines, and even well into the century the island enjoyed a relatively diversified economic base. The sugar plantations were not anywhere as dominant and pervasive as they were in Cuba, and sugar production was one of a number of agricultural activities.[7] In Puerto Rico sugar was not the king it had been in most other islands.

7. Luis M. Diáz Soler, *Historia de la esclavitud negra en Puerto Rico* (Rio Piedras: University of Puerto Rico Press, 1965), pp. 254–55; S. W. Mintz, "The Role of Forced Labor in Nineteenth Century Puerto Rico," *Caribbean Historical Review*, 2 (1951), 134–41.

The labor shortages that forced the Cuban planters to import so many hundreds of thousands of Africans were also felt to a lesser degree in Puerto Rico. Although the numbers of African slaves brought in more than doubled the slave population during the earlier part of the century, yet the proportion of slaves in the labor force gradually diminished. For the intensified economic development around the middle of the century, the planters and employers managed to fulfill their needs adequately, but in order to do so they reorganized their own local population along novel lines. They accentuated the distinctions between the landed and the landless and coerced the landless to labor on the land of those who had it. Curiously enough, all the reorganization of the internal population did not prevent the class of free colored persons from increasing by nearly 100 per cent between the years 1834 and 1860 to a total of 241,000 persons. During the same period, the free colored population of Cuba increased by only about 50 per cent to a total of a little more than 225,000 persons. Puerto Rico also had a relatively high proportion of mulattoes and white, daily-paid workers (jíbaros), and these provided the additional labor required. In 1827, the island had a population of 323,838, of which 50 per cent were white persons, 30 per cent were mulattoes, 9 per cent were free blacks, and 11 per cent were slaves. As the group of free, wage-earning laborers increased, the proportion of slaves decreased. In 1860, slaves represented a mere 7.16 per cent of the total population. By 1872 slaves composed less than 2.0 per cent of the labor force of the island of Puerto Rico, compared to more than 25 per cent in Cuba.[8]

Owing to the nature of the society in Puerto Rico, the slave did not achieve the economic importance he had in Cuba. He was not an indispensable unit in the operation of estates. Moreover, it seems that a fairly large proportion of the slave population in Puerto Rico was composed of Creole slaves rather than imports from Africa, and over a period of time occupations in the island became racially integrated. Free persons of color accounted for more than 33.0 per cent of the landholding group, and both whites and nonwhites participated equally in urban and rural activities. The pernicious distinction between "black man's work" and "white man's work" which plagued most tropical plantation societies became blurred in Puerto Rico, and no occupation had any racial identity. In the long run it became relatively easy for the Puerto Ricans to advocate the total, unindemnified abolition of

8. Díaz Soler, *La esclavitud en Puerto Rico*, pp. 254, 257–59.

slavery, since they were not threatening any entrenched local interests. In a very limited way, the Puerto Rican option for abolition in 1868 in the abortive reform commission meeting in Madrid, and the subsequent abolition of slavery in 1870, was comparable to the decision of the white planters of Antigua to abolish slavery without apprenticeship in 1834. Slavery, of course, had greater significance for the Antiguans, but they realized that the emancipated slaves had very little choice but to continue working on the sugar estates; emancipation would not jeopardize their labor force.

In any event, the case of Puerto Rico dealt a severe blow to the theory that white persons would not exist for long in the tropics if they did manual labor. But even more important, a comparison of developments in both Cuba and Puerto Rico emphasizes the relationship between the economic enterprise and the social structure in the development of race relations, and shows the severe strains placed by the slave plantation society upon Iberian traditions and legal practice.

People of African ancestry were not initially subjected to slavery in the New World on account of their race. Africans had been used on sugar plantations in the Mediterranean basin from as early as the twelfth century, and had been used even more as the sugar plantation migrated along the Atlantic coastal islands to the Americas. And although Africans had perhaps been used ever since the first sugar cane was planted in the New World to nurture the crop to maturity, plantation slavery was merely one facet of slavery in general. But by the end of the eighteenth century, the words "slaves" and "Negroes" began to be interchangeable—the narrow identification of a servile group with a particular race had begun. Nevertheless, seen in historical perspective, Negro slavery was only the last and more efficient phase in a system of slavery which had grown by trial and error. Eric Williams once said that "slavery was not born of racism: rather, racism was the consequences of slavery"—a pithy, if debatable, assertion.[9] In the case of Cuba, it seems indubitable that slavery exacerbated the racism which might have been latent.

9. Eric Williams, *Capitalism and Slavery,* new ed. (New York: Russell and Russell, 1961), pp. 3–29 (quote, p. 7). Some contrary views may be found in Carl Degler, "Slavery and the Genesis of American Race Prejudice," *Comparative Studies in Society and History,* 2 (1959), 49–67; and in Winthrop D. Jordan, *White Over Black: American Attitudes Toward the Negro, 1550–1812* (Chapel Hill: University of North Carolina Press, 1968).

The first Africans arrived in the New World as members of the early expeditions of the Spaniards. People from all parts of northern Africa had already been sold in Europe, and had circulated extensively in the Iberian peninsula. From the ports of Spain and Portugal they left voluntarily or involuntarily on the numerous probing expeditions into the wider world, and this was how at least one African (or person of African descent) had landed in Cuba with the invading forces of Diego Velásquez in 1511. The sixteenth century was a period when slavery also involved Europeans, who were sold as slaves and found service in the galleys of North Africa and the Janissary corps of the Ottoman empire. Slaves and slavery, without distinction of color, were a recognized and often lucrative part of international commerce in which both Europeans and Africans regarded themselves as equals.

Chronologically, the first large-scale attempts at slavery in the New World involved the indigenous Indians. Indian slavery, however, did not prove an adequate solution to the problem of labor recruitment. The Spaniards soon realized that the Indian population of Meso-America suffered calamitously from the disruptive influences of ecological and social dislocation, unfamiliar diseases brought by the Europeans, and in some minor instances, outright cruelty inflicted by the Spaniards. In the English colonies of North America and the Eastern Caribbean, and in Portuguese Brazil, the population density and sociopolitical organization of the Indians did not lend themselves to efficacious enslavement. Spanish, English, and Portuguese colonists, therefore, had to seek other forms of labor.

The Spanish alternative to Indian slavery was African slavery. The arrival of Africans in Mexico, for example, in the late sixteenth and early seventeenth centuries allowed the Indian population to recover from the immediate postconquest decline.[10] In the meantime, the vital occupations of mining and livestock farming continued with the able assistance of black slave-hands. With the recovery of the native population, in most cases largely mesticized, the African slave trade, which had been always expensive and in some cases inconvenient, lost its primacy. Local labor became available once more in satisfactory abundance.

The English colonists on the North Atlantic seaboard and in the

---

10. G. Aguirre Beltrán, *La población negra de México, 1519–1800* (Mexico: Ed. Fuentes Culturales, 1946), pp. 220–22.

Caribbean recruited their labor from Europe, chiefly from the mother country, from a variety of white servants. Three main sources of white labor existed. The largest group of recruits came from servants indented by law to serve a specific period of time in return for the cost of their passage. In the second half of the seventeenth century, large numbers of these white indentured servants went to the West Indies and the North American colonies. They composed one-sixth of Virginia's population in 1683, and two-thirds of all the immigrants to Pennsylvania in the eighteenth century.[11]

From England and the Continent, poor peasants and townsfolk in large numbers were enticed or defrauded into taking ship for the New World—this in addition to the regular traffic in indentured servants. The ranks of white arrivals there were further increased by a substantial influx of convicts, transported for crimes ranging from the trivial picking of a pocket to serious capital offences. "To Barbados" became a popular colloquial expression of the times, reflecting the exodus of white persons overseas.

But the growth of plantations in the South Atlantic demanded a greater supply of laborers than Europe could or would provide. Beginning in Brazil and the Caribbean with the sugar plantations, and continuing in the tobacco and cotton plantations of the mid-Atlantic states, an increasingly large number of Africans were introduced to do the monotonous requirements of plantation agriculture. African slavery developed because it proved more abundant than white servitude, and physically superior to Indian slavery. In the British West Indies, the result of slavery and the growth of plantation agriculture was a massive emigration of the white population, and an abrupt end to the mixed small farming of the earlier colonists.[12]

The rise of the plantation as the supreme economic activity and the adoption of Negro slavery as the method of labor organization had a profound effect on the social system of the regions in which both existed. White servitude had, despite its rigor, certain saving graces. Coming from the same racial stock and the same cultural background as their masters, the servants were usually indistinguishable except by the marks of their profession. Moreover, since the indentured system flourished at a time of abundant land—a milieu of open resources—and since the

11. Williams, *Capitalism and Slavery*, pp. 9–29.
12. Parry and Sherlock, *The West Indies*, pp. 63–80.

period of servitude generally existed only for a definite period of time, the servants could, and often did, aspire to the upper stratum of the society.[13] An example of the type of social mobility prevalent was revealed in the career of Henry Morgan, who started as an indentured servant in Barbados, became a successful, though somewhat savage, buccaneer, and later was knighted by the king of England and made lieutenant-governor of the island-colony of Jamaica.

Cuban slavery, both Indian and Negro, introduced the mutually reinforcing social cleavages of race, color, and occupation. The combination of the three was, of course, accidental. Slavery was itself the response at a particular time to an economic and organizational problem. The passing of time, combined with the economic success of the plantation, led to the proportional reduction of the white dominant stratum, and a corresponding increase of the black subordinate stratum. The upper stratum maintained close contact with Europe and identified with European values. But the rapid rate at which the Africans died and were replaced, as well as their traumatic existence on the plantation, tended to nullify the political and social connections with the African continent.

For the plantation society depended on coercion for its order and stability. The master class formulated an entire system of laws designed both to police the slaves as well as ensure their subordination and exploitation. In order that labor be available when and where it was required, it became necessary to regiment the life of the slaves, and to prohibit escape from the status as far as could be possible. Coercion fomented resentment—frequently explosive—on the part of the slaves. A vicious cycle developed as slave resentment led to fear on the part of the masters (not only of losing their own lives, but also their property), and consequently, increased coercion based on physical force and law.

Nevertheless, the plantation society also derived some stability from the habits and opinions generated by the plantation system. The monotonous repetition which characterized the routine of the slaves drained them of initiative and retarded the development of their skills and intelligence. Inadequate diet and poor hygiene, often a result of the master's determination to maximize profits, further accentuated the process of mental retardation. Confronted with such conditions, the slaves either

13. Herman J. Nieboer, *Slavery as an Industrial System* (The Hague: Nijhoff, 1900), pp. 5–7.

acquiesced in despair, or retaliated in anger by killing their masters, maiming the cattle, burning the canefields, or breaking their tools. The habitual response of the master class was to interpret the behavior of the slaves as a sign of congenital inferiority, an interpretation which reinforced their own ethnocentricity. The end product of the system of slavery was the preposterous postulation of defenders of the system that all blacks were inherently inferior to all whites.

The narrowly drawn racial attitudes in Cuba were, to a great extent, peculiar to the plantation society. For the reinforcing cleavages of race, color, and occupation were neither extensive nor necessary in a community with a mixed economy such as Puerto Rico, where the social order did not rely upon the protection of the privileges of one group at the expense of the opportunities of another. On the plantation, the division was accepted as both justified and "natural." In the late nineteenth century, proslavery Cubans could still use the survival of African cultural traits among their slaves as the basis for arguing that the slaves were "barbarous and uncivilized," and therefore deserved to be enslaved. The argument, however, had none of the theological and philosophical justification found in the famous Las Casas-Sepúlveda debates of the sixteenth century concerning Indian slavery and the Spanish attitude toward non-Spanish peoples. Instead, it was a scarcely veiled appeal to racial purity, which was already prevalent in the English West Indies during the late eighteenth and the early nineteenth centuries.[14]

The difference that the rise of the slave plantations made to the sharpening of racial attitudes may be seen by comparing the development of slavery and society in both Cuba and Puerto Rico at the time. Until the later eighteenth century, both islands had a mixed economy, with relatively amicable relations between the races, and no sharper economic, social, and political deprivation of the nonwhites above and beyond the built-in inequality of Spanish colonial society, based on the purity of blood. But with the rise of sugar cultivation during the nineteenth century, Cuba became a slave plantation society, and Puerto Rico did not.

During the nineteenth century, Puerto Rico intensified and extended its sugar industry, but managed to continue the mixed economy. Even though the landless were regimented, the previous uncomplicated rela-

14. Elsa Goveia, *A Study on the Historiography of the British West Indies* (Mexico: Inst. Panamericano de Geografía e Historia, 1956).

tions between the races were not disrupted—only a massive importation of slaves could have ended the interdependence of the various groups. The island built up its own large intermediate group of free colored persons, akin in culture and language to the elite, which supplied the labor for which African slaves were required in Cuba. But the predominance of mulattoes—as opposed to freed blacks—in the free colored segment meant that "passing as white" was much easier, and the society could level itself upwards. Social mobility in Puerto Rico was possible for most people, who suffered from no practical inequalities and were not visually and culturally distinct from the elite.

The Cuban trend reversed itself once the sugar revolution had brought the flood of Africans to the plantations. The intermediate free colored population not only was swamped by the immigrants, but was restricted to the towns and the eastern part of the island where the opportunities were more abundant. Two consequences of the influx militated against the development of a situation similar to that in Puerto Rico. In the first place, the greater majority of the immigrants, owing to their cultural and linguistic deficiency, were suitable only for the regimented routine of the plantations. It took two generations, generally, for the slave to acquire the language and skills which equipped him for urban life. And while the urban setting afforded more avenues of mobility, the prevalence of the "plantation values" meant that only in the case of the fortunate few with mixed blood was the passage relatively easy. In the second place, the free colored population was predominantly black. Thus the physical characteristics of the majority of this intermediate group distinguished them from the elite and facilitated separatist tendencies.[15]

This later phase of Cuban slavery closely resembled the other West Indian islands while the plantation was the dominant form of economic enterprise. The economic basis of Negro slavery greatly modified the inheritance of culture or the intervention of any religious denomination.[16] Roman Catholicism and the Iberian heritage played no significant role in the variations which developed in the institutions of slavery and race relations in Cuba and Puerto Rico during the nineteenth century.[17] In

15. See H. Hoetink, *The Two Variants in Caribbean Race Relations*, trans. Eva M. Hooykaas (London: Oxford University Press, 1967), esp. pp. 86–97.

16. Eric Williams, *Capitalism and Slavery.*

17. For a contrary view, see Herbert S. Klein, *Slavery in the Americas: A Comparative Study of Virginia and Cuba* (Chicago: University of Chicago Press, 1967); also, Frank Tannenbaum, *Slave and Citizen: The Negro in the Americas* (New York: Knopf, 1946).

fact, as the plantation spread inexorably from Havana eastwards, it took a pattern which had been familiar in Barbados in the middle of the seventeenth century, and in Jamaica, the Leeward Islands, Virginia, and the Carolinas in the eighteenth century. It was less a question of legacy, therefore, than a problem of growth and timing.

Wherever and whenever the plantation superseded small-scale mixed farming, society adjusted itself into basically two groups: the masters and the slaves, or the exploiters and the exploited. And whenever the region lacked a sufficient supply of available labor, slavery was adopted as the best means of labor organization. With certain qualifications, the response of the upper stratum became synonymous and almost predictable in the case of Negro slavery. For by the late eighteenth century, a distinct European ethnocentricity had developed, transcending nationalist lines. "Civilization" became a European monopoly, as the Europeans pitted themselves against the non-European world.

After the eighteenth century, the response of planters in the colonies to humanitarian attacks on the institution of slavery tended to reflect little of any particular culture or religion. Edward Long, writing of the Jamaican slaves in 1774, and Cristóbal Madan, writing of Cuban slaves in 1854, both vividly portray the assumptions and racial prejudice common to the planter elite throughout the Caribbean.[18] Despite the differences in time and circumstances, the institution of plantation slavery had produced almost identical effects on both men.

Many of the inflexibilities which were notable in the system of Cuban slavery towards the middle of the nineteenth century were less prominent prior to the rise of the plantation. And even though the system of slavery had existed for nearly three hundred years before the arrival of the large plantations, the cumulative effect of tradition and habit quickly became corroded by the newer mores of the plantation. Nevertheless, slavery as an industrial system was pregnant with its own disintegration in the nineteenth century. The United States Civil War was the final blow. Yet slavery was as much an issue after the outbreak of the Cuban Ten Years War as it had been during the Civil War in the United States. In the case of Cuba, however, the war dealt some damaging blows not only to the cause of slavery, but also to the pernicious growth of hostile

18. Edward Long, *The History of Jamaica* . . . (3 vols.; London: T. Lowndes, 1774); and [Cristóbal Madan], *Llamamiento de la isla de Cuba a la nación española* . . . (New York: Hallet, 1854).

race relations. Ten years of war convinced many white Cubans that their fear of the African was unfounded, and that given equal opportunities the black person distinguished himself as well as any white. Afro-Cubans found some undeniable heroes of their own as well as a great measure of respect from the wars between 1868 and 1898.

But the war could not eliminate prejudice, just as it could not provide the panacea for national harmony. The black man suffered from practical disabilities in Cuba right up to the middle of the twentieth century. Only revolutions bring the drastic changes which reverse deep-seated biases, and the social effect of plantation slavery existed in Cuba until the advent of Fidel Castro.

The history of slavery in Cuba, by spanning social development from the simple, peasant community to the complex, capitalist plantation, clearly undermines attempts to generalize about the system without reference to a delineated period, or even to a specific geographical zone. One simply cannot accept the proposition that the Cuban participation in and reliance on slavery did not vary through time and from locality to locality. Many writers and propagandists who dealt with Cuban slavery tended to describe a form and a system which, though accurate at some historical moment, was invalid and irrelevant for the actual conditions of the nineteenth century.

It is easy to examine the Spanish *Recopilación de leyes* and the French *Code noir,* and contrast them with the slave laws of the English colonies. Naturally the legal traditions were different, and the English were clearly more exclusionist in their relations with their slaves. Yet this does not get us very far in understanding the systems of slavery in the New World. Legal traditions are one thing. The day-to-day relations between masters and slaves, as the Cuban case of the nineteenth century makes clear, can be quite another thing. And the framework of slave laws or the moral and humanitarian tradition of any European metropolis can be of only limited value in understanding or comparing the nature of the slave plantation societies in tropical America.

Plantation societies in general, and the sugar plantation in particular, do not lend themselves to a great deal of variety or flexibility. Basically, the structural organization of the society and the organization of the sugar estate followed a common pattern from Brazil, through Barbados, St. Domingue, Jamaica, Cuba, Louisiana, or any other place of the Caribbean region, regardless of the timing of the sugar culture or the prevailing metropolitan influences. The mature plantation slave society represented, in Cuba as anywhere else, a relatively short period in the historical span of slavery, and was a consequence of the sugar revolution in the Caribbean and Brazil. Both the nature of the slave society, therefore, as well as the fact of the sugar revolution, must be vital considerations in the comparative study of the slave systems of the Americas. These comparative studies should be concerned less with concurrent time spans and metropolitan institutional differences than with equivalent stages of economic and social growth.

If we begin to see the development of the slave plantation society as a distinct phase in the history of slavery in the Americas, then we may begin to make more meaningful generalizations about slave societies. It is knowledge of the society as a whole with all its economic ramifications, rather than of narrower segments of legal and cultural heritage, which will lead to a better understanding of conditions during and after slavery. For sugar and slavery have had a familiar historical association from Cyprus in the middle of the fifteenth century to Cuba in the middle of the nineteenth century.

# Reference Matter

# Appendix 1

| YEAR | EXPEDITION | NO. OF AFRICANS FOUND |
|------|------------|----------------------|
| 1824 | Relámpago | 150 |
| 1826 | Cayo Verde | 61 |
|      | Campeador | 229 |
|      | Fingal | 58 |
|      | Gergis | 395 |
|      | Mágico | 176 |
|      | Ovestes | 212 |
| 1828 | Firme | 484 |
|      | Intrépido | 135 |
| 1829 | Gallito | 135 |
|      | Josefa | 206 |
|      | Voladura | 231 |
|      | Midas | 281 |
| 1830 | Curilio | 188 |
|      | Santiago | 105 |
| 1832 | Aguila | 604 |
|      | Yndágora | 134 |
|      | Planeta | 238 |
| 1833 | Negrito | 490 |
| 1834 | Rosa | 322 |
|      | Joaquina | 479 |
|      | Manuelita | 200 |
| 1835 | Amalia | 193 |
|      | Carlota | 253 |

| YEAR | EXPEDITION | No. OF AFRICANS FOUND |
|------|------------|------------------------|
|      | Chubasco | 72 |
|      | Holguin | 254 |
|      | Joven Pierna | 341 |
|      | María | 290 |
|      | Marte | 403 |
|      | Julita | 340 |
| 1836 | Fita | 393 |
|      | Diligencia | 205 |
|      | Ninfa | 432 |
|      | Ricomar | 186 |
| 1841 | Portugués | 411 |
| 1842 | Majaves | 150 |
|      | Arelia Felix | 158 |
|      | Demayajabos | 84 |
|      | San Marcos | 47 |
|      | Macambo | 152 |
|      | Yumuri | 90 |
|      | Coleta de Barca | 15 |
|      | Punta de Maya | 10 |
| 1843 | Puerto Escondido | 85 |
| 1846 | Cabañas | 10 |
| 1847 | Trinidad | 134 |
| 1848 | Cabañas, Sn. Diego de Nuñez | 130 |
| 1849 | Cabañas | 85 |
|      | Santa Clara | 172 |
| 1851 | Cárdenas | 402 |
| 1852 | Granavilla | 25 |
| 1853 | Cárdenas y Matanzas | 275 |
|      | Remedios | 52 |
|      | Sagua la Grande | 16 |
|      | Bermeja | 134 |
| 1854 | Caleta del Rosario | 15 |
|      | Cayo Levisa | 261 |
|      | Matanzas | 113 |
|      | Pinar del Rio | 185 |
|      | Ortigosa | 202 |
|      | Güines | 161 |
|      | Manimani | 103 |
|      | Isla de Pinos | 242 |
|      | Mariel-Tiniela Hacha | 70 |
|      | Brujas a Luisa | 589 |
|      | Sti. Spíritus y Trinidad | 743 |
| 1855 | Santa Cruz | 42 |
|      | Pta. de Ganado-Nuevitas | 74 |
|      | Guanajay-Bahia Honda | 93 |
|      | Nuevas Grandes | 25 |

| YEAR | EXPEDITION | NO. OF AFRICANS FOUND |
|------|-----------|:---------------------:|
| 1856 | Bahía Honda | 49 |
| 1857 | Sancti-Espíritus | 55 |
|      | Almendares | 21 |
|      | Jaruco | 91 |
|      | Morro | 85 |
|      | Paez | 356 |
|      | Primer Neptuno | 534 |
|      | Leckiligton | 497 |
|      | Sta. Susasa | 29 |
|      | Jagua Pelada | 3 |
|      | Guadalquizal | 1 |
| 1858 | Lanzanillo | 497 |
|      | Guantánamo | 361 |
|      | Punta de Ganado | 190 |
|      | Venadito | 615 |
| 1859 | Blasco de Garay | 438 |
| 1860 | Gibacoa | 47 |
|      | Luisa | 142 |
|      | Cayo Cadiz | 562 |
|      | 2do Neptuno | 419 |
|      | Cayo Sal | 846 |
|      | Casilda | 371 |
| 1861 | Manatí | 396 |
|      | Juanita | 69 |
|      | Yateras | 40 |
|      | Maniabon | 49 |
|      | Santa Maria | 621 |
| 1862 | Cabo Indio | 281 |
| 1863 | Aguica | 1031 |
|      | Dominica | 353 |
|      | Manaca | 418 |
|      | Canao, Sagua, etc. | 216 |
| 1864 | Guadalquivir | 469 |
|      | Lezo | 365 |
|      | 3er Neptuno | 659 |
| 1865 | Pato | 140 |
| 1866 | Punta Holanda | 278 |
|      | Total | 26,024* |

\* In original, 26,026, erroneously.
Source: AHN, Ultramar, Esclavitud, leg. 3554, 1870.

# Glossary

| | |
|---|---|
| administrador | fulltime overseer of an estate, responsible for operation and management |
| alcabala | sales tax |
| apalencado | runaway slave living in maroon village |
| asiento | license issued by the Spanish crown to an individual or company to engage in colonial trade, especially in slaves |
| barracón | slave market |
| batey | main industrial and residential area of sugar estate |
| bocoy | hogshead |
| bodega | tavern |
| bohío | slave hut |
| boyero | driver of oxcarts |
| bozal | newly imported African |
| caballería | land measurement of 33⅓ acres |
| cabildo | Afro-Cuban club for slaves and exslaves |
| cafetal | coffee plantation |
| capataz de cabildo | leader of a cabildo |
| capitanes de partido | military or judicial commanders of villages |
| carabelas | Africans who had traveled on the same ship across the Atlantic, and who formed social clubs |
| casa de purga | building where the molasses is drained from sugar |
| cepo | stocks for punishment of slaves |
| cimarrón | maroon slave |
| coartación | fixing of price by which slave may gain freedom |
| colonos | small farmers on rented lands |

| | |
|---|---|
| contramayoral | assistant to the white slavemaster—a position often held by a slave or free person of color |
| conuco | small garden plot on which slaves produced for themselves and the Sunday markets |
| criollera | woman who looked after infant slaves |
| criollo | creole |
| emancipado | African declared free by the courts of Mixed Commission |
| espasmo | vomiting sickness |
| furo | funnel-shaped orifice of sugar mold |
| grillete | shackles for punishment of slaves |
| guajíro | white peasant |
| ingenio | sugar estate with factory |
| jíbaro | white daily-paid worker in Puerto Rico |
| ladino | Spanish-speaking slave who has been "broken in" and has served about one year in slavery |
| liberto | slave freed by the Moret Law of 1870 |
| limpieza de sangre | used to describe a Spanish Catholic whose family had no trace of Jewish, Moorish, Indian, or African blood |
| maestro de azúcar | chief supervisor of the boiling house |
| mayoral | supervisor of slaves, often white |
| mayordomo | bookkeeper |
| mercedes | royal grants of land in usufructal tenure |
| moreno | black person |
| mulecón | slave, aged 14–18 years |
| muleque | slave, aged 6–14 years |
| negrero | dealer in slaves |
| novenario | punishment consisting of nine strokes given daily for nine days |
| padriño | white intermediary for runaway slaves |
| palenque | village of maroon slaves |
| pardo | mulatto |
| patrón | trustee |
| potrero | stock farm |
| ranchador | white slavehunter |
| ranchería | small palenque |
| raspadura | crude molasses made by small mills incapable of producing sugar |
| reglamento | administrative regulations implementing a law |
| realengos | crown lands |
| señorios | large estates of the early colonial period |
| síndico procurador | official protector of slaves |

| | |
|---|---|
| tiempo muerto | period after the harvest |
| trapiche | small mill for crushing canes |
| tren jamaiquino | the mechanical complex for boiling, clarifying, and purifying the cane juice to produce sugar |
| tumbadero | punishment area on an estate |
| vega | tobacco farm |
| vecino | Spanish citizen, usually of a particular town |
| vientre libre | measure of Sept. 29, 1868, freeing all slaves born after that date |
| zafra | harvest time for the canes |

# Bibliography

*Bibliographical Guides*

Jones, Cecil K. *A Bibliography of Latin American Bibliographies.* 2nd ed. Washington, D.C.: U.S. Govt. Printing Office, 1942.
Museo Biblioteca de Ultramar, Madrid. *Catálogo de la biblioteca.* Madrid: Impr. de la sucesora de M. Minuesa de los Ríos, 1900.
*Negociado de Ultramar: Registro de documentación de Cuba, Puerto Rico y Filipinas para el Archivo Histórico Militar de Madrid.* Madrid: Biblioteca Nacional, n.d.
Pedreira, Antonio S. *Bibliografía puertorriqueña.* Madrid: Hernando, 1932.
Sánchez, Alonso B. *Fuentes de la historia española e hispano-americana.* 3rd. ed. 3 vols. Madrid: Consejo Superior de Investigaciones Científicas, 1952.
Trelles y Govín, Carlos M. *Biblioteca histórica cubana.* 3 vols. Matanzas, Cuba: J. F. Oliver, 1922.

*Manuscript Sources*

Archivo Histórico Nacional, Madrid. Sección de Estado, Subsección de Esclavitud (1817–60): Legajos 8040–49 and 8057–61.
The information in this section of the Archives varied considerably. A fair proportion of the material dealt with British diplomatic pressure on Spain to terminate the slave trade; to free the so-called emancipados in Cuba; and to grant some measure of religious toleration in the island. The British demands, of course, derived from the formal treaty arrangements concluded with Spain in 1817 and 1835. The correspondence between the two countries is amply represented here both in Spanish and English. At least three entire legajos deal with the accounts and papers of the Sierra Leone Mixed Commission courts. Many other legajos deal with the landing of bozales,

and, sometimes, the confiscation of ships engaged in the slave trade. Legajo 8046 concerns the Spanish protests against the British Consul Crawford, at Havana. Legajos 8053 and 8057 contain protests against the appointment of the British consul, Turnbull, as well as his later "expulsion." The latter legajo also has the inconclusive evidence of the 1844 "revolt" of the free colored people in Cuba.

Archivo Histórico Nacional, Madrid. Sección de Ultramar. Papeles de Ultramar (1827–73).

This archive of the old Colonial Ministry papers was only opened to the general public in 1964, and rests temporarily in the National Archives in Madrid, awaiting transportation to Seville. The uncatalogued—although inventoried—documents of the ministry are divided into many subsections, plus a number of unclassified papers.

The chief value of these two sections of the archives is that they carry the history of colonial Cuba, and especially the history of slavery in Cuba, far into the nineteenth century. The documents at Seville have a terminal point in the early nineteenth century, and so do not support extensive research on this later period of Cuban history. No study of slavery in this later colonial period—in fact, no study of Cuba in the nineteenth century—can be complete without reference to this valuable deposit in Madrid. As far as the Sección de Ultramar was concerned, I found the following subsections and legajos most useful:

Aduanas: Legajo 3512 (1863–66).

Estimates of income from custom duties of the government.

Esclavitud: Legajos 3547–55 (1827–73).

This provided the most important section for my research. These bundles contained a wealth of information on slavery and its relevance to the agricultural and economic development of the island. Information for both slaves and owners, pertaining to the number, distribution, and sexual ratio of the slaves, and the number and distribution of the slaveowners in Cuba, came from the Cédulas de Capitación and Cédulas de Seguridad.

Issued by the government in Havana, this section also included long, informative, often confidential despatches between Havana and Madrid, concerning official policy and public reaction in the island.

Fomento: Legajos 19–81 (1830–70).

This section contains thousands of bundles pertaining to inventions, patents, economic reports, educational surveys, reports on agriculture, banking, and the railroads, as well as numerous copies of Cuban newspapers.

Gobierno: Legajos 4283, 4628–29, 4635, 4645, 4655, 4700–95, 4805–18, 4880–89, 4933–38 (1833–1900).

Among the most important papers here were some anti-Spanish, pro-revolutionary periodicals, printed in New York, Louisiana, and Miami, and circulated clandestinely in the island.

Insurrección: Legajos 4340–4418 (1868–78).

Although this constituted a large subdivision, principally covering the Ten Years War, yet it was in a sense the least helpful. Most of the cases were vague, many of the bundles are depleted—probably deliberately—and a fair amount of the information missing. Nevertheless, this contains a list of the various confiscated estates, records of the arbitrary methods adopted by the Spanish government in the island, and large bundles of notes and letters revealing, at times, the desperate plight of the insurgents.

Presupuestos, gracia y justicia, etc.

These deal with budgets for the island and other internal and legal affairs.

## Selected Books and Articles

Acosta y Albear, Francisco de. *Memoria sobre el estado actual de Cuba.* Havana: A. Pegó, 1874. Pamphlet.

Acosta y Quintero, José. *José J. Acosta y su tiempo.* Puerto Rico: Impr. Sucesión J. I. Acosta, 1899.

*The African Slave Trade.* New York: n.p., n.d. [ca. 1869]. Pamphlet.

Aguirre Beltrán, G. *La población negra de México, 1519–1800.* Mexico: Ed. Fuentes Culturales, 1946.

Aimes, Hubert H. S. "Coartación: A Spanish Institution for the Advancement of Slaves into Freedmen," *Yale Review,* 17(1909), 412–31.

———. *A History of Slavery in Cuba, 1511–1868.* New York: G. P. Putnam's Sons, 1907.

Alcalá y Henke, Augustín. *La esclavitud de los negros en la América española.* Madrid: J. Pueyo, 1919.

Alcazar, José de. *Historia de España en América (Isla de Cuba).* Madrid: Herres, 1898.

Alcázar Molina, Cayetano. *Los virreinatos en el siglo XVIII.* 2nd. ed. Madrid: Salvat, 1959.

Alonso y Sanjurjo, Eugenio. *Apuntes sobre los proyectos de la esclavitud en las islas de Cuba y Puerto Rico.* Madrid: Bibl. de Instrucción y Recreo, 1874. Pamphlet.

Altamira y Crevea. Rafael. *A History of Spain from the Beginnings to the Present Day.* Trans. Muna Lee. New York: Van Nostrand, 1949.

Amer, Carlos. *Cuba y la opinión pública.* Madrid: H. Gómez, 1897. Pamphlet.

Andueza, J. M. de. *Isla de Cuba, pintoresca, histórica, política, literaria, mercantil é industrial.* Madrid: Boix, 1841.

*Las Antillas ante el parlamento español en 1872.* Madrid: Dubrull, 1873.

*Apuntes sobre la cuestión de la reforma política y de la introducción de africanos en las islas de Cuba y Puerto-Rico.* Madrid: Fortanet, 1866.

Arango y Parreño, Francisco de. *Obras.* New ed. Havana: Dirección de Cultura, 1952.

Archer, William. *Through Afro-America: An English Reading of the Race Problem.* London: Chapman & Hall, 1910.

Armas y Céspedes, Francisco de. *De la esclavitud en Cuba.* Madrid: Fortanet, 1866.

————. *Regimen político de las Antillas españolas.* Palma: Biblioteca Popular, 1882.

Armas y Céspedes, José de, et al. *The Cuban Revolution: Notes from the Diary of a Cuban.* New York: n.p., 1869.

Atkins, Edwin F. *Sixty Years in Cuba.* Cambridge: Private printing at the Riverside Press, 1926.

Atkinson, William C. *A History of Spain and Portugal.* Baltimore, Md.: Penguin Books, 1960.

Ballesteros y Bereta, Antonio. *Historia de España y su influencia en la historia universal.* 11 vols. Barcelona: Salvat, 1944–56.

Balmes, Jaime. *El Protestantismo comparado con el Catolicismo en sus relaciones con la civilización europea.* Barcelona: Biblioteca Balmes, 1925.

*Bando de gobernación y policía de la isla de Cuba espedido por el Excmo. Sr. D. Gerónimo Valdés, Gobernador y Capitan-General.* Havana: Impr. del Gobierno, 1842.

Barras y Prado, Antonio de las. *Memorias, La Habana a mediados del siglo XIX.* Madrid: Ciudad Lineal, 1925.

Bartlett, Christopher J. "British Reaction to the Cuban Insurrection of 1868–1878," *Hispanic American Historical Review,* 37(1957), 296–312.

Beachey, Robert W. *The British West Indies Sugar Industry in the Late 19th Century.* Oxford: Blackwell, 1957.

Becker y González, Jerónimo. *España y Inglaterra.* Madrid: n.p., 1906.

————. *La Historia política y diplomática de España desde la independencia de los Estados Unidos hasta nuestros días, 1776–1895.* Madrid: Romero, 1897.

————. *La historia de las relaciones exteriores de España durante el siglo XIX.* 4 vols. Madrid: J. Ratès Martín, 1924.

————. *La política española en las Indias.* Madrid: J. Ratès Martín, 1920.

Benoist, Charles. *Cánovas del Castillo, la restauración renovadora.* Madrid: Ed. Literarias, 1931.

Betancourt, José R. *Las dos banderas: Apuntes históricos sobre la insurrección de Cuba.* Seville: Círculo liberal, 1870.

Bethell, Leslie M. "The Mixed Commissions for the Suppression of the Transatlantic Slave Trade in the Nineteenth Century," *The Journal of African History,* 12(1966), 79–93.

Blanco Herrero, Miguel. *Isla de Cuba: Su situación actual y reformas que reclama.* Madrid: Jubera, 1876. Pamphlet.

————. *Política de España en ultramar.* Madrid: Sucesores de Rivadeneyra, 1888.

*El boletín de la revolución, Cuba y Puerto Rico.* No. 1. New York, Thursday, December 10, 1868. Pamphlet.

Bremer, Fredrika. *The Homes of the New World: Impressions of America.* Trans. Mary Howitt. 2 vols. New York: Harper & Bros., 1853.

Buenrostro, Francisco. *Biografía de la fiebre Amarilla.* Havana: Impr. del Tiempo, 1858.

Butland, Gilbert J. *Latin America, A Regional Geography.* London: Longmans, 1960.

Calcagno, Francisco. *Diccionario biográfico cubano.* New York: N. Ponce de Leon, 1878.

Callahan, James M. *Cuba and International Relations.* Baltimore: Johns Hopkins, 1899.

Cancio Villa-Amil, Mariano. *Communicación . . . sobre las causas que influyen en la depreciación del billete del Banco.* Havana: El Iris, 1874. Pamphlet.

Canet Alvarez, Gerardo A. *Atlas de Cuba.* Cambridge: Harvard University Press, 1949.

Cánovas del Castillo, Antonio. *Historia de la decadencia de España desde el advenimiento de Felipe III al trono hasta la muerte de Carlos II.* Madrid: J. Ruiz, 1910; 1st. ed., 1854.

————. *La paz de Cuba. Discursos . . . en el congreso de los diputados el día 8 de mayo de 1878.* Madrid: Hernández, 1878. Pamphlet.

Cantero, Justo Germán. *Los ingenios, colección de vistas de los principales ingenios de azúcar de la isla de Cuba.* Havana: Marquier, 1857. Luxury edition with unnumbered pages.

Carbonell, Néstor, and Emeterio S. Santovenia. *Guaírmaro . . . .* Havana: Seoane y Fernández, 1919.

Carr, Raymond. *Spain 1808–1939.* Oxford: Clarendon, 1966.

*Cartilla práctica del manejo de ingenios ó fincas destinadas á producir azúcar. Escrito por un montuno . . . .* Irun: Impr. de la Elegancia, 1862.

Ceballos y Vargas, Francisco de. *Plan de campaña para pacificación de Cuba presentado al gobierno . . . .* Havana: n.p., 1872. Pamphlet.

Cepero Bonilla, Raul. *Obras históricas.* Havana: Inst. de Historia, 1963.

Céspedes y Quesada, Carlos M. *Manuel de Quesada y Loynaz.* Havana: El Siglo XX, 1925.

Chadwick, French E. *The Relations of the United States and Spain: The Spanish-American War.* New York: C. Scribner's Sons, 1911.

Chapman, Charles E. *A History of the Cuban Republic.* New York: Macmillan, 1927.

Christelow, Allan. "Contraband Trade between Jamaica and the Spanish Main, and the Free Port Act of 1766," *Hispanic American Historical Review,* 22(1942), 309–43.

Cisneros y Betancourt, S. *A los cubanos de Occidente.* Holguin: n.p. 1873. Pamphlet.

Clark, William J. *Commercial Cuba: A Book for Businessmen.* New York: C. Scribner's Sons, 1898.

Coggeshall, George. *Thirty Six Voyages to Various Parts of the World, Made Between the Years 1799 and 1841.* New York: G. P. Putnam, 1858.

*Colección de los fallos de pronunciados por una sección de la comisión militar establecida en la ciudad de Matanzas para conocer de la causa de conspiración de la gente de color.* Matanzas: n.p., 1844.

*Comunicaciones de la cámara de representantes desde el día 10 de abril de 1869 hasta el día 10 de junio del mismo año.* Havana: La Universal, 1919. Pamphlet.

Conrad, Alfred H. and John R. Meyer. *The Economics of Slavery, and Other Stories in Econometric History.* Chicago: Aldine Publishing Co., 1964.

Conrado y Asprer, Antonio. *Cartas sobre emigración y colonias.* Madrid: Dubrull, 1881.

*Constitution of the Republic of Cuba, April 10, 1869 at Guáimaro, Provisional Capital of the Republic.* New York: Wynkoop & Hallenbeck, 1869.

Corbitt, Duvon C. "Immigration in Cuba," *Hispanic American Historical Review,* 22(1942), 219–30.

————. "Mercedes and Realengos: A Survey of the Public Land System in Cuba," *Hispanic American Historical Review,* 19(1939), 262–85.

Corwin, Arthur F. *Spain and the Abolition of Slavery in Cuba, 1817–1886.* Austin: University of Texas Press, 1967.

Crespo de la Serna, León. *Informe sobre las reformas políticas, sociales y económicas que deben introducirse en la isla de Cuba.* Paris: Impr. hispano-americana, 1879. Pamphlet.

Cuba. *Colección de reales ordenes y disposiciones de las autoridades . . . 1856.* Havana: Impr. del Gobierno, 1857.

Cuba, Census. *Resumen del censo de población de la isla de Cuba . . . 1841. . . .* Havana: Impr. del Gobierno, 1842.

*Cuba desde 1850 á 1873, colección de informes, memorias, etc. . . .* Madrid: Impr. Nacional, 1873.

*Cuba española.* Madrid: Universal, 1869. Pamphlet.

*Cuba y la hacienda española: Cuestión palpitante.* Paris: n.p., 1873. Pamphlet.

Curtin, Philip D. *The Atlantic Slave Trade: A Census.* Madison: University of Wisconsin Press, 1969.

————. *The Image of Africa: British Ideas and Action, 1780–1850.* Madison: University of Wisconsin Press, 1964.

————, and Jan Vansina. "Sources of the Nineteenth Century Atlantic Slave Trade," *Journal of African History,* 5(1964), 185–208.

Dana, Richard H., Jr. *To Cuba and Back: A Vacation Voyage.* Boston: Ticknor and Fields, 1859; new ed., Carbondale: Southern Illinois University Press, 1966.

Daniel-Rops, Henri. *The Church in an Age of Revolution 1789–1870.* Trans. John Warrington. 2 vols. New York: Doubleday, 1967.

Davidson, Basil. *Black Mother: The Years of the African Slave Trade.* Boston: Little, Brown, 1961.

Davis, David B. *The Problem of Slavery in Western Culture.* Ithaca: Cornell University Press, 1966.

Deerr, Noël. *The History of Sugar.* 2 vols. London: Chapman & Hall, 1949–50.

Degler, Carl. "Slavery and the Genesis of American Race Prejudice," *Comparative Studies in Society and History,* 2(1959), 49–67.

Díaz Soler, Luis M. *La historia de la esclavitud negra en Puerto Rico.* 2nd ed. Rio Piedras: University of Puerto Rico Press, 1965.

Donnan, Elizabeth, ed. *Documents Illustrative of the History of the Slave Trade to America.* 4 vols. Washington: Carnegie Institute, 1930–35; repr. New York: Octagon, 1965.

Dulce, Domingo. *Informe al Ministro de Ultramar.* Madrid: Impr. Nacional, 1867. Pamphlet.

Elkins, Stanley M. *Slavery: A Problem in American Institutional and Intellectual Life.* Chicago: University of Chicago Press, 1959.

Ely, Roland T. *Cuando reinaba su majestad el azúcar: Estudio histórico-sociológico de una tragedia latino-americana.* Buenos Aires: Ed. Sudamericana, 1963.

Entralgo, Elias José. *La insurrección de los diez años. . . .* Havana: Depto. de Intercambio Cultural, 1950.

*España y el tráfico de negros. . . .* London: British and Foreign Antislavery Society, 1862. Pamphlet.

Ettinger, Amos A. *The Mission to Spain of Pierre Soulé, 1853–1855.* New Haven: Yale University Press, 1932.

*Fact Book: Agricultural Cuba.* New Orleans: Banker's Loan, 1916.

*Facts about Cuba.* Published under the authority of the N.Y. Cuban Junta. New York: Sun Job, 1870.

Fagg, John E. *Latin America: A General History.* New York: Macmillan, 1963.

Feijóo de Sotomayor, Urbano. *Isla de Cuba. Inmigración de trabajadores españoles. . . .* Madrid: J. Peña, 1855.

Ferrer de Couto, José. *Cuba May Become Independent: A Political Pamphlet Bearing upon Current Events.* Trans. Charles Kirchhoff. New York: El Cronista, 1872.

———. *Los negros en sus diversos estados y condiciones. . . .* New York: Hallet, 1864.

Figuera, Fermín. *Estudios sobre la isla de Cuba: La cuestión social.* Madrid: Colegio de sordos-mudos y de ciegos, 1866. Pamphlet.

Fladeland, Betty. "Abolitionist Pressures on the Concert of Europe, 1814–22," *Journal of Modern History,* 38(1966), 355–73.

Foner, Laura, and Eugene D. Genovese, eds. *Slavery in the New World: A Reader in Comparative History.* New Jersey: Prentice-Hall, 1969.

Foner, Philip S. *A History of Cuba and Its Relations with the United States.* 2 vols. New York: International Publishers, 1962–63.

Franco, José L. *Afroamérica.* Havana: Junta Nac. de Arq., 1961.

———. *La Vida heróica y ejemplar de Antonio Maceo.* Havana: Inst. de Historia, 1963.

Frías y Jacott, Francisco de, conde de Pozos Dulces. *La isla de Cuba: Colección de escritos sobre agricultura, industria, ciencias. . . .* Paris: Kugelman, 1860.

Friedlaender, Heinrich E. *Historia económica de Cuba*. Havana: Montero, 1944.

Gallenga, Antonio C. *The Pearl of the Antilles*. London: Chapman & Hall, 1873.

García de Arboleya, José. *Manual de la isla de Cuba*. . . . 2nd ed. Havana: Impr. del Tiempo, 1859.

————. *Tres cuestiones sobre la isla de Cuba*. . . . Havana: Impr. del Tiempo, 1869. Pamphlet.

Genovese, Eugene D. *The Political Economy of Slavery*. New York: Pantheon Books, 1965.

Gibson, Charles. *Spain in America*. New York: Harper & Row, 1966.

Gómez y Báez, Máximo. *Diario de campaña*. Havana: Centro superior tecnológico, 1940.

González del Valle y Ramírez, Francisco. *La Habana en 1841*. . . . Havana: Municipio de la Habana, 1947.

————. "El clero en la revolución cubana," *Cuba Contemporánea*, 18 (1918), 140–205.

Gordon, R. A. "Slavery and the Comparative Study of Social Structure," *American Journal of Sociology*, 66(1960), 184–86.

Goveia, Elsa V. *Slave Society in the British Leeward Islands at the End of the Eighteenth Century*. New Haven: Yale University Press, 1965.

————. *A Study on the Historiography of the British West Indies*. Mexico: Inst. Panamericano de Geografía e Historia, 1956.

————. "The West Indian Slave Laws of the Eighteenth Century," *Revista de Ciencias Sociales*, 4 (1960), 75–105.

Great Britain, Parliament, House of Commons. *Accounts and Papers*, 1844–73.

————. *Correspondence Respecting the Slave Trade and Other Matters, Jan. 1. 1869*. London, 1870.

Grupo Cubano de Investigaciones Económicas. *A Study on Cuba*. Florida: University of Miami Press, 1965.

Guerra y Sánchez, Ramiro. *Guerra de los diez años 1868–1878*. Havana: Cultural, 1950.

————, et al., eds. *Historia de la nación cubana*. 10 vols. Havana: Ed. Hist. de la Nación Cubana, 1952.

————. *Manual de historia de Cuba (económica, social y política)*. Havana: Cultural, 1938.

————. *Sugar and Society in the Caribbean: An Economic History of Cuban Agriculture*. Trans. Marjorie M. Urquidi. New Haven: Yale University Press, 1964.

Gutierrez de la Concha y de Irigoyen, José, marqués de la Habana. *Memoria sobre la guerra de la isla de Cuba y sobre su estado político y económico desde . . . 1871 . . . 1874*. Madrid: R. Labajos, 1875.

————. *Memorias sobre el estado político, gobierno y administración de la isla de Cuba*. Madrid: J. Trujillo, 1853.

Halstead, Murat. *The Story of Cuba*. . . . Chicago: Werner, 1896.

Haring, Clarence. *The Spanish Empire in America.* New York: Oxford University Press, 1947.

Harris, Marvin. *Patterns of Race in the Americas.* New York: Walker, 1964.

Hart, Francis Russell. *The Siege of Havana, 1762.* London: Allen & Unwin, 1931.

Hazard, Samuel. *Cuba with Pen and Pencil.* Hartford, Conn.: Hartford Pub. Co., 1871.

Helps, Arthur. *The Spanish Conquest in America, and Its Relation to the History of Slavery and to the Government of Colonies.* Rev. ed. London: J. Lane, 1900–1904; first published in 4 vols., 1855–61.

Hennessy, Charles A. M. *The Federal Republic in Spain: Pí y Margall and the Federal Republican Movement, 1868–74.* Oxford: Clarendon, 1962.

Hernández Iglesias, Fermín. *La esclavitud y el señor Ferrer de Couto.* Madrid: Universal, 1866. Pamphlet.

Herr, Richard. *The Eighteenth-Century Revolution in Spain.* Princeton: Princeton University Press, 1958.

Herskovits, Melville J. *The Myth of the Negro Past.* Boston: Beacon Press, 1958.

Hoetink, H. *The Two Variants in Caribbean Race Relations.* Trans. by Eva M. Hooykaas. London: Oxford University Press for Institute of Race Relations, 1967.

Horrego Estuch, Leopoldo. *Juan Gualberto Gómez, un gran inconforme.* 2nd. ed. Havana: El Siglo XX, 1954.

———. *Maceo, héroe y carácter.* Havana: La Milagrosa, 1952.

———. *El sentido revolucionario del 68, historia de un proceso ideológico.* Havana: Montero, 1945.

Humboldt, Alexander. *The Island of Cuba.* Trans. J. S. Thrasher. New York: Derby & Jackson, 1856.

Humphreys, Robert A. and John Lynch, eds. *The Origins of Latin American Revolutions, 1808–1826.* New York: Knopf, 1965.

[Hurlbert, William Henry]. *Gan-Eden: or, Pictures of Cuba.* Boston: Jewett, 1854.

Ibañez, Francisco F. *Observaciones sobre la utilidad . . . del establecimiento . . . de grandes ingenios centrales . . .* Havana: Obispo, 1880. Pamphlet.

Infiesta, Ramon. *Historia constitutional de Cuba.* Havana: Ed. Selecta, 1942.

———. *Máximo Gómez.* Havana: El Siglo XX, 1937.

*Información: Reformas de Cuba y Puerto Rico.* 2 vols. New York: Hallet, 1867.

*Informe presentado a la junta informativa de ultramar. . . .* Madrid: J. Peña, 1869. Pamphlet.

*Informe sobre la abolición inmediata de la esclavitud en la isla de Puerto Rico, presentado en la junta de información . . . el 10 de abril de 1867 por los comisionados de la expresada isla. . . .* Madrid: n.p. 1870.

Jameson, Russell P. *Montesquieu et l'esclavage.* Paris: Hachette, 1911.

Jenks, Leland. *Our Cuban Colony: A Study in Sugar.* New York: Vanguard, 1928.

Jensen, Merrill, ed. *English Historical Documents, IX. American Colonial Documents to 1776.* Oxford: Eyre & Spottiswoode, 1964.

Jiménez Pastrana, Juan. *Los chinos en las luchas por la liberación cubana (1847–1930).* La Havana: Inst. de Historia, 1963.

Johnston, Sir Harry H. *The Negro in the New World.* London: Methuen, 1910.

Jordan, Winthrop D. *White over Black: American Attitudes Toward the Negro, 1550–1812.* Chapel Hill: University of North Carolina Press, 1968.

Just, Ramon. *Las aspiraciones de Cuba.* Paris: Mourgues, 1859. Pamphlet.

Klein, Herbert S. "Anglicanism, Catholicism and the Negro Slave," *Comparative Studies in Society and History,* 8(1966), 295–327.

——. *Slavery in the Americas: A Comparative Study of Virginia and Cuba.* Chicago: University of Chicago Press, 1967.

Labra y Cadrana, Rafael M. de. *La abolición de la esclavitud en las Antillas españolas.* Madrid: Morete, 1869.

——. *La abolición de la esclavitud en el orden económico.* Madrid: Noguera, 1873.

——. *La autonomía colonial.* Madrid: Alaría, 1883. Pamphlet.

——. *La brutalidad de los negros.* Havana: Avon, 1950. 1st. ed., 1875.

——. *Cuestión de Puerto Rico.* Madrid: Morete, 1870. Pamphlet.

——. *La Cuestión de ultramar. . . .* Madrid: Noguera, 1871. Pamphlet.

——. *España y América, 1812–1912.* Madrid: Sindicato de Publicidad, 1912.

——. *La política colonial y la revolución española de 1868.* Madrid: Sindicato de Publicidad, 1915.

——. *La reforma política de ultramar 1868–1900.* Madrid: Alonso, 1902.

Le Riverend Brusone, Julio, "Sobre la industria azucarera de Cuba durante el siglo XIX," *El Trimestre Económico,* 11 (1944), 52–70.

*Ley de cuatro de julio de 1870 sobre abolición de la esclavitud y reglamento para su ejecución en las islas de Cuba y Puerto Rico.* Havana: Impr. del Gobierno, 1873. Pamphlet.

*Ley y reglamento de la abolición de la esclavitud de 13 de febrero y 8 de mayo de 1880.* Havana: Impr. del Gobierno, 1880.

Llorente, Antonio G. P. de. *Cuba y el actual ministro de ultramar.* Madrid: Arejas, 1872. Pamphlet.

Lloyd, Christopher. *The Navy and the Slave Trade.* London: Longmans Green, 1949.

Long, Edward. *The History of Jamaica.* 3 vols. London: T. Lowndes, 1774.

López de Letona, Antonio. *Isla de Cuba: Reflexiones sobre su estado social, político y económico.* Madrid: Ducazal, 1865.

Mackellar, Patrick. *A Correct Journal of the Landing of His Majesty's Forces on the Island of Cuba . . . August 13, 1762.* London: n.p., 1762.

[Madan, Cristóbal]. *Llamamiento de la isla de Cuba a la nación española. . . .* New York: Hallet, 1854.

[——]. *El trabajo libre y el libre cambio en Cuba.* Paris: n.p., 1864. Pamphlet.

Madariaga, Salvador de. *The Fall of the Spanish American Empire*. London: Hollis & Carter, 1947; rev. ed. New York: Collier, 1963.

———. *Spain: A Modern History*. New York: Praeger, 1958.

Madden, Robert R. *The Island of Cuba: Its Resources, Progress, and Prospects*. London: Gilpin, 1849.

———. *Poems by a Slave on the Island of Cuba*. . . . London: Ward, 1840.

Mannix, Daniel P., and Malcolm Cowley. *Black Cargoes: A History of the Atlantic Slave Trade, 1518–1865*. New York: Viking, 1962.

María, Jacinto. *Los voluntarios de Cuba y el obispo de la Habana*. Madrid: Pérez Dubrull, 1871. Pamphlet.

Martínez de Campos y Serrano, Carlos, duque de la Torre. *España bélica, el siglo XIX*. Madrid: Aguilar, 1961.

Mathieson, William L. *British Slavery and Its Abolition, 1832–1838*. London: Longmans Green, 1926.

———. *Great Britain and the Slave Trade, 1839–1865*. London: Longmans Green, 1929.

Mellafe, Rolando. *La esclavitud en Hispanoamérica*. Buenos Aires: Editorial Universitaria, 1964.

Menéndez, Carlos R. *Historia del . . . comercio de indios, vendidos a los esclavistas de Cuba . . . 1848 hasta 1861*. Mérida: Revista de Yucatan, 1923.

Merritt, J. E. "The Triangular Trade," *Business History*, 3(1960), 1–7.

Mintz, Sidney W. "Labor and Sugar in Puerto Rico and in Jamaica, 1800–1850," *Comparative Studies in Society and History*, 1(1958–59), 273–83.

———. "The Role of Forced Labor in Nineteenth Century Puerto Rico," *Caribbean Historical Review*, 2(1951), 134–41.

———. "Slavery and Emergent Capitalisms," in Foner and Genovese, eds., *Slavery in the New World* (q.v.) (reprint of the author's review of Stanley M. Elkins's *Slavery*, which first appeared in the *American Anthropologist*, 63[1961], 579–87).

Moller, Herbert, ed. *Population Movements in Modern European History*. New York: Macmillan, 1964.

Montalvo y Castillo, José. *Tradado sobre la crisis mercantil en el año de 1837 que abraza las causas de la decadencia del precioso fruto del azúcar*. . . . Havana: Impr. del Comercio, 1937. Pamphlet.

Montaos y Robillard, Francisco. *Proyecto de emancipación de la esclavitud en la isla de Cuba*. Madrid: Ducazal, 1865. Pamphlet.

Morales Carrión, Arturo. *Puerto Rico and the Non-Hispanic Caribbean: A Study in the Decline of Spanish Exclusivism*. Rio Piedras: University of Puerto Rico Press, 1952.

Morales y Morales, Vidal. *Hombres del 68*. Havana: Rambla y Bouza, 1904.

———. *Iniciadores y primer mártires de la revolución cubana*. New ed. 3 vols. Havana: Consejo Nacional de Cultura, 1963.

Moreno Fraginals, Manuel. *El ingenio: El complejo económico social cubano del azúcar. Tomo I, 1760–1860*. Havana: Unesco, 1964.

———. "Nación o plantación (el dilema político cubano visto a través de

José Antonio Saco," in Julio Le Riverend, et al., eds. *Estudios históricos americanos*. Mexico: El Colegio de Mexico, 1953, pp. 241–72.

Mörner, Magnus. *Race Mixture in the History of Latin America*. Boston: Little, Brown, 1967.

Nelson, Bernard H. "The Slave Trade as a Factor in British Foreign Policy," *Journal of Negro History*, 27(1942), 192–209.

Nelson, Lowry. *Rural Cuba*. Minneapolis: University of Minnesota Press, 1950.

Nevins, Allan. *Hamilton Fish: The Inner History of the Grant Administration*. Rev. ed. New York: Frederick Ungar, 1957.

Nichols, Lawrence R. "The Bronze Titan . . . Antonio Maceo." Unpublished Ph.D. dissertation, Duke University, 1954.

Nieboer, Herman J. *Slavery as an Industrial System*. The Hague: Nijoff, 1900.

[Nobel, Adeline M.] *Rambles in Cuba*. New York, 1870.

Norman, Benjamin M. *Rambles by Land and Water, or Notes of Travel in Cuba and Mexico.* . . . New York: Paine & Burgess, 1845.

*Nuevos papeles sobre la toma de la Habana por los ingleses en 1762*. Havana: Publ. del Archivo Nacional, 1951.

O'Kelly, James. *The Mambi-Land or, Adventures of a Herald Correspondent in Cuba.* Philadelphia: J. B. Lippincott, 1874.

*Opúsculo. Cuba y Puerto Rico. Medios de conservar estas dos Antillas en su estado de esplendor. Por un negrófilo concienzudo*. Madrid: J. Cruzado, 1866.

Ortiz Fernández, Fernando. "Los cabildos afro-cubanos," *Revista Bimestre Cubana*, 16(1921), 5–39.

————. *Cuban Counterpoint: Tobacco and Sugar*. Trans. Harriet de Onís. New York: Knopf, 1947.

————. "La fiesta afro-cubana del día de reyes," *Revista Bimestre cubana*, 15(1920), 5–26.

————. *Hampa afro-cubana, los negros esclavos*. Havana: Revista Bimestre Cubana, 1916.

————. *José Antonio Saco y sus ideas cubanas*. Havana: Universo, 1929.

Page, Charles Albert. "The Development of Organized Labor in Cuba." Unpublished Ph.D. dissertation, University of California, 1952.

*Paralelos: Independencia de Cuba 1821–1869* New York: Hallet Green, 1869. Pamphlet.

*El partido liberal de Cuba*. Madrid: Alaria, n.d. [ca. 1879]. Pamphlet.

Parry, John H. *The Spanish Seaborne Empire*. New York: Knopf, 1966.

————, and P. M. Sherlock. *A Short History of the West Indies*. London: Macmillan, 1956.

Patterson, Orlando. *The Sociology of Slavery*. London: MacGibbon & Kee, 1967.

Perez Cabrera, José M. *Los primeros esbozos biográficos de Céspedes*. Havana: El Siglo XX, 1947.

Pérez de la Riva, Juan. "Documentos para la historia de las gentes sin historia. El tráfico de culies chinos," *Revista de la Biblioteca Nacional José Martí*, 6 (1965), 77–90.

Pérez de la Riva y Pons, Francisco. *El café: Historia de su cultivo y explotación en Cuba.* Havana: Montero, 1944.

———. *Origen y régimen de la propiedad territorial en Cuba.* Havana: El Siglo XX, 1946.

Pérez Moris, José et al. *Historia de la insurrección de Lares. . . .* Barcelona: Ramirez, 1872.

Perojo, José de. *Cuestiones coloniales.* Madrid: Fernando Fe, 1883. Pamphlet.

Perry, John A. *Thrilling Adventures of a New Englander. Travels, Scenes and Sufferings in Cuba, Mexico, and California.* Boston: Redding, 1853.

Pezuela y Lobo, Jacobo de la. *Crónica de las Antillas.* Madrid: Rubio, Grilo y Vitturi, 1871.

———. *Diccionario geográfico, estadístico, histórico de la isla de Cuba.* 4 vols. Madrid: Mellado, 1863–66.

———. *Historia de la isla de Cuba.* 4 vols. Madrid: Baillière Hermanos, 1868–78.

Phelan, John L. "Authority and Flexibility in the Spanish Imperial Bureaucracy," *Administrative Science Quarterly*, 5(1960), 47–65.

———. *The Kingdom of Quito in the Seventeenth Century.* Madison: University of Wisconsin Press, 1967.

Philalethes, Demoticus [pseud.]. *Yankee Travels Through the Island of Cuba. . . .* New York: Appleton, 1856.

Piñyero, Enrique. *Como acabó la dominación de España en America.* Paris: Garnier Hermanos, 1908.

Pirala y Criado, Antonio. *Anales de la guerra de Cuba.* 4 vols. Madrid: F. González Rojas, 1895–98.

Pitt-Rivers, Julian. "Race, Color and Class in Central America and the Andes," *Daedalus*, 96(1967), 542–59.

Pí y Margall, Francisco. *Las grandes conmociones políticas del siglo XIX en España.* 6 vols. Barcelona: Casa Editorial, 1934.

Polavieja y del Castillo, Camillo García de, Marqués de Polavieja. *Relación documentada . . . de mi política in Cuba.* Madrid: Minuesa, 1898.

Pons y Umbert, Adolfo. *Cánovas del Castillo.* Madrid: Hernández, 1901.

Ponte Dominguez, Francisco J. *Arango Parreño, el estadista colonial.* Havana: Ed. Trópico, 1937.

———. *Historia de la guerra de los diez años. . . .* 2 vols. Havana: El Siglo XX, 1944–58.

———. *La Masonería en la independencia de Cuba 1809–1869.* Havana: Masonic World, 1944.

———. *La Personalidad Política de José Antonio Saco.* Havana: Melina, 1931.

Portell Vilá, Herminio. *Céspedes, el padre de la patria cubana.* Madrid: Espasa-Calpe, 1931.

————. *Historia de Cuba en sus relaciones con los Estados Unidos y España.* 4 vols. Havana: Montero, 1938–41.

————. *Narciso López y su época 1848–1850.* 3 vols. Havana: Cultural, 1930–58.

Porter, Robert P. *Industrial Cuba; Being a Study of Present Commercial and Industrial Conditions.* New York: G. P. Putnam's Sons, 1899.

Pritchard, Walter. "The Effects of the Civil War on the Louisiana Sugar Industry," *Journal of Southern History,* 5(1939), 316–20.

Ragatz, Lowell J. *The Fall of the Planter Class in the British Caribbean, 1763–1833.* New York: Century, 1928.

Rauch, Basil. *American Interest in Cuba, 1848–1855.* New York: Columbia University Press, 1948.

Rebello, Carlos. *Estados relativos a la producción azucarera de la isla. . . .* Havana: Impr. del Gobierno, 1860.

————. *The Pith of the Sugar Question.* Trans. from the Spanish. New York: Hallet, 1879. Pamphlet.

*Recopilación de las leyes de los reynos de las Indias.* 3 vols. New ed. Madrid: Consejo de Hispanidad, 1943.

Reed, William. *The History of Sugar and Sugar Yielding Plants. . . .* London: Longmans, Green, 1866.

*Reglamento sobre la educación, trato y ocupaciones que deben dar a sus esclavos los dueños o mayordomos de esta isla.* San Juan, Puerto Rico: Impr. del Gobierno, 1826.

Ribó, José J. *Historia de los voluntarios cubanos. . . .* 2 vols. Madrid: González, 1872.

Ricard, Robert. *The Spiritual Conquest of Mexico.* Trans. Lesley B. Simpson. Berkeley: University of California Press, 1966.

Rodriques Aldave, Alfonso. *La política ultramarina de la república de '73.* Havana: Nuestra España, 1940. Pamphlet.

Rodriguez, José Ignacio. *Estudio histórico sobre . . . la anexión . . . de Cuba a los Estados Unidos de América.* Havana: La Propaganda Literaria, 1900.

Rodriguez Ecay, Francisco. *Compendido de la geografía de la isla de Cuba.* Havana: Miguel de Villa, 1881.

Roig de Leuchsenring, Emilio. *Cuba y los Estados Unidos 1805–1898.* Havana: Sociedad Cubana de Estudios Históricos y Internacionales, 1949.

————. *La guerra libertadora cubana de los treinta años, 1868–1898.* Havana: Oficina del Historiador de la Ciudad de la Habana, 1952.

————. *Máximo Gómez: El libertador de Cuba.* Havana: Oficina del Historiador de la Ciudad de la Habana, 1959.

Rosenblat, Angel. *La población indígena y el mestizaje en América.* Buenos Aires: Nova, 1954.

Saco, José Antonio. *Contra la anexión.* 2 vols. Havana: Cultural, 1928.

————. *Colección de papeles científicos, históricos, políticos sobre la isla de Cuba.* Paris: d'Aubusson, 1859.

————. *La esclavitud en Cuba y la revolución en España.* Madrid: La política, 1868. Pamphlet.

Saco, José Antonio. *Historia de la esclavitud de la raza africana en el nuevo mundo.* . . . 4 vols. Havana: Cultural, 1938.

————. *Ideario reformista.* Havana: Talleres de Cultural, 1935.

————. *Réplica a la contestación.* . . . Madrid: La Publicidad, 1847. Pamphlet.

Sagra, Ramón de la. *Estudios coloniales con aplicación a la isla de Cuba.* Madrid: Hidalgo, 1845. Pamphlet.

Sanromá, Joaquín María. *La esclavitud en Cuba.* Madrid: T. Fortanet, 1872. Pamphlet.

————. *Mis Memorias 1828–1868.* 2 vols. Madrid: Hernández, 1887, 1894.

Santa Cruz, Mercedes de, condesa de Merlin. "Les esclaves dans les colonies espagnoles," *Revue des Deux Mondes,* XXVI, 4a, 1841.

Santovenia y Echaide, Emeterio. *Bartolomé Masó.* Havana: El Siglo XX, 1930.

————. *Las constituciones cubanas de Guáimaro (1869), Jimaguayu (1895), y la Yaya (1897).* Havana: La Universal, 1926.

————. *Cuba y su historia.* 2 vols. Miami: Rema Press, 1965.

————. *Estudios, biografías y ensayos.* Havana: Comisión Organizadora del Homenaje al Dr. Emeterio S. Santovenia, 1957.

————. *Gómez El Máximo.* Havana: El Siglo XX, 1936.

————. *Lincoln in Martí: A Cuban View of Abraham Lincoln.* Trans. Donald F. Fogelquist. Chapel Hill: University of North Carolina Press, 1953.

————. *Prim, el caudillo estadista.* Madrid: Espasa-Calpe, 1933.

Sedano, Carlos de. *Estudios políticas.* Madrid: Hernández, 1872.

Seeber, Edward D. *Anti-Slavery Opinion in France during the Second Half of the Eighteenth Century.* Baltimore: Johns Hopkins, 1937.

Serrano, Francisco, duque de la Torre. *Informe al Sr. Ministro de Ultramar.* Madrid: Impr. de la Biblioteca Universal Económica, 1868. Pamphlet.

Shafer, Robert J. *The Economic Societies in the Spanish World (1763–1821).* New York: Syracuse University Press, 1958.

Sio, Arnold A. "Interpretations of Slavery: The Slave Status in the Americas," *Comparative Studies in Society and History,* 7(1965), 289–308.

Sitterson, J. Carlyle. *Sugar Country: The Sugar Cane Industry in the South, 1753–1950.* Lexington: University of Kentucky Press, 1953.

Smith, Rhea M. *Spain: A Modern History.* Ann Arbor: University of Michigan Press, 1965.

Soto Paz, Rafael. *La falsa cubanidad de Saco, Luz y Del Monte.* Havana: Ed. Alfa, 1941.

Soulsby, Hugh G. *The Right of Search and the Slave Trade in Anglo-American Relations, 1814–1862.* Baltimore: Johns Hopkins Press, 1933.

Spain, Instituto Geográfico y Estadístico. *Censo . . . 1860.* . . . Madrid: Impr. Nacional, 1863.

————. *Censo de la población de España . . . 1887.* . . . Madrid: Inst. Geog. y Estadístico, 1891.

Strode, Hudson. *The Pageant of Cuba.* New York: Smith and Haas, 1934.

Suárez Argudín, José. *Cuestión social.* Havana: n.p., 1870. Pamphlet.

Suárez Inclán, Estanislao. *El gobierno del ministerio presidio . . . con respeto a la administración de las provincias de ultramar.* Madrid: Fortanet, 1884.

Suárez y Romero, Anselmo. *Colección de artículos* (Havana: La Antilla, 1859.

————. *Francisco. El ingenio o las delicias del campo.* New ed. Havana: Ministro de Educación, 1947.

Sypher, Wylie. *Guinea's Captive Kings: British Anti-Slavery Literature of the XVIIIth Century.* Chapel Hill: University of North Carolina Press, 1942.

Tacón y Rosique, Miguel. *Memoria.* . . . Havana: Impr. del Gobierno, 1838.

————. *Relacion del gobierno superior.* . . . Havana: Impr. del Gobierno, 1838.

Tannenbaum, Frank. *Slave and Citizen: The Negro in the Americas.* New York: Knopf, 1946.

Taylor, John Glanville. *The United States and Cuba: Eight Years of Change and Travel.* London: Bentley, 1851.

Torrente, Mariano. *Bosquejo económico político de la isla de Cuba.* 2 vols. Madrid: M. Pita, 1852–53.

————. *Cuestion importante sobre la esclavitud.* Madrid: Viuda de Jordan, 1841. Pamphlet.

Tuñón de Lara, Manuel. *La España del siglo XIX (1808–1914).* Paris: Club del Libro Español, 1961.

Turnbull, David. *Travels in the West. Cuba, with Notices of Porto Rico and the Slave Trade.* London: Longman, Orme, Brown, Green, and Longmans, 1840.

[Tyng, C. D.]. *The Stranger in the Tropics: . . . a hand-book and guide book.* . . . New York: American News, 1868.

Urban, Stanley C. "The Africanization of Cuba Scare 1853–1855," *Hispanic American Historical Review,* 37(1957), 29–45.

Vandama y Calderón, E. *Colección de artículos sobre el instituto de voluntarios de la isla de Cuba.* Havana: Cultural, 1897.

Vásquez Queipo, Vicente. *Breves observaciones sobre las principales cuestiones . . . de las provincias ultramarinas.* Madrid: n.p. 1873.

[————]. *Informe fiscal sobre fomento de la población blanca en la isla de Cuba.* Madrid: Alegria, 1845.

————. *La crisis monetaria española.* Madrid: n.p. 1866. Pamphlet.

Vera y González, Enrique. *La esclavitud en sus relaciones con el estado social de los pueblos.* Toledo: Fando, 1881.

Villaverde, Cirilo. *Cecilia Valdés or Angel's Hill.* Trans. Sydney Gest. New York: Vintage Press, 1962. First published in 1882.

Vitier, Medardo. *Las ideas en Cuba . . . durante el siglo XIX.* 2 vols. Havana: Editorial Trópico, 1938.

Walton, Gary M. "New Evidence on Colonial Commerce," *Journal of Economic History,* 28(1968), 363–89.

Whitaker, Arthur P., ed. *Latin America and the Enlightenment.* (Ithaca, N.Y.: Great Seal Books, 1961.

Williams, Eric. *Capitalism and Slavery.* Chapel Hill: University of North Carolina Press, 1944; new ed., New York: Russell and Russell, 1961.

————. *History of the People of Trinidad and Tobago.* Port-of-Spain, Trinidad: PNM Publ. Co., 1962.

Woodruff, William. *Impact of Western Man: A Study of Europe's Role in the World Economy, 1750–1960.* New York: St Martin's, 1967.

[Wurdemann, J. G. F.] *Notes on Cuba.* Boston: Munroe, 1844.

Zamora y Coronado, José M., comp. *Biblioteca de legislación ultramarina.* 7 vols. Madrid: Alegría y Charlain, 1844–49.

Zaragoza, Justo. *Las insurrecciones en Cuba.* . . . 2 vols. Madrid: Hernández, 1872–73.

# Index